CONTENTS

200⁺ *Best-Selling Homes for Sloping Lots*

ON THE COVER

Main Cover Photo: Plan CDG-4001, page 164
Design: Columbia Design Group
Photo by: Mark Englund/HomeStyles

IN THIS ISSUE:

HOW TO ORDER BLUEPRINTS

President Jeffrey B. Heegaard
Publisher Roger W. Heegaard
Associate Publishers Mark Englund, Wendy Schroeder
Editor Dianne Talmage
Associate Editors Pamela Robertson, Eric Englund, Matthew Arthurs
Sales Operations Supervisor Wayne Ramaker
Marketing Associates Gene Tubbs, Mary Gehlhar, Carrie Morrison
Controller Nancy Ness
Financial Analysts Barbara Marquardt, Jeanne Marquardt, Tom Klauer
Information Systems Analyst John Herber
Information Systems Associates Mary Oelke, Kevin Gellerman, Jeffrey Tindillier
Blueprint Manager Chuck Lantis
Staff: Barb Brueggeman, Shirley Holmes, April Liljedahl, Karen Liljedahl, Sarah McCadden, Debe McEnelly, Monita Mohammadian, Michelle Olofson, Cindy Pai, Kellie Pierce, Scott Woelm, Karen Zambory

Home Designs for Sloping Lots, a publication of the HomeStyles Group, is published by HomeStyles Publishing and Marketing, Inc., Roger F. Heegaard, Chairman; Jeffrey B. Heegaard, President; Roger W. Heegaard, Publisher; Robert L. Pool, Executive Vice President.

Massive, Windowed Great Room I-1354-B, p. 41

Great for Narrow, Sloping Lot P-529, p. 82

Panoramic Views H-855, p. 93

Expandable One-Story S-41792, p. 167

Design for Steep Terrain CDG-2009, p. 212

Simple Exterior, Luxurious Interior

- Modest and unassuming on the exterior, this design provides an elegant and spacious interior.
- Highlight of the home is undoubtedly the vast Great Room/ Dining area, with its vaulted ceiling, massive hearth and big bay windows.
- An exceptionally fine master suite is also included, with a large sleeping area, luxurious bath and big walk-in closet.
- A beautiful kitchen is joined by a bright bay-windowed breakfast nook; also note the large pantry.
- The lower level encompasses two more bedrooms and a generously sized game room and bar.

MAIN FLOOR

49'3"
50'8"

RAILING
DECK
HOT TUB
MASTER 19/0x14/0
VAULTED GREAT RM. 21/6x17/6
PLNTR.
SUNKEN TUB
DRESSING
LIN
VAULTED DINING 14/4x10/6
WALK IN WARDROBE
BATH
SKYLIGHT
PANTRY
REF
VAULTED ENTRY
KITCHEN 13/6x10/6
DW
GARAGE 21/4x21/8
NOOK 10/0x10/0

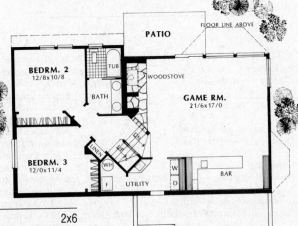

FLOOR LINE ABOVE
PATIO
BEDRM. 2 12/8x10/8
TUB
WOODSTOVE
BATH
GAME RM. 21/6x17/0
BEDRM. 3 12/0x11/4
LINEN
WH
F
UTILITY
W D
BAR

BASEMENT

Plan P-6595-3D

Bedrooms: 3	Baths: 2½

Space:
Main floor:	1,530 sq. ft.
Lower level:	1,145 sq. ft.
Total living area:	2,675 sq. ft.
Garage:	462 sq. ft.

Exterior Wall Framing: 2x6

Foundation options:
Daylight basement only.
(Foundation & framing conversion diagram available — see order form.)

Blueprint Price Code: D

11,989 CHOICES. AND EVERY ONE IS PERFECT.

When you're building a house, you want windows that reflect your personal taste. And you shouldn't have to compromise. With Louisiana-Pacific, you can have your windows any way you like. Our wood windows give you thousands of choices—from special shapes and grille options, to energy-saving high-performance glass. And they're all available with a low-maintenance aluminum-clad exterior that doesn't need painting, or a fully primed wood exterior that offers unlimited finishing options.

Of course, L-P windows are carefully engineered for energy-efficiency and years of smooth, trouble-free operation. And while they're rated among the very best, they actually cost as much as 15% less than other top-quality wood windows.

Call us today at **(216) 745-1661**. We'd be happy to send you information about the rest of our 11,989 choices.

Crown two slender pentagons with a diamond inset for a one-of-a-kind room.

Louisiana-Pacific
Windows & Doors
America looks through us.®

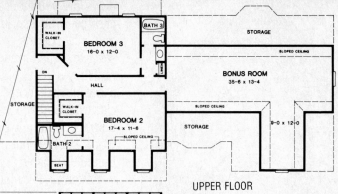

UPPER FLOOR

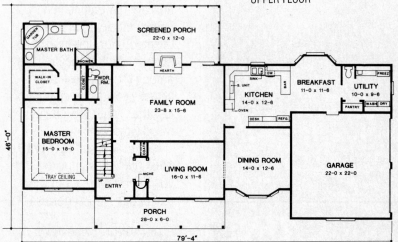

MAIN FLOOR

Deluxe Main-Floor Master Suite

- Traditional-style exterior with modern floor plan. Dormers and stone add curb appeal to this home.
- Formal entry with staircase leads to formal living or large family room.
- Large kitchen is conveniently located between formal dining room and secluded breakfast nook with bay window.
- Private master suite has tray ceiling and walk-in closet. Master bath has corner tub, shower, and dual vanities.
- Large screened porch off family room is perfect for outdoor living.
- Large utility room with pantry and toilet are conveniently located off the garage.
- Second floor features two large bedrooms with walk-in closets and two full baths.
- Optional bonus room (624 sq. ft.) can be finished as a large game room, bedroom, office, etc.

Plan C-8915

Bedrooms: 3	Baths: 3½

Space:

Upper floor:	832 sq. ft.
Main floor:	1,927 sq. ft.
Bonus area:	624 sq. ft.
Total living area:	**3,383 sq. ft.**
Basement:	1,674 sq. ft.
Garage:	484 sq. ft.

Exterior Wall Framing:	2x4

Ceiling Heights:

First floor:	9'
Second floor:	8'

Foundation options:
Daylight basement.
Crawlspace.
(Foundation & framing conversion diagram available — see order form.)

Blueprint Price Code:	E

2.6 Million Windows Say We're Right.

At one time, vinyl windows were only thought of as replacement windows. Today builders know that nothing meets the tough new energy codes better than vinyl. That's why 2.6 million vinyl windows are expected to be used in *new* construction in 1994, double that of three years ago*. For new construction or replacement, L-P windows are the best choice in vinyl.

L-P's vinyl windows don't just meet the codes, they exceed them. They're made with attention to every energy-saving detail: chambers of insulating air that keep out winter cold and summer heat, a watertight and airtight fusion-welded frame and sash, and optional high-performance glass. They also come in all the basic styles and virtually any custom shape.

Call us at **800-358-2954** in Barberton, Ohio. And find out why 2.6 million windows say L-P's vinyl windows are right.

*American Architectural Manufacturer's Association Industry Statistical Review and Forecast 1993.

**Louisiana-Pacific
Windows & Doors**
Doing something about it.™

Photo by Mark Englund/HomeStyles

UPPER FLOOR

**NOTE:
The above photographed home may have been modified by the homeowner. Please refer to floor plan and/or drawn elevation shown for actual blueprint details.

PLAN P-7579-2D
WITH DAYLIGHT BASEMENT

Three Fireplaces for a Hot Plan

- Fireplaces in the sunken living and family rooms as well as in the master suite help to make this an extra hot plan.
- A traditional tudor exterior envelopes a spacious, open-feeling interior.
- The two-story entry opens to the sunken living room and the formal dining room with covered patio beyond through sliding glass doors.
- The island kitchen overlooks a breakfast eating area with sliders to a rear patio and the sunken family room.
- There are three bedrooms upstairs including an exciting master suite with private covered deck off the master bath.

Plan P-7579-2A,-2D

Bedrooms: 4	Baths: 2 ½
Space:	
Main floor	1,500 sq. ft.
Upper floor	1,061 sq. ft.
Total Living Area	**2,561 sq. ft.**
Basement	1,500 sq. ft.
Garage	456 sq. ft.
Exterior Wall Framing	2x4
Foundation options:	**Plan #**
Crawlspace	P-7579-2A
Daylight Basement	P-7579-2D
(Foundation & framing conversion diagram available—see order form.)	
BLUEPRINT PRICE CODE:	**D**

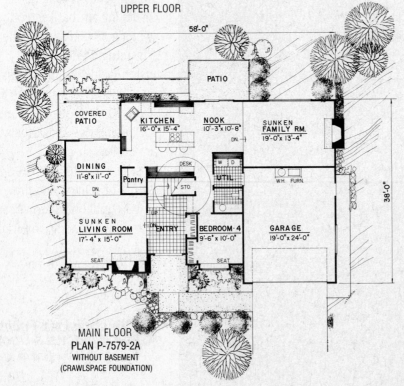

MAIN FLOOR
PLAN P-7579-2A
WITHOUT BASEMENT
(CRAWLSPACE FOUNDATION)

TO ORDER THIS BLUEPRINT,
CALL TOLL-FREE 1-800-547-5570

Plan P-7579-2A, -2D

PRICES AND DETAILS
ON PAGES 12-15

Tudor-Inspired Hillside Design

- The vaulted entry opens to a stunning living room with a high ceiling and massive fireplace.
- The dining room, five steps higher, overlooks the living room for a dramatic effect.
- Double doors lead into the informal family area, which consists of a beautifully integrated kitchen, nook and family room.
- The magnificent master suite, isolated downstairs, includes a sumptuous bath, enormous wardrobe and double-door entry.
- The upstairs consists of three more bedrooms, a bath and balcony hallway open to the entry below.
- Three-car garage is tucked under the family room/dining room area.

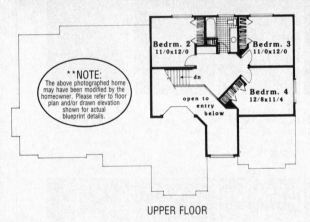

**NOTE:
The above photographed home may have been modified by the homeowner. Please refer to floor plan and/or drawn elevation shown for actual blueprint details.

Bedrm. 2
11/0x12/0

Bedrm. 3
11/0x12/0

dn

open to entry below

Bedrm. 4
12/8x11/4

UPPER FLOOR

Plan R-4001

Bedrooms: 4	Baths: 2½
Living Area:	
Upper floor	709 sq. ft.
Main floor	2,388 sq. ft.
Total Living Area:	**3,097 sq. ft.**
Garage	906 sq. ft.
Exterior Wall Framing:	2x6

Foundation Options:

Crawlspace
(Typical foundation & framing conversion diagram available—see order form.)

BLUEPRINT PRICE CODE:	E

68'-6"

43'-0"

PATIO

Nook
10/0x10/0

Kit.

bar

w.s.

Family
20/2x18/0

Dining
12/0x13/0

Living
13/4x17/6

Entry

sewing

laundry

wardrobe

dressing

tub

up

dn

up

Master
13/10x16/6

MAIN FLOOR

w.h.

up

Garage
32/0x28/4

TO ORDER THIS BLUEPRINT,
CALL TOLL-FREE 1-800-547-5570

Plan R-4001

PRICES AND DETAILS
ON PAGES 12-15

Free Home Tour Video Offer!

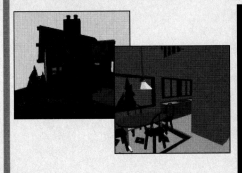

You won't believe the
Views
you're going to get
Free!

*HomeStyles' exclusive 3-D computer-animated **VideoGraphic Home Tours** video allows you to visually tour highlights of each home inside and out on your own TV! You'll get a real feel for the size and shape of your dream home!*

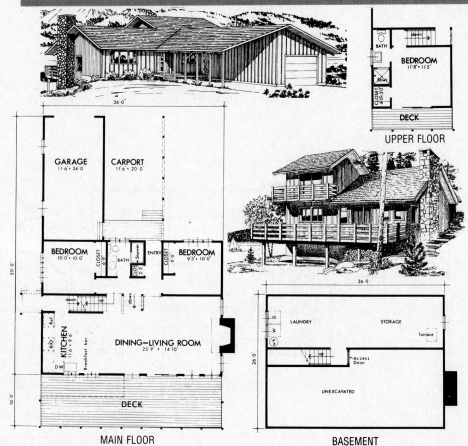

UPPER FLOOR

MAIN FLOOR

BASEMENT

Rustic Styling, Comfortable Interior

- Front-to-back split level with large decks lends itself to steep sloping site, particularly in a scenic area.
- Compact, space-efficient design makes for economical construction.

Plan H-25-C

Bedrooms: 3	Baths: 2
Space:	
Upper floor:	222 sq. ft.
Main floor:	936 sq. ft.
Basement:	365 sq. ft.
Total living area:	1,523 sq. ft.
Garage:	276 sq. ft.
Exterior Wall Framing:	2x4

Foundation options:
Daylight basement only.
(Foundation & framing conversion diagram available — see order form.)

Blueprint Price Code:	B

Luxuries Abound

- This design is filled with luxuries, beginning with the front door. Sidelights and a large transom flood the vaulted, raised entry hall with light.
- Straight ahead, French doors and windows in the living room provide a stunning view of the backyard.
- The formal dining room is elegantly capped with an arched ceiling.
- Vaulted ceilings further expand the combination kitchen, eating nook and family room. This entire area opens to a four-season porch, which gives way to a deck for even more space for outdoor entertainment.
- The fabulous main-floor master suite showcases a bath with a tray ceiling, a luxurious whirlpool tub and double-door access to the backyard.
- Upstairs, a versatile loft and a balcony hall lead to three bedrooms and a compartmentalized bath.
- The home features 9-ft. ceilings throughout the main floor, unless otherwise noted.

**NOTE:
The above photographed home may have been modified by the homeowner. Please refer to floor plan and/or drawn elevation shown for actual blueprint details.

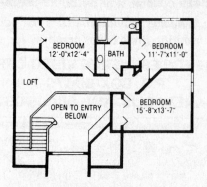

UPPER FLOOR

Plan AH-3230

Bedrooms: 4	Baths: 2½
Living Area:	
Upper floor	890 sq. ft.
Main floor	2,340 sq. ft.
Total Living Area:	**3,230 sq. ft.**
Daylight basement	2,214 sq. ft.
Garage	693 sq. ft.
Exterior Wall Framing:	2x6

Foundation Options:

Daylight basement

(All plans can be built with your choice of foundation and framing. A generic conversion diagram is available. See order form.)

BLUEPRINT PRICE CODE:	E

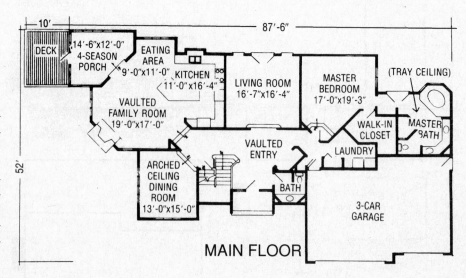

MAIN FLOOR

WHAT OUR PLANS INCLUDE

"SOURCE 1" construction blueprints are detailed, clear and concise. All blueprints are designed by licensed architects or members of the A.I.B.D. (American Institute of Building Design), and each plan is designed to meet nationally recognized building codes (either the Uniform Building Code, Standard Building Code or Basic Building Code) at the time and place they were drawn.

The blueprints for most home designs include the following elements, but the presentation of these elements may vary depending on the size and complexity of the home and the style of the individual designer:

1. *Exterior Elevations* show the front, rear and sides of the house, including exterior materials, details and measurements.

2. *Foundation Plans* include drawings for a full, daylight or partial basement, crawlspace, slab, or pole foundation. All necessary notations and dimensions are included. (Foundation options will vary for each plan. If the home you want does not have the type of foundation you desire, a foundation conversion diagram is available from "SOURCE 1".)

3. *Detailed Floor Plans* show the placement of interior walls and the dimensions for rooms, doors, windows, stairways, etc., of each level of the house.

4. *Cross Sections* show details of the house as though it were cut in slices from the roof to the foundation. The cross sections specify the home's construction, insulation, flooring and roofing details.

5. *Interior Elevations* show the specific details of cabinets (kitchen, bathroom, and utility room), fireplaces, built-in units, and other special interior features, depending on the nature and complexity of the item. **Note:** *For cost savings and to accommodate your own style and taste, we suggest contacting local cabinet and fireplace distributors for sizes and styles.*

6. *Roof Details* show slope, pitch and location of dormers, gables and other roof elements, including clerestory windows and skylights. These details may be shown on the elevation sheet or on a separate diagram. **Note:** *If trusses are used, we suggest using a local truss manufacturer to design your trusses to comply with your local codes and regulations.*

7. *Schematic Electrical Layouts* show the suggested locations for switches, fixtures and outlets. These details may be shown on the floor plan or on a separate diagram.

8. *General Specifications* provide general instructions and information regarding structure, excavating and grading, masonry and concrete work, carpentry and wood, thermal and moisture protection, and specifications about drywall, tile, flooring, glazing, caulking and sealants.

PLANS PACKAGE

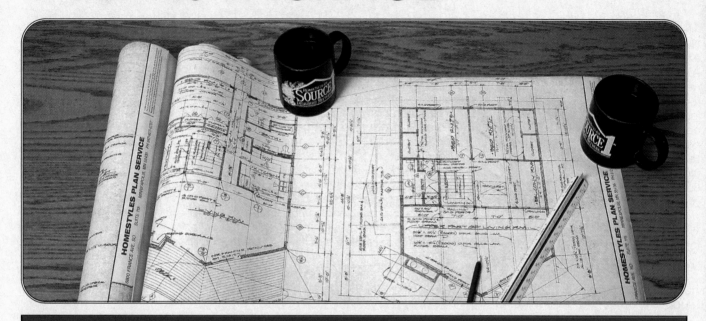

OTHER HELPFUL BUILDING AIDS

Every set of plans that you order will contain the details your builder needs. However, "Source 1" provides additional guides and information that you may order, as follows:

1. *Reproducible Blueprint Set* is useful if you will be making changes to the stock home plan you've chosen. This set consists of original line drawings produced on erasable, reproducible paper for the purpose of modification. When alterations are complete, working copies can be made.

2. *Mirror Reversed Plans* are used when building the home in reverse of the illustrated floor plan. Reversed plans are available for an additional one-time surcharge. Since the lettering and dimensions will read backwards, we recommend that you order only one or two reversed sets in addition to the regular-reading sets.

3. *Itemized List of Materials* details the quantity, type and size of materials needed to build your home. (This list is helpful in acquiring an accurate construction estimate.)

4. *Description of Materials* describes the type and quality of materials suggested for the home. This form may be required for obtaining FHA or VA financing.

5. *Typical "How-To" Diagrams — Plumbing, Wiring, Solar Heating, and Framing and Foundation Conversion Diagrams.* Each of these diagrams details the basic tools and techniques needed to plumb, wire and install a solar heating system, convert plans with 2 x 4 exterior walls to 2 x 6 (or vice versa), or adapt a plan for a basement, crawlspace or slab foundation. ***Note: These diagrams are general and not specific to any one plan.**

NOTE: Due to regional variations, local availability of materials, local codes, methods of installation, and individual preferences, it is impossible to include much detail on heating, plumbing, and electrical work on your plans. The duct work, venting, and other details will vary depending on the type of heating and cooling system (forced air, hot water, electric, solar) and the type of energy (gas, oil, electricity, solar) that you use. These details and specifications are easily obtained from your builder, contractor, and/or local suppliers.

PLEASE READ BEFORE YOU ORDER

WHO WE ARE

"Source 1" is a consortium of 45 of America's leading residential designers. All the plans presented in this book are designed by licensed architects or members of the A.I.B.D. (American Institute of Building Designers), and each plan is designed to meet nationally recognized building codes (either the Uniform Building Code, Standard Building Code or Basic Building Code) in effect at the time and place that they were drawn.

BLUEPRINT PRICES

Our sales volume allows us to offer quality blueprints at a fraction of the cost it takes to develop them. Custom designs cost thousands of dollars, usually 5 to 15% of the cost of construction. Design costs for a $100,000 home, for example, can range from $5,000 to $15,000.

Our pricing schedule is based on "Total heated living space." Garages, porches, decks and unfinished basements are not included.

Number of Sets	Price Code Based on Square Feet						
	A under 1,500	B 1,500-1,999	C 2,000-2,499	D 2,500-2,999	E 3,000-3,499	F 3,500-3,999	G 4,000 & up
1	$265	$300	$335	$370	$405	$440	$475
4	$310	$345	$380	$415	$450	$485	$520
7	$340	$375	$410	$445	$480	$515	$550
Reproducible Set	$440	$475	$510	$545	$580	$615	$650

ARCHITECTURAL AND ENGINEERING SEALS

The increased concern over energy costs and safety has prompted many cities and states to require an architect or engineer to review and "seal" a blueprint prior to construction. There may be a fee for this service. Please contact your local lumber yard, municipal building department, Builders Association, or local chapter of the AIBD or AIA (American Institute of Architecture).

Note: (Plans for homes to be built in Nevada may have to be re-drawn and sealed by a Nevada-licensed design professional.)

RETURNS AND EXCHANGES

HomeStyles blueprints are satisfaction-guaranteed. If, for some reason, the blueprints you ordered cannot be used, we will be pleased to exchange them within 30 days of the purchase date. Please note that a handling fee will be assessed for all exchanges. For more information, call us toll-free. **Note: Reproducible Sets cannot be exchanged or returned.**

ESTIMATING BUILDING COSTS

Building costs vary widely depending on style, size, type of finishing materials you select, and the local rates for labor and building materials. A local average cost per square foot of construction can give you a rough estimate. To get the average cost per square foot in your area, you can call a local contractor, your state or local Builders Association, the National Association of Home Builders (NAHB), or the AIBD. A more accurate estimate will require a professional review of the working blueprints and the types of materials you will be using.

FOUNDATION OPTIONS AND EXTERIOR CONSTRUCTION

Depending on your location and climate, your home will be built with either a slab, crawlspace or basement foundation; the exterior walls will either be 2x4 or 2x6. Most professional contractors and builders can easily adapt a home to meet the foundation and exterior wall requirements that you desire.

If the home that you select does not offer the foundation or exterior wall requirements that you prefer, HomeStyles offers a typical foundation and framing conversion diagram. (See order form.)

HOW MANY BLUEPRINTS SHOULD I ORDER?

A single set of blueprints is sufficient to study and review a home in greater detail. However, if you are planning to get cost estimates or are planning to build, you will need a minimum of 4 sets. If you will be modifying your home plan, we recommend ordering a Reproducible Blueprint Set.

To help determine the exact number of sets you will need, please refer to the Blueprint Checklist below:

BLUEPRINT CHECKLIST

____**Owner (1 Set)**
____**Lending Institution (usually 1 set for conventional mortgage; 3 sets for FHA or VA loans)**
____**Builder (usually requires at least 3 sets)**
____**Building Permit Department (at least 1 set)**

REVISIONS, MODIFICATIONS AND CUSTOMIZING

The tremendous variety of designs available from "SOURCE 1" allows you to choose the home that best suits your lifestyle, budget and building site. Through your choice of siding, roof, trim, decorating, color, etc., your home can be customized easily.

Minor changes and material substitutions can be made by any professional builder without the need for expensive blueprint revisions. However, if you will be making major changes, we strongly recommend that you order a Reproducible Blueprint Set and seek the services of an architect or professional designer.

**Every state, county and municipality has its own codes, zoning requirements, ordinances, and building regulations. Modifications may be necessary to comply with your specific requirements -- snow loads, energy codes, seismic zones, etc.

COMPLIANCE WITH CODES

Depending on where you live, you may need to modify your plans to comply with local building requirements -- snow loads, energy codes, seismic zones, etc. All "SOURCE 1" plans are designed to meet the specifications of seismic zones I or II. "SOURCE 1" authorizes the use of our blueprints expressly conditioned upon your obligation and agreement to strictly comply with all local building codes, ordinances, regulations, and requirements -- including permits and inspections at the time of construction.

LICENSE AGREEMENT, COPY RESTRICTIONS, COPYRIGHT

When you purchase a "SOURCE 1" blueprint, we, as Licensor, grant you, as Licensee, the right to use these documents to construct a single unit. All of the plans in this publication are protected under the Federal Copyright Act, Title XVII of the United States Code and Chapter 37 of the Code of Federal Regulations. Each "Source 1" designer retains title and ownership of the original documents. The blueprints licensed to you cannot be resold or used by any other person, copied or reproduced by any means. **This does not apply to Reproducible Blueprints.** When you purchase a Reproducible Blueprint Set, you reserve the right to modify and reproduce the plan.

BLUEPRINT ORDER FORM

Ordering your dream home plans is as easy as 1-2-3!

Complete this order form in just 3 easy steps. Then mail in your order, or call 1-800-547-5570 for faster service!

Thank you for your order and good luck with your new home!

1. BLUEPRINTS & ACCESSORIES

BLUEPRINT CHART   **SAVE $60!**   **SAVE $135!**

Price Code	1 Set	4 Sets	7 Sets	Reproducible Set*
A	$265	$310	$340	$440
B	$300	$345	$375	$475
C	$335	$380	$410	$510
D	$370	$415	$445	$545
E	$405	$450	$480	$580
F	$440	$485	$515	$615
G	$475	$520	$550	$650

Prices subject to change.

*A Reproducible Set is produced on erasable paper for the purpose of modification. Available for plans with prefix: AG, AGH, AH, AHP, APS, AX, B, BOD, C, CPS, DD, DW, E, EOF, FB, GL, GML, GSA, H, HDS, HFL, J, K, KLF, LMB, LRD, M, NW, OH, PH, PI, PM, S, SDG, THD, UDG, V.

ADDITIONAL SETS: Additional sets of the plan ordered are $35 each. Save $60 to $135 when you order the 4-set or 7-set package shown above!

MIRROR REVERSED SETS: $40 Surcharge. From the total number of sets you ordered above, choose the number of these that you want to be reversed. Pay only $40. *Note: All writing on mirror reversed plans is backwards. We recommend ordering only one or two reversed sets in addition to the regular-reading sets.*

ITEMIZED LIST OF MATERIALS: Available for $40; each additional set is $10. Details the quantity, type and size of materials needed to build your home.

DESCRIPTION OF MATERIALS: Sold only in a set of two for $40. (For use in obtaining FHA or VA financing.)

TYPICAL HOW-TO DIAGRAMS: One set $12.50. Two sets $23. Three sets $30. All four sets only $35. General guides on plumbing, wiring, and solar heating, plus information on how to convert from one foundation or exterior framing to another.
Note: These diagrams are not specific to any one plan.

2. SHIPPING AND HANDLING

Add shipping and handling costs according to chart below:

	1-3 Sets	4-6 Sets	7 Sets or more	Reproducible Set
U.S. Regular (4-6 working days)	$12.50	$15.00	$17.50	$15.00
U.S. Express (2 working days)	$25.00	$27.50	$30.00	$27.50
Canada Regular (2-3 weeks)	$12.50	$15.00	$17.50	$15.00
Canada Express (4-6 working days)	$25.00	$30.00	$35.00	$30.00
Overseas/Airmail (7-10 working days)	$50.00	$60.00	$70.00	$60.00

3. PAYMENT INFORMATION

Choose the method of payment you prefer. Send check, money order or credit card information, along with name and address to:

---

1. COMPLETE THIS FORM

Plan Number_____   **Price Code**_____

Foundation_____
(Carefully review the foundation option(s) available for your plan -- basement, crawlspace, pole, pier, or slab. If several options are offered, choose only one.)

No. of Sets:
- ☐ One Set
- ☐ Four Sets
- ☐ Seven Sets
- ☐ One Reproducible Set

$_____ (See Blueprint Chart at left)

ADDITIONAL SETS_____ (Quantity) $_____ ($35 each)

MIRROR REVERSED SETS_____ (Quantity) $_____ ($40 Surcharge)

ITEMIZED LIST OF MATERIALS_____ (Quantity) $_____ ($40; $10 for each additional)
(Available on plans with prefix: AH, AHP, APS*, AX, B*, C, CAR, CDG*, CPS, DD*, DW, E, FB, GSA, H, HFL, I, J, K, LMB*, LRD, N, NW*, P, PH, R, S, THD, U, UDG, VL.)
*Not available on all plans. *Please call before ordering.*

DESCRIPTION OF MATERIALS $_____ ($40 for two sets)
(Available on plans with prefix: AHP, C, DW, H, HFL, J, K, LMB, N, P, PH, VL.)

TYPICAL HOW-TO DIAGRAMS $_____ (All four only $35)
(One set $12.50. Two sets $23. Three sets $30.)
- ☐ Plumbing   ☐ Wiring   ☐ Solar Heating   ☐ Framing & Foundation Conversion

SUBTOTAL $_____

SALES TAX* $_____ (*MN residents add 6.5% sales tax)

2. SHIPPING & HANDLING $_____ (See chart at left)

GRAND TOTAL $_____

3.
- ☐ Check/Money Order enclosed (in U.S. funds)
- ☐ VISA   ☐ MASTERCARD   ☐ DISCOVER   ☐ AMEX

Credit Card#_____   **Exp. Date**_____

Name_____

Address_____

City_____ **State**_____ **Country**_____

Zip_____ **Daytime Phone(__)**_____

Check if you are a builder: ☐   **Home Phone(__)**_____

Mail coupon to:	HomeStyles Plan Service P.O. Box 50670 Minneapolis, MN 55405	Or Fax to: (612)338-1626

FOR FASTER SERVICE CALL 1-800-547-5570

FOR FASTER SERVICE CALL 1-800-547-5570   PGW32

15

Gracious Open-Concept Floor Plan

- A striking and luxurious contemporary, this home offers great space and modern styling.
- A covered entry leads to a spacious foyer, which flows into the sunken dining and Great Room area.
- The vaulted Great Room boasts a spectacular two-story-high fireplace, dramatic window walls and access to a rear deck or patio.
- A bright nook adjoins the open kitchen, which includes a corner window above

the sink.
- The den, which could be a guest bedroom, features a bay window overlooking the deck.
- The majestic master bedroom on the second floor offers a 10-ft.-high coved ceiling, a splendid bath, a large closet and a private deck.
- Two other upstairs bedrooms share a second bath and a balcony hallway overlooking the Great Room and entry below.

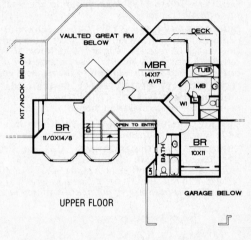

UPPER FLOOR

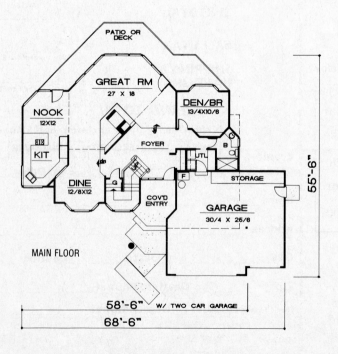

MAIN FLOOR

58'-6" w/ TWO CAR GARAGE

68'-6"

Plan S-41587

Bedrooms: 3-4	Baths: 3
Living Area:	
Upper floor:	1,001 sq. ft.
Main floor	1,550 sq. ft.
Total Living Area:	**2,551 sq. ft.**
Basement	1,550 sq. ft.
Garage (three-car)	773 sq. ft.
Exterior Wall Framing:	2x6

Foundation Options:
Daylight basement
Standard basement
Crawlspace
Slab
(Typical foundation & framing conversion diagram available—see order form.)

BLUEPRINT PRICE CODE:	D

Compact Plan Fits Narrow Building Site

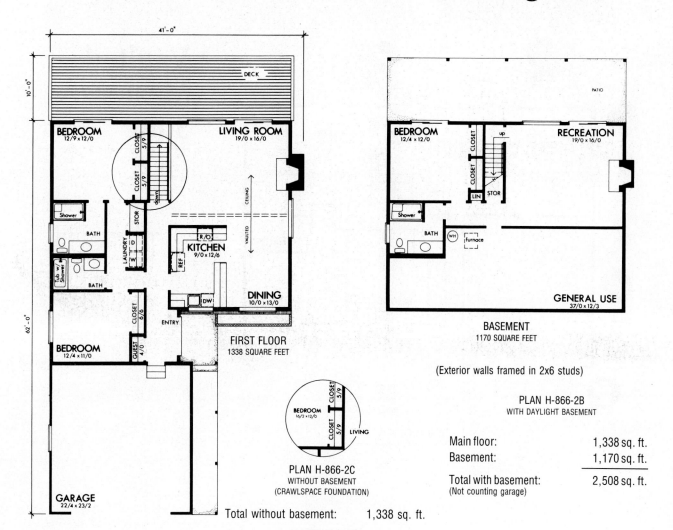

FIRST FLOOR
1338 SQUARE FEET

BEDROOM
12/9 x 12/0

LIVING ROOM
19/0 x 16/0

CLOSET 5/9

CLOSET 5/9

DECK

Shower

BATH

Tub w/ Shower

BATH

STOR

LAUNDRY

D

W

KITCHEN
9/0 x 12/6

R/O

REF

VAULTED CEILING

DW

DINING
10/0 x 13/0

CLOSET 6/6

GUEST 4/0

ENTRY

BEDROOM
12/4 x 11/0

GARAGE
22/4 x 23/2

41'-0"

10'-0"

62'-0"

PLAN H-866-2C
WITHOUT BASEMENT
(CRAWLSPACE FOUNDATION)

BEDROOM
16/2 x 12/0

CLOSET 5/9

CLOSET 5/9

LIVING

Total without basement: 1,338 sq. ft.

BASEMENT
1170 SQUARE FEET

BEDROOM
12/4 x 12/0

RECREATION
19/0 x 16/0

CLOSET

CLOSET

up

LIN

STOR

Shower

BATH

WH

furnace

GENERAL USE
37/0 x 12/3

PATIO

(Exterior walls framed in 2x6 studs)

PLAN H-866-2B
WITH DAYLIGHT BASEMENT

Main floor: 1,338 sq. ft.
Basement: 1,170 sq. ft.
Total with basement: 2,508 sq. ft.
(Not counting garage)

Blueprint Price Code D With Basement
Blueprint Price Code A Without Basement

TO ORDER THIS BLUEPRINT,
CALL TOLL-FREE 1-800-547-5570

Plans H-866-2B & -2C

PRICES AND DETAILS
ON PAGES 12-15   **17**

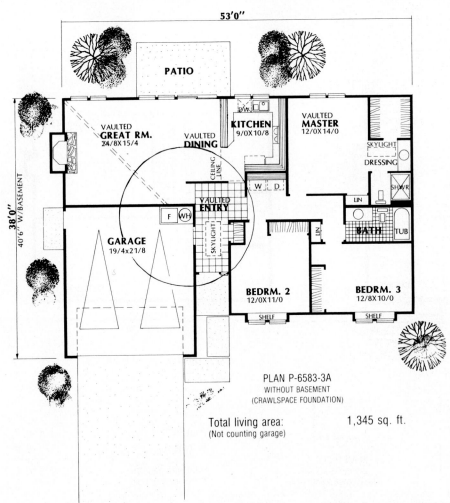

53'0"

PATIO

VAULTED **GREAT RM.** 24/8X15/4

VAULTED **DINING**

CEILING LINE

KITCHEN 9/0X10/8

DW.

VAULTED **MASTER** 12/0X14/0

SKYLIGHT

DRESSING

SHWR

LIN

W D

VAULTED **ENTRY**

SKYLIGHT

F WH

GARAGE 19/4x21/8

LIN

BATH TUB

38'0"

40'6" W/BASEMENT

BEDRM. 2 12/0X11/0

BEDRM. 3 12/8X10/0

SHELF

SHELF

PLAN P-6583-3A
WITHOUT BASEMENT
(CRAWLSPACE FOUNDATION)

Total living area: 1,345 sq. ft.
(Not counting garage)

Vaulted
Master
Suite

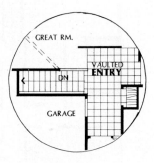

GREAT RM.

DN

VAULTED **ENTRY**

GARAGE

PLAN P-6583-3D
WITH DAYLIGHT BASEMENT

Main floor: 1,380 sq. ft.
(Not counting garage)
Basement level: 1,380 sq. ft.

Blueprint Price Code A

Plans P-6583-3A & -3D

PRICES AND DETAILS
ON PAGES 12-15

Handsome Chalet Design Features View

- Roomy floor plan will make this chalet something you'll yearn for all year long.
- Massive fireplace in living room is a pleasant welcome after a day in the cold outdoors.
- Open kitchen has two entrances for smoother traffic.
- Generous laundry facilities and large bath are unexpected frills you'll appreciate.
- Upper floor bedrooms feature sloped ceilings and plenty of storage space.
- Optional basement plan affords more storage and general use space.

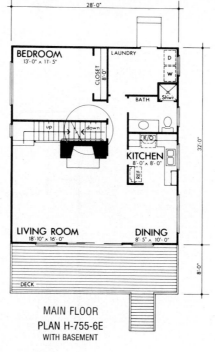

MAIN FLOOR
PLAN H-755-6E
WITH BASEMENT

UPPER FLOOR

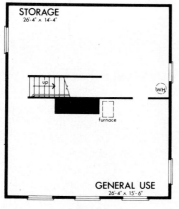

BASEMENT

PLAN H-755-5E
WITHOUT BASEMENT

WATER HEATER & FURNACE
LOCATED IN LAUNDRY RM.

Plans H-755-5E & -6E

Bedrooms: 3	**Baths:** 2

Space:	
Upper floor:	454 sq. ft.
Main floor:	896 sq. ft.

Total without basement:	1,350 sq. ft.
Basement:	896 sq. ft.

Total with basement:	2,246 sq. ft.

Exterior Wall Framing:	2x4

Foundation options:
Daylight basement (Plan H-755-6E).
Crawlspace (Plan H-755-5E).
(Foundation & framing conversion diagram available — see order form.)

Blueprint Price Code:	
Without basement:	A
With basement:	C

Vaulted Design for Narrow Lot

- Vaulted living spaces add to the spacious feel of this narrow-lot home.
- The focal point is a large fireplace flanked by windows that give views of a lovely patio and the yard beyond.
- The dining room offers access to a secluded courtyard, while the bayed kitchen overlooks a front garden.
- The master suite features a sitting room with sliders to the patio. The master bath leads to a large walk-in closet.
- The two remaining bedrooms share the hall bath.

Plans P-6588-2A & -2D

Bedrooms: 3	Baths: 2

Living Area:

Main floor (non-basement version)	1,362 sq. ft.
Main floor (basement version)	1,403 sq. ft.
Total Living Area:	**1,362/1,403 sq. ft.**
Daylight basement	1,303 sq. ft.
Garage	427 sq. ft.
Exterior Wall Framing:	2x6

Foundation Options:	**Plan #**
Daylight basement	P-6588-2D
Crawlspace	P-6588-2A

(Typical foundation & framing conversion diagram available—see order form.)

BLUEPRINT PRICE CODE:	**A**

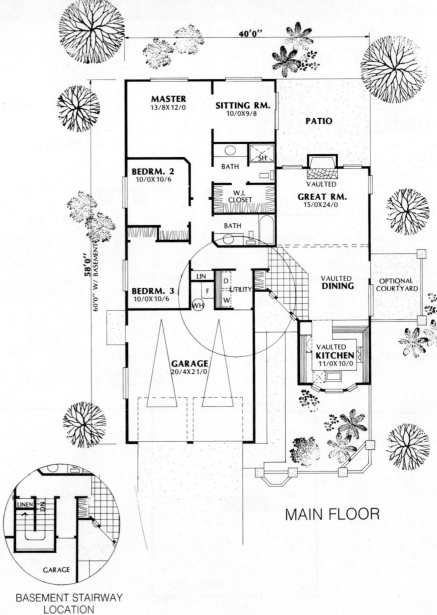

MAIN FLOOR

BASEMENT STAIRWAY
LOCATION

Plans P-6588-2A & -2D

PRICES AND DETAILS
ON PAGES 12-15

Garden Home

- This thoroughly modern plan exhibits beautiful traditional touches in its exterior design.
- A gracious courtyard-like area leads visitors to a side door with a vaulted entry.
- A delightful kitchen/nook area is just to the right of the entry, and includes abundant window space and a convenient utility room.
- The vaulted living and dining areas join together to create an impressive space for entertaining and family living.
- The master suite boasts a large closet and a private bath.
- The daylight-basement option adds almost 1,500 square feet of space to the home.

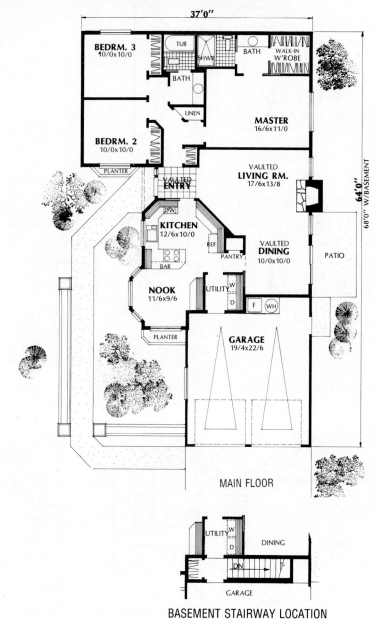

MAIN FLOOR

BASEMENT STAIRWAY LOCATION

Plans P-6598-2A & -2D

Bedrooms: 3	Baths: 2
Living Area:	
Main floor (without basement)	1,375 sq. ft.
Main floor (with basement)	1,470 sq. ft.
Total Living Area:	**1,375/1,470 sq. ft.**
Daylight basement	1,470 sq. ft.
Garage	435 sq. ft.
Exterior Wall Framing:	2x4
Foundation Options:	**Plan #**
Daylight basement	P-6598-2D
Crawlspace	P-6598-2A
(Typical foundation & framing conversion diagram available—see order form.)	
BLUEPRINT PRICE CODE:	**A**

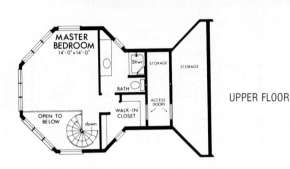

UPPER FLOOR

Octagonal Vacation Retreat

- Octagonal shape offers a view on all sides.
- Living, dining, and meal preparation are combined in a single Great Room, interrupted only by a provocative spiral staircase.
- Winding staircase allows continuous observance of activities below.
- Extraordinary master suite is bordered by glass, a private bath, and dressing room.
- Attached garage has room for boat, camper, or extra automobile.

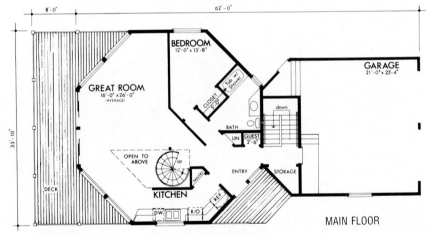

MAIN FLOOR

Plans H-964-1A & -1B

Bedrooms: 2-3	Baths: 2-3

Space:	
Upper floor:	346 sq. ft.
Main floor:	1,067 sq. ft.

Total living area:	1,413 sq. ft.
Basement:	approx. 1,045 sq. ft.
Garage:	512 sq. ft.
Storage (2nd floor):	134 sq. ft.

Exterior Wall Framing:	2x6

Foundation options:
Daylight basement (Plan H-964-1B).
Crawlspace (Plan H-964-1A).
Foundation & framing conversion diagram available — see order form.)

Blueprint Price Code:
Without basement:	A
With basement:	C

BASEMENT

(Alternate, included in blueprints)

Distinctive Contemporary Offers Two Exterior Designs

An open-arbor entry porch, boxed chimney, horizontal board siding and semihipped rooflines lend a custom look to the exterior of this contemporary ranch home. And the home's 1,415 sq. ft. interior is equally distinctive.

The front entry hall, which separates the spacious, open living area from the comfortably sized bedroom wing, has a vaulted ceiling with skylight for a dramatic first impression. The great room also has a vaulted ceiling, plus a long window wall (with sliding-glass door off the dining area opening onto a partly covered patio) and large fireplace.

There's an efficient U-shaped kitchen with pantry storage and an adjacent utility room. (In the daylight basement version, the utility room is replaced by stairs, and the entry to the garage is relocated.) A large master bedroom suite also has a vaulted ceiling with a skylight in the wardrobe/dressing area.

Floor plan labels

49'0''

PATIO

VAULTED MASTER 12/8x13/0

VAULTED DRESSING

VAULTED GREAT RM. 25/4x16/0

EXPOSED BEAMS

VAULTED DINING RM.

8'0'' WALL

SKYLIGHT

SH/WR

CEILING LINE

PANTRY

BAR

TUB LIN

VAULTED ENTRY SKYLIGHT

KITCHEN 10/8x11/4

DW.

UTIL. W D

BEDRM. 2 10/4x10/4

BEDRM. 3 10/4x10/2

WH F

51'0''

GARAGE 19/4x22/8

ENTRY

KITCHEN

DN

GARAGE

PLAN P-6584-4D
WITH DAYLIGHT BASEMENT

Main floor   1,458 sq. ft.
Lower floor   1,413 sq. ft.

PLAN P-6584-4A
WITHOUT BASEMENT

Total living area: 1,415 sq. ft.
(Not counting garage)

Blueprint Price Code A

Plans P-6584-4A & 4D

TO ORDER THIS BLUEPRINT,
CALL TOLL-FREE 1-800-547-5570

PRICES AND DETAILS
ON PAGES 12-15   23

All-Season Chalet

A guided tour from the front entry of this home takes you into the central hallway that serves as the hub of traffic to the main floor level. From here, convenience extends in every direction and each room is connected

in a step-saving manner. Besides the master bedroom with twin closets, a full bathroom with stall shower is placed adjacent to a common wall that also serves the laundry equipment.

The living room and dining area are connected to allow for the expandable use of the dining table should the need arise for additional seating. The kitchen is open ended onto the dining area and has all the modern conveniences and built-in details.

A raised deck flanks the gable end of the living zone and extends outward for a distance of 8'.

A full basement is reached via a stairway connecting with the central hallway. The basement provides ample storage plus room for the central heating system. Another interesting feature is the garage placed under the home where the owner may not only store his automobile but such things as a boat and trailer and other sporting equipment.

First floor:	1,008 sq. ft.
Second floor:	462 sq. ft.
Total living area:	1,470 sq. ft.
(Not counting basement or garage)	

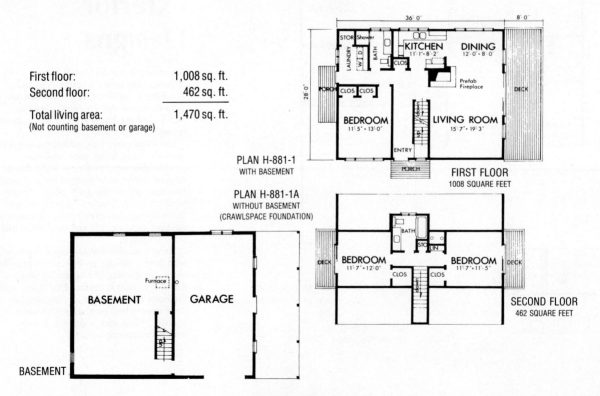

PLAN H-881-1
WITH BASEMENT

PLAN H-881-1A
WITHOUT BASEMENT
(CRAWLSPACE FOUNDATION)

FIRST FLOOR
1008 SQUARE FEET

SECOND FLOOR
462 SQUARE FEET

BASEMENT

Blueprint Price Code A

Plans H-881-1 & -1A

TO ORDER THIS BLUEPRINT,
CALL TOLL-FREE 1-800-547-5570

PRICES AND DETAILS
ON PAGES 12-15

Eye-Catching Prow-Shaped Chalet

- Steep pitched roof lines and wide cornices give this chalet a distinct alpine appearance.
- Prowed shape, large windows, and 10' deck provide view and enhancement of indoor/outdoor living.
- Functional division of living and sleeping areas by hallway and first floor full bath.

- Laundry facilities conveniently located near bedroom wing.
- U-shaped kitchen and spacious dining/living areas make the main floor perfect for entertaining.

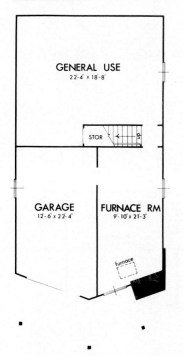

BASEMENT

GENERAL USE
22'-4" x 18'-8"

STOR

GARAGE
12'-6" x 22'-4"

FURNACE RM
9'-10" x 21'-3"

furnace

MAIN FLOOR

23'-8"

4'-0"

BEDROOM
8'-10" x 11'-0"

BEDROOM
10'-0" x 13'-10"

CLOSET
5'-0"

W D

CLOSET
4'-0"

CLOSET
4'-0"

LIN

BATH

44'-0"

DW Ref
KITCHEN
7'-1" x 8'-3"

R/O

DINING LIVING
22'-7" x 22'-10"

10'-0"

UPPER FLOOR

BEDROOM
12'-11" x 13'-10"

STORAGE

STORAGE

Shower

LIN

CLOSET
7'-9"

BATH

down

STORAGE

BALCONY
12'-10" x 9'-7"

STORAGE

Handrail

Plans H-886-3 & -3A

Bedrooms: 3	Baths: 2

Space:	
Upper floor:	486 sq. ft.
Main floor:	994 sq. ft.

Total without basement:	1,480 sq. ft.
Basement:	approx. 715 sq. ft.
Garage:	279 sq. ft.

Exterior Wall Framing:	2x6

Foundation options:
Daylight basement (Plan H-886-3).
Crawlspace (Plan H-886-3A).
(Foundation & framing conversion diagram available — see order form.)

Blueprint Price Code:	A

Unique and Dramatic

- This home's unique interior and dramatic exterior make it perfect for a sloping, scenic lot.
- An expansive and impressive Great Room, warmed by a woodstove, flows into an island kitchen that's completely open in design.
- The passive-solar sun room is designed to collect and store heat from the sun, while providing a good view of the surroundings.
- Upstairs, you'll see a glamorous, skylighted master suite with a private bath and a huge walk-in closet.
- A skylighted hall bath serves the bright second bedroom.
- The daylight basement adds a sunny sitting room, a third bedroom and a large recreation room.

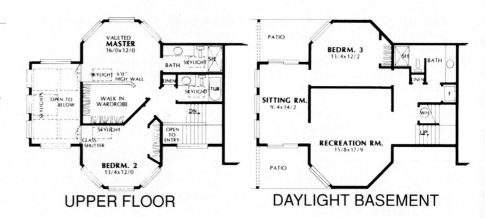

UPPER FLOOR   DAYLIGHT BASEMENT

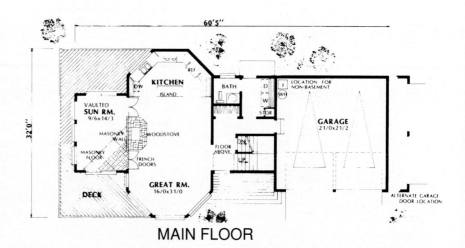

MAIN FLOOR

Plans P-536-2A & -2D

Bedrooms: 2+	Baths: 2½-3½
Living Area:	
Upper floor	642 sq. ft.
Main floor	863 sq. ft.
Daylight basement	863 sq. ft.
Total Living Area:	**1,505/2,368 sq. ft.**
Garage	445 sq. ft.
Exterior Wall Framing:	2x6
Foundation Options:	**Plan #**
Daylight basement	P-536-2D
Crawlspace	P-536-2A

(All plans can be built with your choice of foundation and framing. A generic conversion diagram is available. See order form.)

BLUEPRINT PRICE CODE:	**B/C**

Photo courtesy of Piercy & Barclay Designers

Quality Design for a Narrow, Sloping Lot

Multi-pitched rooflines, custom window treatments and beveled board siding add a distinctive facade to this two-level home of only 1,516 sq. ft. Its slim 34′ width allows it to fit nicely on a narrow lot while offering ample indoor and outdoor living areas.

The enclosed entry courtyard is a pleasant area for al fresco breakfasts or spill-over entertaining. The wide, high-ceilinged entry hall opens directly into the sweeping Great Room and dining area. This room is warmed by a large fireplace and has a door to a large wood deck. Also off the entry hall is the morning room with a vaulted ceiling and a matching arched window overlooking the courtyard. A half-bath and utility room is on the other side of the entry.

An open-railed stairway leads from the entry to the bedrooms on the second level. The master suite has a high dormer with peaked windows, a walk-in closet and a private bathroom. The larger of the other bedrooms could be used as a den, and it also overlooks the morning room and entry hall. If additional room is required, this plan is available with a daylight basement.

**NOTE: The above photographed home may have been modified by the homeowner. Please refer to floor plan and/or drawn elevation shown for actual blueprint details.

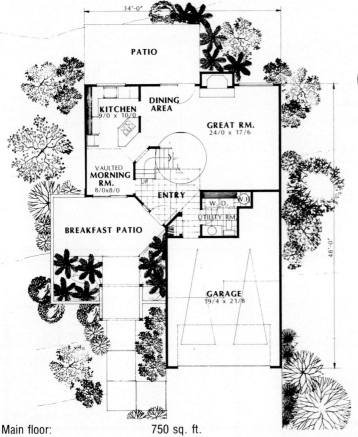

PLAN P-6563-4A
WITHOUT BASEMENT

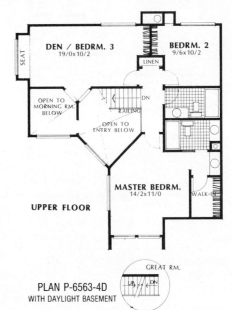

UPPER FLOOR

PLAN P-6563-4D
WITH DAYLIGHT BASEMENT

Main floor:	750 sq. ft.
Upper floor:	766 sq. ft.
Total living area:	1,516 sq. ft.
Basement level:	809 sq. ft.

Blueprint Price Code B

Plans P-6563-4A & -4D

Split-Level Vacation Home

By opting for a smaller than average lot, a family choosing a split-level design such as this will benefit from the space-savings and their attending cost savings. Notice, for example, the overall width of 68' includes the projection of the double-sized garage on one side and the location of a sun deck that flanks the sliding doors of the den. Since most leisure home building sites have some slope, the three-level design of this dwelling will fit many situations.

This plan is an example of a design for seclusion, with all the primary living areas oriented to the rear of the home. Notice how the living room, dining area and U-shaped kitchen face the rear wall and have access to the spacious raised deck. The recreation room at the basement level and a third bedroom also face the rear garden.

The main floor area of 1,200 sq. ft. is actually on two elevations. The entry hall is on the same level as the adjacent den and bedroom with bath. A dramatic effect is achieved by the placement of the living room four steps below. The soaring height

of the vaulted ceiling, with exposed beams extending from the central ridge to the exterior wall, adds to the feeling of openness to the outdoors, framed by the window wall and sliding glass doors.

The kitchen itself is convenient to both the dining area and informal portions of the home, and has a work-saving U-shaped design.

The spacious master bedroom suite offers the unencumbered view of an eagle's nest, and also boasts a walk-in

closet and private bath with shower stall. Another added luxury is the 4' cantilevered sun deck, accessible through sliding glass doors. This raised portion of the home that includes the master bedroom contains 320 additional sq. ft.

Other features which should be pointed out include the two massive fireplaces. One is located in the recreation room and the other is the focal point of the end wall of the living room. A third full bath is also placed at the basement level.

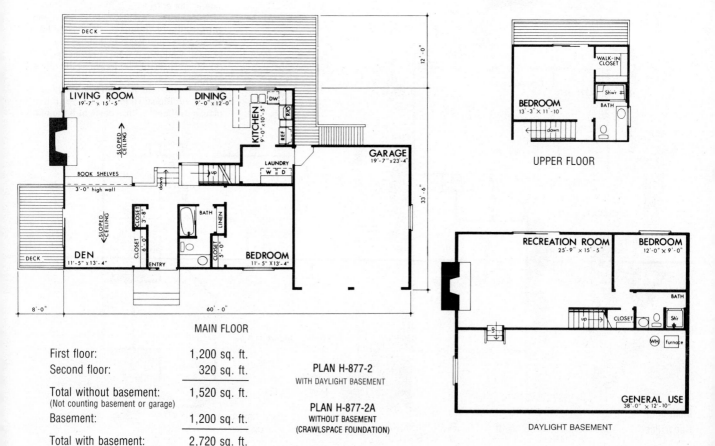

MAIN FLOOR

First floor:	1,200 sq. ft.
Second floor:	320 sq. ft.
Total without basement: (Not counting basement or garage)	1,520 sq. ft.
Basement:	1,200 sq. ft.
Total with basement:	2,720 sq. ft.

PLAN H-877-2
WITH DAYLIGHT BASEMENT

PLAN H-877-2A
WITHOUT BASEMENT
(CRAWLSPACE FOUNDATION)

UPPER FLOOR

DAYLIGHT BASEMENT

Blueprint Price Code D With Basement
Blueprint Price Code B Without Basement

Plans H-877-2 & -2A

TO ORDER THIS BLUEPRINT,
CALL TOLL-FREE 1-800-547-5570

PRICES AND DETAILS
ON PAGES 12-15

Vaulted Living Room Featured

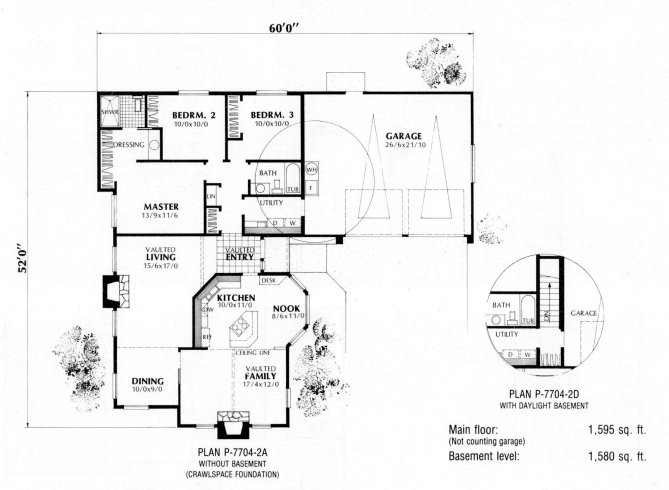

60'0"

52'0"

SHWR
DRESSING

BEDRM. 2
10/0x10/0

BEDRM. 3
10/0x10/0

GARAGE
26/6x21/10

MASTER
13/9x11/6

BATH

WH

TUB

F

LIN

UTILITY

D   W

VAULTED
LIVING
15/6x17/0

VAULTED
ENTRY

DESK

KITCHEN
10/0x11/0

NOOK
8/6x11/0

DW

REF

CEILING LINE

DINING
10/0x9/0

VAULTED
FAMILY
17/4x12/0

PLAN P-7704-2A
WITHOUT BASEMENT
(CRAWLSPACE FOUNDATION)

Total living area: 1,535 sq. ft.
(Not counting garage)

BATH

TUB

UTILITY

GARAGE

D   W

PLAN P-7704-2D
WITH DAYLIGHT BASEMENT

Main floor: 1,595 sq. ft.
(Not counting garage)
Basement level: 1,580 sq. ft.

Blueprint Price Code B

Economical Design

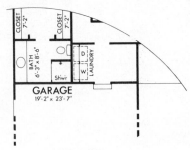

FRONT VIEW

MAIN FLOOR
PLAN H-868-1A
WITHOUT BASEMENT

GARAGE
19'-2" × 23'-7"

- Uninterrupted glass and a full, rear deck afford a sweeping view of the outdoors.
- Rear orientation provides a seclusion from street and neighbors.

- Open, flexible family living areas allow for efficient traffic flow.
- Optional daylight basement plan offers recreation room, additional bedroom and third bath.

Plans H-868-1 & -1A	
Bedrooms: 3-4	**Baths:** 2-3

Space:	
Main floor:	1,525 sq. ft.

Total living area:	1,525 sq. ft.
Basement:	1,420 sq. ft.
Garage:	426 sq. ft.

Exterior Wall Framing:	2x4

Foundation options:
Daylight basement (Plan H-868-1).
Crawlspace (Plan H-868-1A).
(Foundation & framing conversion diagram available — see order form.)

Blueprint Price Code:
Without basement	B
With basement	D

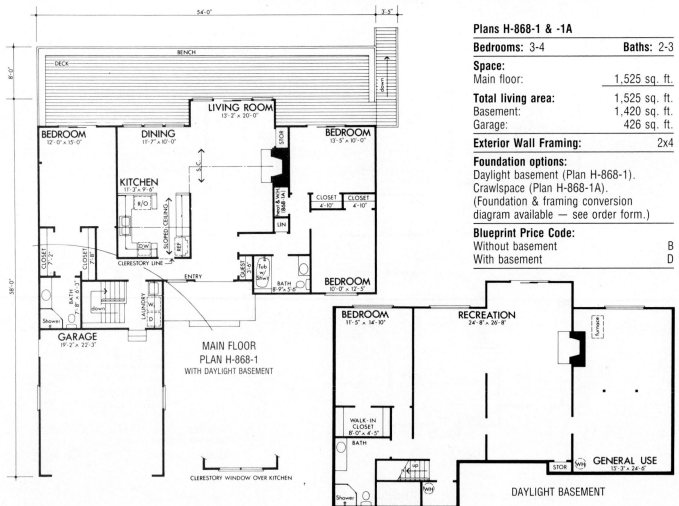

MAIN FLOOR
PLAN H-868-1
WITH DAYLIGHT BASEMENT

CLERESTORY WINDOW OVER KITCHEN

DAYLIGHT BASEMENT

TO ORDER THIS BLUEPRINT,
CALL TOLL-FREE 1-800-547-5570

Plans H-868-1 & -1A

**PRICES AND DETAILS
ON PAGES 12-15**

Rustic Home Offers Comfort, Economy

- Rustic and compact, this home offers economy of construction and good looks.
- The homey front porch, multi-paned windows, shutters and horizontal siding combine to create a rustic exterior.
- An L-shaped kitchen is open to the dining room and also to the living room to create a Great Room feel to the floor plan.
- The living room includes a raised-hearth fireplace.
- The main-floor master suite features a large walk-in closet and a double vanity in the master bath.
- An open two-story-high foyer leads to the second floor, which includes two bedrooms with walk-in closets and a full bath with two linen closets.

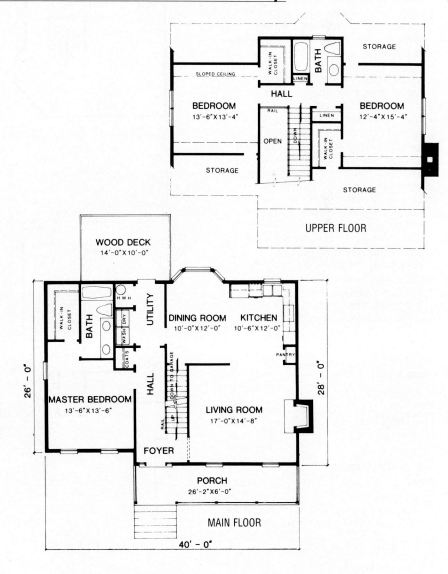

Plan C-8339

Bedrooms: 3	Baths: 2
Space:	
Upper floor	660 sq. ft.
Main floor	1,100 sq. ft.
Total Living Area	**1,760 sq. ft.**
Basement	approx. 1,100 sq. ft.
Garage	Included in basement
Exterior Wall Framing	2x4

Foundation options:

Daylight Basement
(Foundation & framing conversion diagram available—see order form.)

Blueprint Price Code	**B**

Instant Impact

- Bold rooflines, interesting angles and unusual window treatments give this stylish home lots of impact.
- Inside, high ceilings and an open floor plan maximize the home's square footage. At only 28 ft. wide, the home also is ideal for a narrow lot.
- A covered deck leads to the main entry, which features a sidelighted door, angled glass walls and a view of the striking open staircase.
- The Great Room is stunning, with its vaulted ceiling, energy-efficient woodstove and access to a large deck.
- A flat ceiling distinguishes the dining area, which shares an angled snack bar/cooktop with the step-saving kitchen. A laundry/mudroom is nearby.
- Upstairs, the master suite offers a sloped ceiling and a clerestory window. A walk-through closet leads to the private bath, which is enhanced by a skylighted, sloped ceiling.
- Linen and storage closets line the hallway leading to the smaller bedrooms, one of which has a sloped ceiling and double closets.

Plans H-1427-3A & -3B

Bedrooms: 3	Baths: 2½
Living Area:	
Upper floor	880 sq. ft.
Main floor	810 sq. ft.
Total Living Area:	**1,690 sq. ft.**
Daylight basement	810 sq. ft.
Garage	409 sq. ft.
Exterior Wall Framing:	2x4
Foundation Options:	**Plan #**
Daylight basement	H-1427-3B
Crawlspace	H-1427-3A
(All plans can be built with your choice of foundation and framing. A generic conversion diagram is available. See order form.)	
BLUEPRINT PRICE CODE:	**B**

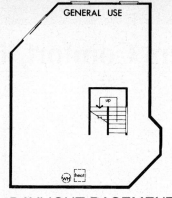

DAYLIGHT BASEMENT

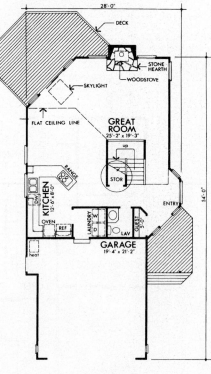

MAIN FLOOR

UPPER FLOOR

STAIRWAY AREA IN CRAWLSPACE VERSION

A-Frame Offered in Three Versions

Why is the A-frame so popular? One reason may be that the spirit of the A-frame is a complete opposite of most of our full time box houses, and its soaring, free, unfettered lines carry with it an unusual appeal.

Its simplicity is another reason for its popularity.

To make this home all the more desirable, we have designed three ways for you to build it. A plan with a standard basement and no garage is Plan H-726-3. A plan without any basement whatsoever is Plan H-726-3A. If you would like a daylight basement and a garage you should then order Plan H-726-3B.

First floor:	720 sq. ft.
Second floor:	250 sq. ft.
Total living area:	970 sq. ft.
(Not counting basement or garage)	

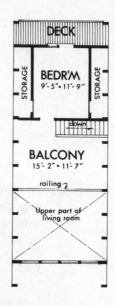

FIRST FLOOR
LIVING AREA — 720 SQ. FT.
FLOORED AREA — 912 SQ. FT.

26'-0"
DECK
wash dry
BATH
Shwr
KITCHEN 9'-9" x 8'-0"
refr
CLOSET
up
rge
Stairs down for Plan 726-3 Closet for Plan 726-3A
breakfast
STORAGE
BEDROOM 9'-0" x 10'-0"
STORAGE
36'-0"
52'-6"
balcony line above
prefab fireplace
LIVING ROOM 19'-2" x 20'-7"
DECK

SECOND FLOOR
LIVING AREA — 250 SQ. FT.
FLOORED AREA — 370 SQ. FT.

DECK
STORAGE
BEDR'M 9'-5" x 11'-9"
STORAGE
down
BALCONY 15'-2" x 11'-7"
railing
Upper part of living room

PLAN H-726-3
WITH STANDARD BASEMENT (NO GARAGE)

PLAN H-726-3A
WITHOUT BASEMENT (CRAWLSPACE FOUNDATION)

PLAN H-726-3B
WITH DAYLIGHT BASEMENT & GARAGE

wh
furnace
up
GARAGE 12'-2" x 35'-0"
BASEMENT 12'-2" x 35'-0"
THIS AREA IS GARAGE ON PLAN H-726-3B AND ADD'L BASEMENT SPACE ON PLAN H-726-3

PLAN H-726-3B BASEMENT

Casual Flexibility

- This beautifully designed vacation or year-round home is spacious and flexible.
- The interior is brightened by an abundance of windows.
- The open, vaulted living room boasts a central fireplace that makes a great conversation place or a cozy spot for spending cold winter evenings.
- The kitchen opens to the dining room and the scenery beyond through the dramatic window wall with half-round transom.
- The sleeping room and loft upstairs can easily accommodate several guests or could be used as multi-purpose space.

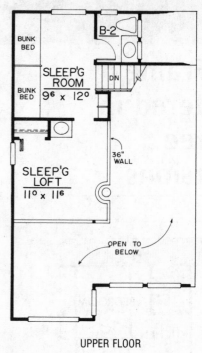

UPPER FLOOR

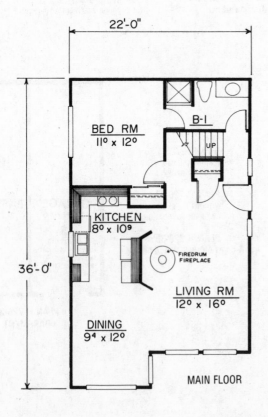

MAIN FLOOR

Plan I-1032-A

Bedrooms: 2-3	**Baths:** 1½
Living Area:	
Upper floor	288 sq. ft.
Main floor	744 sq. ft.
Total Living Area:	**1,032 sq. ft.**
Exterior Wall Framing:	2x6

Foundation Options:

Crawlspace
(Typical foundation & framing conversion diagram available—see order form.)

BLUEPRINT PRICE CODE: A

High Ceilings, Large Spaces!

- This affordable home is filled with large spaces that are further enhanced by high ceilings and lots of windows.
- The charming exterior is complemented by a combination of lap siding and brick, a covered front porch with a column and a sidelighted entry door.
- Inside, the first area to come into view is the huge family room, which features a vaulted ceiling and a space-saving corner fireplace. Sliding glass doors open up the room to the backyard.

- The family room flows into the spacious breakfast room and kitchen. A picture window or an optional bay window brightens the breakfast room, while the kitchen offers a window above the sink and a convenient laundry closet that hides the clutter.
- The master suite leaves out nothing. A tray ceiling in the sleeping area gives way to the vaulted master bath, which is accented with a plant shelf above the entrance. A roomy walk-in closet is also included. The two smaller bedrooms share a hall bath.
- The optional basement doubles the home's size, providing ample expansion space.

Plan FB-1070	
Bedrooms: 3	**Baths:** 2
Living Area:	
Main floor	1,070 sq. ft.
Total Living Area:	**1,070 sq. ft.**
Daylight basement	1,070 sq. ft.
Garage	484 sq. ft.
Exterior Wall Framing:	2x4

Foundation Options:
Daylight basement
Crawlspace
Slab
(All plans can be built with your choice of foundation and framing. A generic conversion diagram is available. See order form.)

BLUEPRINT PRICE CODE:	A

MAIN FLOOR

48'-0"

36'-0"

OPT. BAY WINDOW

Kitchen
D.
D.W.
REF.
W.
Stor.

Breakfast

OPT. STAIRS TO BSMT.

Vaulted Family Room
13³x20¹⁰

VAULT VAULT VAULT

FPL.

Garage

Covered Porch

COATS

Bedroom 2
10'x10⁰

TUB
Vaulted M. Bath
W.i.c.

PLANT SHELF

TRAY CLG.

Master Suite
14⁶x12⁰

W.H.

LIN.

Bedroom 3
11'x10⁰

Extra-Special Ranch-Style

- Repeating gables, wood siding and brick adorn the exterior of this ranch-style home, which offers numerous extras inside.
- The entry leads directly into the vaulted family room, an ideal entertainment area accented by a corner fireplace and a French door to the backyard.
- A serving bar joins the family room to the efficient kitchen, with its walk-in pantry, ample counter space and sunny breakfast room.
- The luxurious master suite boasts a tray ceiling, a large bank of windows and a walk-in closet. The private master bath features a garden tub.
- Two additional bedrooms, one with a vaulted ceiling, share another full bath.
- A two-car garage provides convenient access to the kitchen and laundry area.

Plan FB-1104

Bedrooms: 3	Baths: 2
Living Area:	
Main floor	1,104 sq. ft.
Total Living Area:	**1,104 sq. ft.**
Daylight basement	1,104 sq. ft.
Garage	400 sq. ft.
Exterior Wall Framing:	2x4

Foundation Options:
Daylight basement
Crawlspace
(Typical foundation & framing conversion diagram available—see order form.)

BLUEPRINT PRICE CODE: A

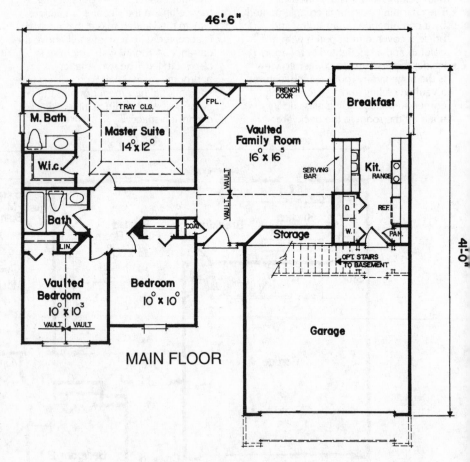

46'-6"

41'-0"

M. Bath

TRAY CLG.

Master Suite
14⁰ x 12⁰

W.i.c

Bath

LIN.

Vaulted
Bedroom
10⁰ x 10³

VAULT VAULT

Bedroom
10⁰ x 10⁰

FPL.

FRENCH
DOOR

Vaulted
Family Room
16⁰ x 16⁵

VAULT VAULT

COAT

SERVING
BAR

Breakfast

Kit.
RANGE

REF.

D.

W.

PAN.

Storage

OPT. STAIRS
TO BASEMENT

Garage

MAIN FLOOR

The Simple & Economical Housing Solution

- This compact plan could serve as a second home or a primary residence for a small family.
- Spacious Great Room features woodstove and a large adjoining deck.
- Efficent kitchen is close to storage and laundry area.
- Large, overlooking loft offers infinite possibilities, such as extra sleeping quarters, a home office, art studio, or recreation room.
- Clerestory window arrangement and sloped-ceilings top the loft for added light.

Plan H-963-2A

Bedrooms: 1	Baths: 1
Space:	
Loft:	432 sq. ft.
Main floor:	728 sq. ft.
Total living area:	**1,160 sq. ft.**
Lower level/garage:	728 sq. ft.
Exterior Wall Framing:	2x4

Foundation options:
Slab.
(Foundation & framing conversion diagram available — see order form.)

Blueprint Price Code:	A

LOFT
25'-3" x 16'-2"

←SLOPED CEILING→

down → RAILING   S. C.

CLERESTORY LINE   S. C.

OPEN TO GREAT ROOM

SKYLIGHTS →

LOFT

CLERESTORY WINDOWS OVER LOFT AND STAIRS

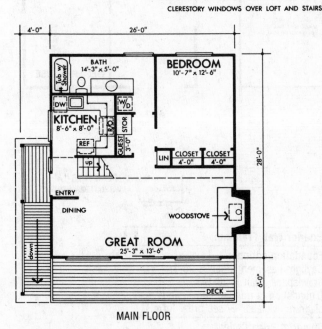

4'-0"   26'-0"

BATH
14'-3" x 5'-0"

BEDROOM
10'-7" x 12'-6"

Tub w/ Shower

DW

KITCHEN
8'-6" x 8'-0"

W/D

GUEST STOR 3'-0"

REF

UP

LIN   CLOSET 4'-0"   CLOSET 4'-0"

28'-0"

ENTRY

DINING

WOODSTOVE →

down

GREAT ROOM
25'-3" x 13'-6"

6'-0"

DECK

MAIN FLOOR

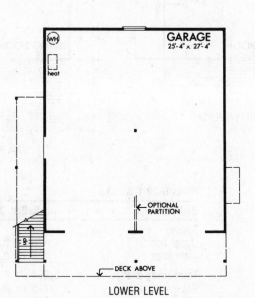

WH

heat

GARAGE
25'-4" x 27'-4"

OPTIONAL PARTITION

DECK ABOVE

LOWER LEVEL

Simple and Economical Chalet

- This home away from home is relatively simple to construct; it is also an enjoyable reason to spend your weekends in the mountains or at the beach.
- The main level is largely devoted to open living space, other than the kitchen and master bedroom, which could also be used as a study or hobby room.
- Second-floor bedrooms are larger and share a full bath and large storage areas.

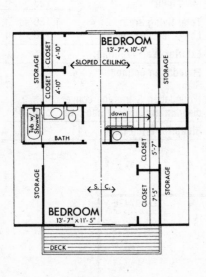

UPPER FLOOR

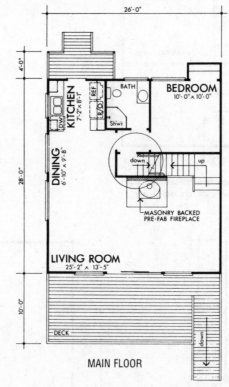

MAIN FLOOR

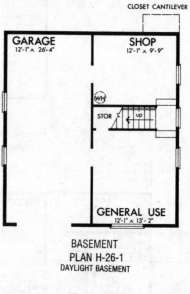

BASEMENT
PLAN H-26-1
DAYLIGHT BASEMENT

PLAN H-26-1A
WITHOUT BASEMENT

Plans H-26-1 & -1A

Bedrooms: 3	Baths: 2

Space:	
Upper floor:	476 sq. ft.
Main floor:	728 sq. ft.
Total living area:	**1,204 sq. ft.**
Basement:	410 sq. ft.
Garage:	318 sq. ft.

Exterior Wall Framing:	2x4

Foundation options:
Daylight basement (Plan H-26-1).
Crawlspace (Plan H-26-1A).
(Foundation & framing conversion diagram available — see order form.)

Blueprint Price Code:	A

Plans H-26-1 & -1A

PRICES AND DETAILS
ON PAGES 12-15

Eye-Catching Details

- This handsome home features an eye-catching exterior and an exciting floor plan that maximizes square footage.
- A covered porch leads into a vaulted foyer with an angled coat closet. Straight ahead, the vaulted Great Room combines with the dining room and kitchen to create one huge, well-integrated living and entertaining area.
- The Great Room includes a fireplace and access to the backyard. The vaulted, galley-style kitchen is bordered by the vaulted dining room on one side and a breakfast area with a laundry closet on the other.
- The isolated master suite boasts a tray ceiling and a vaulted bath with a garden tub, a separate shower, a vanity with knee space and a walk-in closet.
- The two remaining bedrooms are located on the opposite side of the home and share a full bath. A plant shelf is an attention-getting detail found here.

Plan FB-1289

Bedrooms: 3	Baths: 2
Living Area:	
Main floor	1,289 sq. ft.
Total Living Area:	**1,289 sq. ft.**
Daylight basement	1,289 sq. ft.
Garage	430 sq. ft.
Exterior Wall Framing:	2x4

Foundation Options:
Daylight basement
Crawlspace
Slab
(Typical foundation & framing conversion diagram available – see order form.)

BLUEPRINT PRICE CODE: A

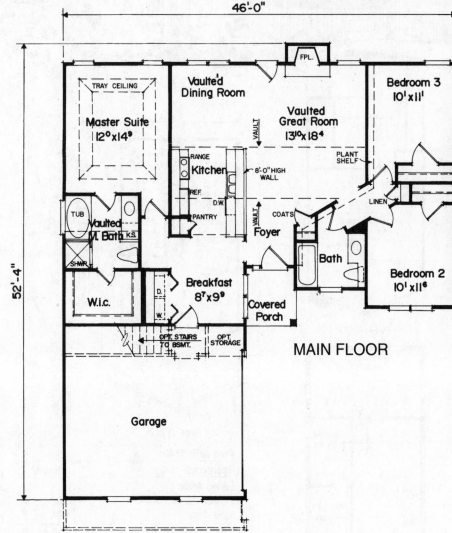

MAIN FLOOR

A Chalet for Today

- This new, up-to-date chalet design is ideal for recreational living, whether year-round or part-time. The home's rustic appeal and soaring windows are ideally suited to scenic sites.
- The living and dining rooms are combined to take advantage of the dramatic cathedral ceiling, the view through the spectacular windows and the rugged stone fireplace.
- A quaint balcony adds to the warm country feeling of the living area, which is further expanded by a wrap-around deck. The open, peninsula kitchen includes a breakfast bar that connects it to the living area.
- The first-floor study or den is an added feature rarely found in a home of this size and style.
- A convenient main-floor laundry is adjacent to two bedrooms and a full bath.
- The master bedroom retreat takes up the entire second floor. Cathedral ceilings, sweeping views from the balcony and a private bath with spa tub are highlights here.
- The optional basement plan calls for a tuck-under garage, a large family room, plus utility and storage space.

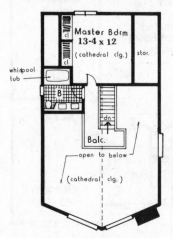

UPPER FLOOR

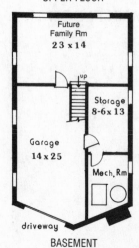

BASEMENT

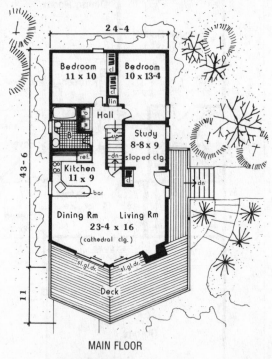

MAIN FLOOR

Plan AHP-9340

Bedrooms: 3-4	Baths: 2
Living Area:	
Upper floor	332 sq. ft.
Main floor	974 sq. ft.
Total Living Area:	**1,306 sq. ft.**
Basement	624 sq. ft.
Garage	350 sq. ft.
Exterior Wall Framing:	2x4 or 2x6

Foundation Options:

Daylight basement
Standard basement
Crawlspace
Slab
(Typical foundation & framing conversion diagram available—see order form.)

BLUEPRINT PRICE CODE: A

Windowed Great Room

- This attractive, open design can function as a cabin, mountain retreat or permanent residence.
- The main level of the home is entered via a split-landing, wraparound deck.
- The kitchen and Great Room merge to form a large family activity area; an open balcony loft above offers an elevated view of the massive front window wall.
- Two quiet main-floor bedrooms share a hall bath.
- A third sleeping room upstairs could be split into two smaller bedrooms.

Plan I-1354-B

Bedrooms: 2+	Baths: 2
Living Area:	
Upper floor	366 sq. ft.
Main floor	988 sq. ft.
Total Living Area:	**1,354 sq. ft.**
Daylight basement	658 sq. ft.
Tuck-under garage	260 sq. ft.
Exterior Wall Framing:	2x6

Foundation Options:

Daylight basement

(All plans can be built with your choice of foundation and framing. A generic conversion diagram is available. See order form.)

BLUEPRINT PRICE CODE:	A

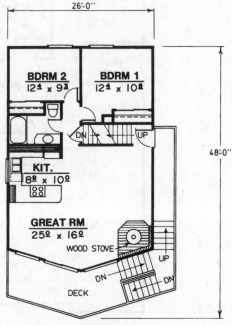

MAIN FLOOR

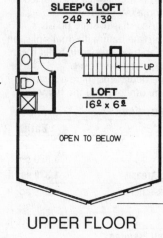

UPPER FLOOR

Distinctive Inside and Out

- A decorative columned entry, shuttered windows and a facade of stucco and stone offer a distinct look to this economical one-story home.
- The focal point of the interior is the huge, central family room. The room is enhanced with a dramatic corner fireplace, a vaulted ceiling and a neat serving bar that extends from the kitchen and includes a wet bar.
- A decorative plant shelf adorns the entrance to the adjoining breakfast room, which features a lovely bay window. The kitchen offers a pantry and a pass-through to the serving bar.
- The formal dining room is easy to reach from both the kitchen and the family room, and is highlighted by a raised ceiling and a tall window.
- The secluded master suite boasts a vaulted private bath with dual sinks, an oval garden tub, a separate toilet room and a large walk-in closet.
- Two more bedrooms share a second bath at the other end of the home.

Plan FB-5001-SAVA

Bedrooms: 3	Baths: 2
Living Area:	
Main floor	1,379 sq. ft.
Total Living Area:	**1,379 sq. ft.**
Daylight basement	1,379 sq. ft.
Garage	250 sq. ft.
Storage	14 sq. ft.
Exterior Wall Framing:	2x4

Foundation Options:
Daylight basement
Crawlspace
Slab
(Typical foundation & framing conversion diagram available—see order form.)

BLUEPRINT PRICE CODE: A

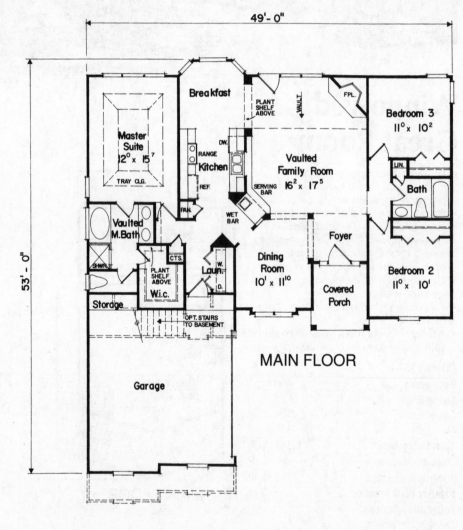

MAIN FLOOR

TO ORDER THIS BLUEPRINT, CALL TOLL-FREE 1-800-547-5570

Plan FB-5001-SAVA

PRICES AND DETAILS ON PAGES 12-15

Sunken Living Room Centers on Fireplace

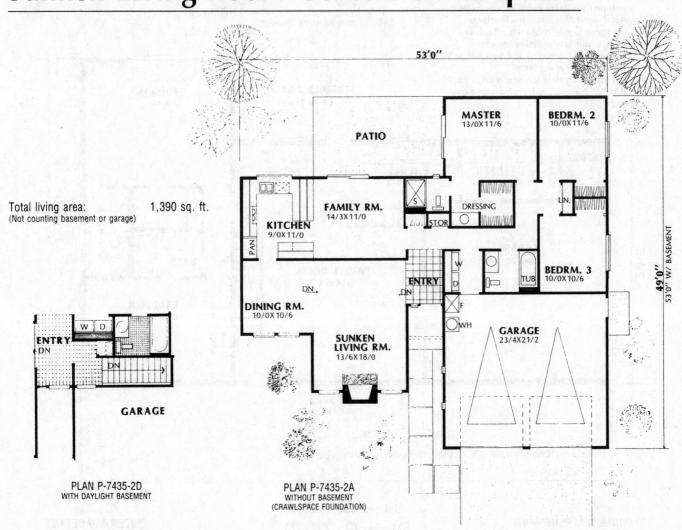

Total living area: 1,390 sq. ft.
(Not counting basement or garage)

53'0"

49'0"
53'0" W/ BASEMENT

MASTER
13/0X11/6

BEDRM. 2
10/0X11/6

PATIO

FAMILY RM.
14/3X11/0

KITCHEN
9/0X11/0

PAN

S

DRESSING

STOR

LIN.

W
D

BEDRM. 3
10/0X10/6

TUB

ENTRY

DN

F

WH

DINING RM.
10/0X10/6

DN

GARAGE
23/4X21/2

SUNKEN LIVING RM.
13/6X18/0

ENTRY
DN

W   D

DN

GARAGE

PLAN P-7435-2D
WITH DAYLIGHT BASEMENT

PLAN P-7435-2A
WITHOUT BASEMENT
(CRAWLSPACE FOUNDATION)

Blueprint Price Code A

Two-Bedroom Country Cottage

A covered veranda and screened rear porch provide extra living spaces in this modest-sized ranch design. The large all-purpose family room has a built-in fireplace and bright dining corner.

Two roomy bedrooms and two full baths make up the sleeping wing.

An efficient galley kitchen is adjacent to utility room (with pantry) and side-entry garage.

Total living area: 1,420 sq. ft.
(Not counting basement or garage)

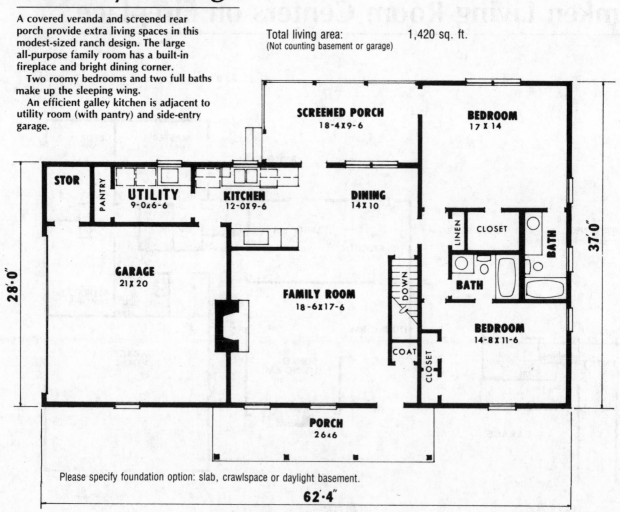

STOR

PANTRY

UTILITY 9-0x6-6

KITCHEN 12-0x9-6

SCREENED PORCH 18-4x9-6

BEDROOM 17 X 14

DINING 14x10

LINEN

CLOSET

BATH

BATH

GARAGE 21x20

FAMILY ROOM 18-6x17-6

DOWN

BEDROOM 14-8x11-6

COAT

CLOSET

PORCH 26x6

28'-0"

37'-0"

62'-4"

Please specify foundation option: slab, crawlspace or daylight basement.

Blueprint Price Code A
Plan C-7520

PRICES AND DETAILS ON PAGES 12-15

Split-Foyer Has Room for Expansion

- This popular split-foyer design provides space for expansion with the inclusion of an unfinished family room in the lower level. The garage and laundry room also share the lower level.
- A vaulted ceiling highlights both the living room and the dining room; the living room also offers a warming fireplace and a view to the backyard deck, which is accessible through the dining room.
- The roomy kitchen features an angled countertop, a pantry and an eat-in kitchen.
- Secluded to the rear, the spacious master suite features two closets, a corner window and a generous bath with a step-up tub and separate shower.
- The two additional bedrooms share a second full bath.

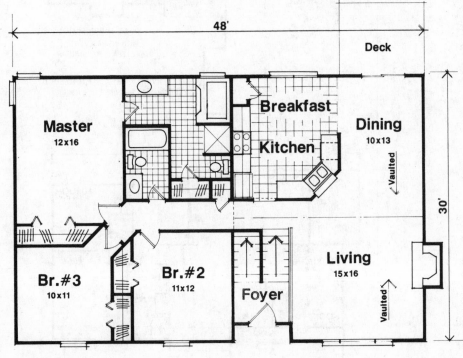

Plan APS-1410

Bedrooms: 3	Baths: 2

Living Area:

Main floor	1,428 sq. ft.

Total Living Area:	**1,428 sq. ft.**

Daylight basement	458 sq. ft.
Garage	480 sq. ft.

Exterior Wall Framing: 2x4

Foundation Options:

Daylight basement

(Typical foundation & framing conversion diagram available—see order form.)

BLUEPRINT PRICE CODE: A

Options for Sloping or Flat Lots

With less than 1,450 square feet of living area on the main floor, this contemporary three-bedroom home stretches available space to make way for many conveniences.

The plan also features flexibility and can be adapted to a flat or a sloping lot. Plan 2088-1C is designed without a basement, on a crawlspace foundation, and works well for relatively flat lots. Plan 2088-1D has a lower level that is well suited for lots with front-to-rear slopes. The patio becomes a deck, and sliding glass doors in the basement open to the backyard. The basement also includes a rec room and plenty of space for expansion.

Special touches inside and out set this house apart from others. The roof of the street-facing garage is extended on one side to create a "bridge" from which to hang a welcoming light or plants. The irregular shape of the garage creates a storage nook on the inside and a sheltered alcove outside the front entry. Further interest is added by the deep overhang that shields the entry, the vertical trim around doors and windows, and the bumped-out window.

Inside, a 6-ft.-high divider wall screens the dining room from the entry. In the non-basement version, the dining room has a built-in china hutch, and a laundry room is between the garage and the kitchen. In the basement version, the kitchen is right off the garage.

The large living room has a window wall facing the backyard, and a sliding glass door opens onto either a concrete patio or a wood deck. The pre-fab fireplace is framed by shelves.

The main bath is off the two smaller bedrooms, while the master bedroom has its own bath with a corner shower. Double closets and a window seat make this room even more functional and cozy.

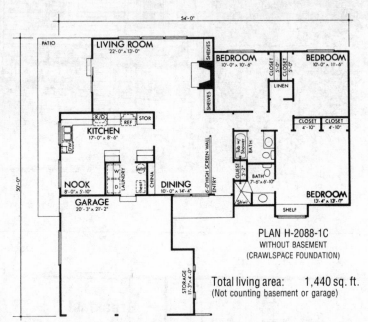

PLAN H-2088-1C
WITHOUT BASEMENT
(CRAWLSPACE FOUNDATION)

Total living area: 1,440 sq. ft.
(Not counting basement or garage)

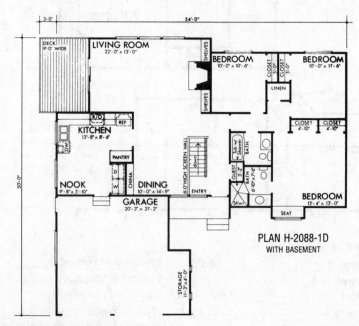

PLAN H-2088-1D
WITH BASEMENT

Blueprint Price Code A

TO ORDER THIS BLUEPRINT, CALL TOLL-FREE 1-800-547-5570

Plans H-2088-1C & -1D

PRICES AND DETAILS ON PAGES 12-15

Charming Three-Bedroom

- A covered front porch and shuttered windows lend an authentic charm to this two-story home.
- The main-floor living areas are oriented around stairways that access the basement and the upper floor. The spacious family room shows off a dramatic centered fireplace and an array of surrounding windows. A French door opens to the backyard.
- The nice-sized kitchen is nestled between the sunny vaulted breakfast room and the formal dining room.
- A convenient main-floor laundry closet is neatly positioned off the breakfast room and near the garage entrance.
- The upper floor houses three bedrooms, including a large master bedroom with a tray ceiling, a huge walk-in closet and a private vaulted bath with an oval tub.

Plan FB-5013-LYNW

Bedrooms: 3	Baths: 2½
Living Area:	
Upper floor	681 sq. ft.
Main floor	771 sq. ft.
Total Living Area:	**1,452 sq. ft.**
Daylight basement	771 sq. ft.
Garage	420 sq. ft.
Storage	20 sq. ft.
Exterior Wall Framing:	2x4

Foundation Options:

Daylight basement
(Typical foundation & framing conversion diagram available—see order form.)

BLUEPRINT PRICE CODE: A

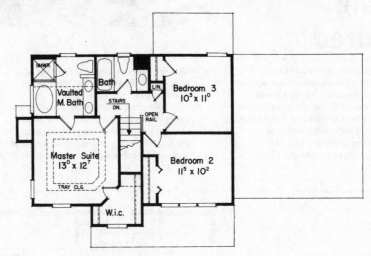

UPPER FLOOR

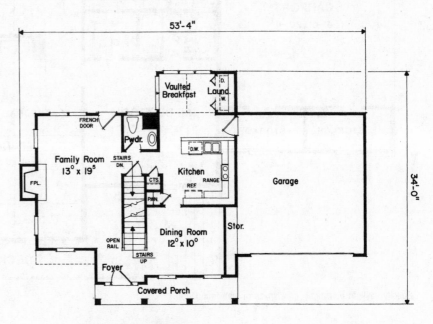

MAIN FLOOR

Cathedral Ceiling Featured

The open floor plan of this modified A-Frame design virtually eliminates wasted hall space. The centrally located Great Room features a 15'4" cathedral ceiling with exposed wood beams and large areas of fixed glass on both front and rear. Living and dining areas are visually separated by a massive stone fireplace.

The isolated master suite features a walk-in closet and sliding glass doors opening onto the front deck.

A walk-thru utility room provides easy access from the carport and outside storage area to the compact kitchen. On the opposite side of the Great Room are two additional bedrooms and a second full

bath. All this takes up only 1,454 square feet of heated living area. A full length deck and vertical wood siding with stone accents on the corners provide a rustic yet contemporary exterior.

Total living area: 1,454 sq. ft.
(Not counting basement or garage)

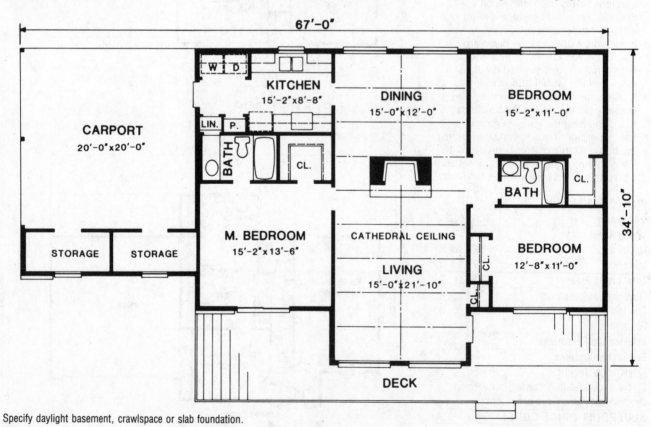

67'-0"

34'-10"

CARPORT
20'-0"x20'-0"

STORAGE   STORAGE

W   D

KITCHEN
15'-2"x8'-8"

LIN.   P.

BATH

CL.

M. BEDROOM
15'-2"x13'-6"

DINING
15'-0"x12'-0"

CATHEDRAL CEILING

LIVING
15'-0"x21'-10"

CL.

BEDROOM
15'-2"x11'-0"

BATH   CL.

CL.

BEDROOM
12'-8"x11'-0"

DECK

Specify daylight basement, crawlspace or slab foundation.

Blueprint Price Code A

Plan C-7360

TO ORDER THIS BLUEPRINT,
CALL TOLL-FREE 1-800-547-5570

PRICES AND DETAILS
ON PAGES 12-15

Compact Contemporary With Clerestory

This 1,457 square foot contemporary design features a large family room with a stone fireplace, double doors to the rear patio, dining area, open stairwell to the full basement and a vaulted ceiling with exposed wood beams and triple clerestory windows. The master suite includes two walk-in closets and a private bath. Both front bedrooms have a walk-in closet and share a second full bath. The eat-in kitchen includes access from the dining area as well as the front opening garage. Additional features include a coat closet off the foyer, vertical wood siding with stone, and a recessed entry with a front porch.

Total living area: 1,457 sq. ft.
(Not counting basement or garage)

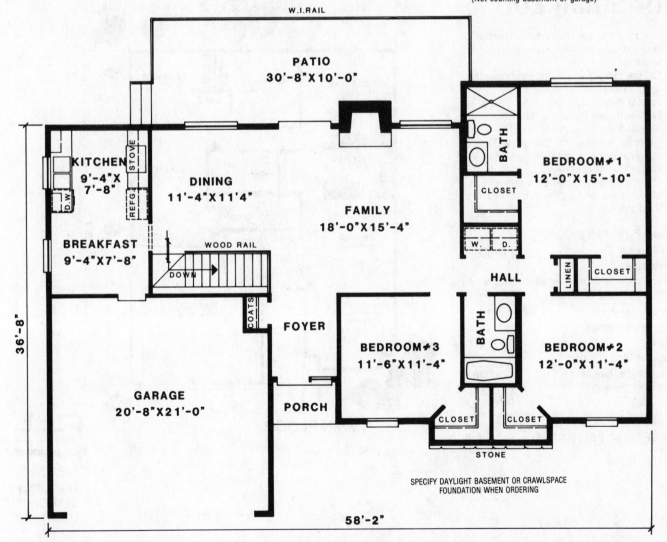

SPECIFY DAYLIGHT BASEMENT OR CRAWLSPACE FOUNDATION WHEN ORDERING

Blueprint Price Code A

Plan C-8356

Compact Plan for Small Lot

- Luxury is not forgotten in this compact one-story home, which is perfect for a small lot.
- Off the entry, the vaulted living room with a boxed-out window joins the formal dining area, which features a half-wall opening to the hallway.
- The kitchen is separated from the family room by a functional eating bar. The family room is brightened by sliding glass doors that open to a patio.
- The master bedroom offers generous closet space and a private bath with a dual-sink vanity.

Plans P-7699-2A & -2D

Bedrooms: 3	Baths: 2
Living Area:	
Main floor (crawlspace version)	1,460 sq. ft.
Main floor (basement version)	1,509 sq. ft.
Total Living Area:	**1,460/1,509 sq. ft.**
Daylight basement	1,530 sq. ft.
Garage	383 sq. ft.
Exterior Wall Framing:	2x4
Foundation Options:	**Plan #**
Daylight basement	P-7699-2D
Crawlspace	P-7699-2A

(All plans can be built with your choice of foundation and framing. A generic conversion diagram is available. See order form.)

BLUEPRINT PRICE CODE:	**A/B**

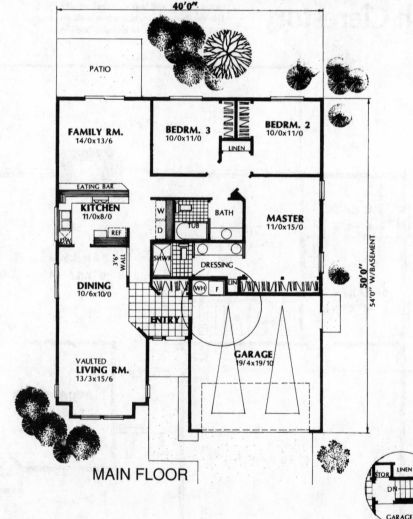

MAIN FLOOR

BASEMENT STAIRWAY LOCATION

Contemporary Blends with Site

The striking contemporary silhouette of this home paradoxically blends with the rustic setting. Perhaps it is the way the shed rooflines repeat the spreading limbs of the surrounding evergreens, or the way the foundation conforms to the grade much as do the rocks in the foreground. Whatever the reason, the home "belongs."

Aesthetics aside, one must examine the floor plan to determine genuine livability. From the weather-protected entry there is access to any part of the house without annoying cross traffic. Kitchen, dining and living room, the active "waking-hours" section of the residence, are enlarged and enhanced by the convenient outdoor deck. Laundry and bath are located inconspicuously along the hall leading to the main floor bedroom. A huge linen closet is convenient to this area. The additional bedrooms are located upstairs on the 517 sq. ft. second level. A romantic feature of the second floor is the balcony overlooking the living area.

Plans including a full basement are available at your option. A large double garage completes the plan and is an important adjunct, especially if the home is built without a basement, because it can provide much needed storage space.

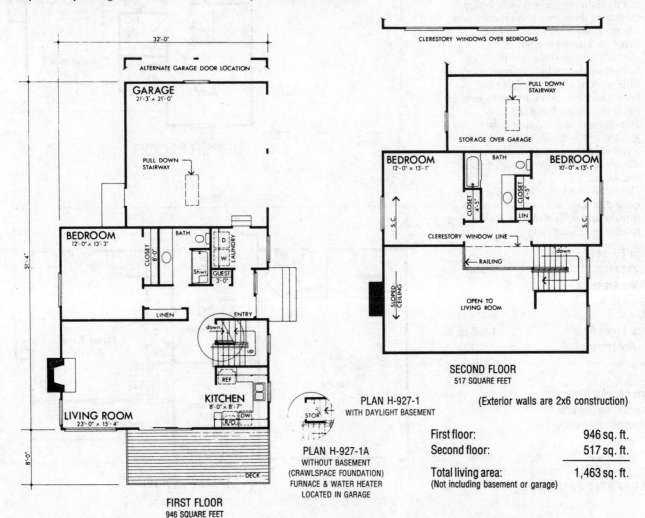

(Exterior walls are 2x6 construction)

First floor:	946 sq. ft.
Second floor:	517 sq. ft.
Total living area: (Not including basement or garage)	1,463 sq. ft.

Blueprint Price Code A

Plans H-927-1 & -1A

PRICES AND DETAILS ON PAGES 12-15

Pleasantly Peaceful

- You'll enjoy relaxing on the covered front porch of this pleasant two-story traditional home.
- Off the open foyer is an oversized family room, drenched with sunlight streaming through a French door and windows on three sides. A nice fireplace also adds warmth.
- A neatly arranged kitchen is conveniently nestled between a formal dining room and a sunny, casual breakfast room. A pantry and a powder room adjoin the breakfast room.
- The stairway to the upper floor is located in the family room. Closets and a sizable laundry room isolate the master suite from the two secondary bedrooms.
- The master bedroom features a tray ceiling, a huge walk-in closet and a private bath with a vaulted ceiling and a separate tub and shower.

Plan FB-1466

Bedrooms: 3	Baths: 2½
Living Area:	
Upper floor	703 sq. ft.
Main floor	763 sq. ft.
Total Living Area:	**1,466 sq. ft.**
Daylight basement	763 sq. ft.
Garage	426 sq. ft.
Storage	72 sq. ft.
Exterior Wall Framing:	2x4

Foundation Options:
Daylight basement
Crawlspace
(Typical foundation & framing conversion diagram available—see order form.)

BLUEPRINT PRICE CODE:	A

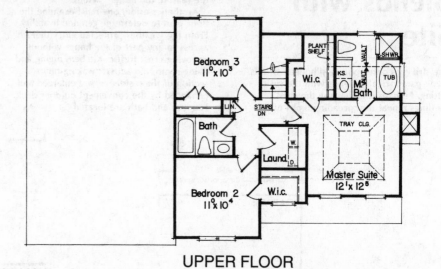

UPPER FLOOR

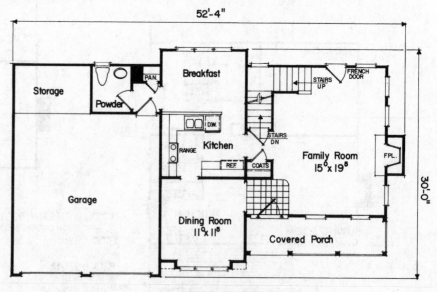

MAIN FLOOR

TO ORDER THIS BLUEPRINT, CALL TOLL-FREE 1-800-547-5570

Plan FB-1466

PRICES AND DETAILS ON PAGES 12-15

All the Options

- Attention-getting gables and decorative window details characterize this spacious home, which features an optional bonus room for future expansion possibilities.
- A two-story foyer leads into the main living areas. The vaulted family room is warmed by a fireplace and has French-door access to the backyard. The adjoining dining room leads to a bright breakfast area, where another French door opens to a covered porch.
- The centrally located kitchen services the entire living area, with a convenient serving bar to the breakfast area and a pass-through to the dining room.
- The elegant master suite is distinguished with a tray ceiling and a vaulted bath. The luxurious bath offers a garden tub, a separate shower and a deluxe walk-in closet adorned with a plant shelf.
- Upstairs, two bedrooms share a full bath. A balcony overlook provides a stunning view of the family room. The huge bonus room with a sloped ceiling is a nice option.

Plan FB-1469

Bedrooms: 3+	Baths: 2½
Living Area:	
Upper floor	409 sq. ft.
Main floor	1,060 sq. ft.
Optional bonus room	251 sq. ft.
Total Living Area:	**1,720 sq. ft.**
Daylight basement	1,060 sq. ft.
Garage	420 sq. ft.
Exterior Wall Framing:	2x4

Foundation Options:

Daylight basement
(Typical foundation & framing conversion diagram available—see order form.)

BLUEPRINT PRICE CODE: B

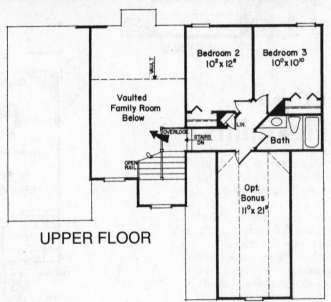

UPPER FLOOR

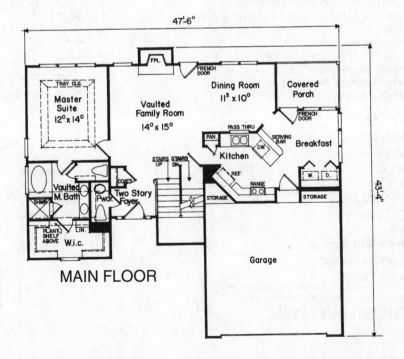

MAIN FLOOR

TRADITIONAL

CONTEMPORARY

Split-Level with Flexibility

- Choose a contemporary or a traditional facade for this roomy split-level plan. Both options are included in the blueprints.
- A covered entry opens into the Great Room, which boasts a vaulted ceiling, a fireplace and access to a rear deck.
- The open kitchen offers a snack counter and a handy pantry. It also has a view of the Great Room as well as a window overlooking the charming plant shelf.
- The master bedroom features built-in shelves, a walk-in closet and a private bath. Two more bedrooms share another full bath.
- The bonus space on the lower level is ideal as a playroom, study, office or entertainment area. A convenient half-bath is nearby.

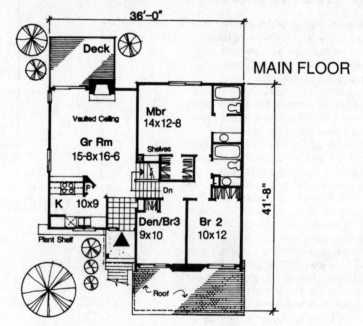

MAIN FLOOR

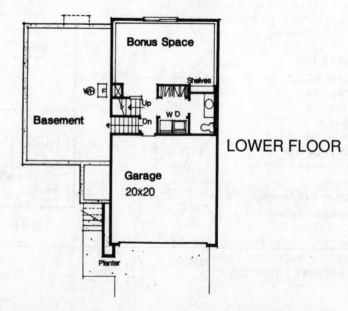

LOWER FLOOR

Plan B-8321

Bedrooms: 2+	Baths: 2½
Living Area:	
Main floor	1,096 sq. ft.
Lower floor	400 sq. ft.
Total Living Area:	**1,496 sq. ft.**
Partial basement	405 sq. ft.
Garage	400 sq. ft.
Exterior Wall Framing:	2x4
Foundation Options:	

Partial basement
(All plans can be built with your choice of foundation and framing. A generic conversion diagram is available. See order form.)

BLUEPRINT PRICE CODE: **A**

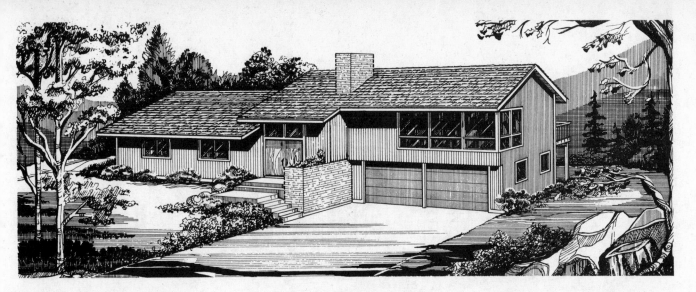

Four-Bedroom Tri-Level for Sloping Lot

The average building site today may slope in almost any direction. This, along with the high cost of real estate, has generated the need for multiple level plans. This design is a good example. Actually, the home has four levels and is designed to fit on a site that slopes in at least one, if not two, directions.

The entry is on the same level as the three upper bedrooms. From there, a stairway leads up to the living room, dining room and kitchen area. These two upper levels combined total 1,516 sq. ft. Another stairway from the entry level leads down to the garage, or to the 1,034 sq. ft. lower level (if basement option is chosen.) The entry hall's spatial variety is expressed in the double-door entry as well as the open balustrade of the staircase leading to the living room above. It also connects with the central hall of the three-bedroom wing and serves as an easy access to the other two lower levels. Well lighted by clerestory windows, the entry is also within view of the living room.

The generous-sized living room is divided from the entry by a massive fireplace that includes a log-sized opening. The L-shaped living-dining combination serves as a functional arrangement for expanding the dining table. A kitchen nook provides a second dining area. The kitchen-dining areas also face a rear deck, elevated above the garden. Back yard access is provided by a staircase from the outdoor deck. Multiple bathrooms are provided on the bedroom wing off the laundry.

The lowest level of the basement version provides another spacious bedroom with walk-in closet and bath, and the house-spanning recreation room features a second fireplace. An open staircase connects to the floor above.

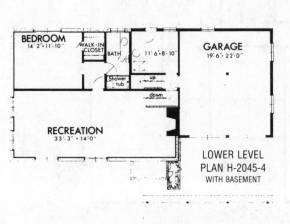

LOWER LEVEL
PLAN H-2045-4
WITH BASEMENT

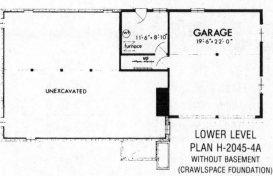

LOWER LEVEL
PLAN H-2045-4A
WITHOUT BASEMENT
(CRAWLSPACE FOUNDATION)

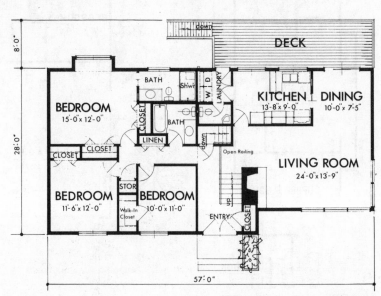

UPPER LEVELS — BOTH VERSIONS
(Exterior walls are 2x6 construction)

Two upper levels:	1,516 sq. ft.
Lower level (opt):	1,034 sq. ft.
Total living area: (Not counting garage)	2,550 sq. ft.

Blueprint Price Code D With Basement
Blueprint Price Code B Without Basement

Vaulted Master Suite Upstairs

UPPER FLOOR

PLAN P-6490-2D
WITH DAYLIGHT BASEMENT

MAIN FLOOR

PLAN P-6490-2A
WITHOUT BASEMENT
(CRAWLSPACE FOUNDATION)

Main floor:	1,173 sq. ft.
Upper floor:	345 sq. ft.
Total living area:	1,518 sq. ft.
(Not counting basement or garage)	

Blueprint Price Code B

Plans P-6490-2A & -2D

PRICES AND DETAILS
ON PAGES 12-15

REAR VIEW

For Vacation or Year-Round Casual Living

- More than 500 square feet of deck area across the rear sets the theme of casual outdoor living for this compact plan.
- The living/dining/kitchen combination is included in one huge, 15' x 39' Great Room, which is several steps down from the entry level for an even more dramatic effect.
- Two large downstairs bedrooms share a bath. Upstairs, a hideaway bedroom includes a private bath, a walk-in closet and a romantic private deck.
- A utility room is conveniently placed in the garage entry area.
- The optional basement features a large recreation room with a fireplace and sliders to a patio underneath the rear deck.
- A fourth bedroom and a third bath in the basement would be ideal for guests.
- At the front of the basement is a large area that could be used for a hobby room or a children's play area.

Plans H-877-1 & -1A

Bedrooms: 3-4	Baths: 2-3
Living Area:	
Upper floor	320 sq. ft.
Main floor	1,200 sq. ft.
Daylight basement	1,200 sq. ft.
Total Living Area:	**1,520/2,720 sq. ft.**
Garage	155 sq. ft.
Exterior Wall Framing:	2x6
Foundation Options:	**Plan #**
Daylight basement	H-877-1
Crawlspace	H-877-1A
(Typical foundation & framing conversion diagram available—see order form.)	
BLUEPRINT PRICE CODE:	**B/D**

UPPER FLOOR

BASEMENT STAIRWAY LOCATION

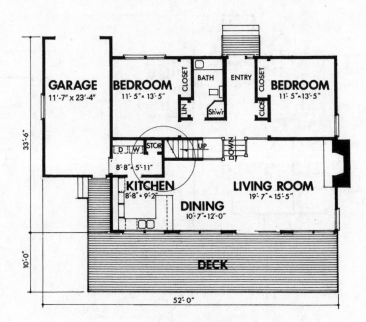

MAIN FLOOR

Main-Floor Master Suite!

- The refined exterior detailing of this attractive three-bedroom home includes eye-catching gables, brick trim and half-round louvers.
- The vaulted foyer is brightened by an upper-level window and accented with a plant shelf. The dining room merges with the wonderful family room, separated only by a graceful column.
- The family room is made even more spacious by a vaulted ceiling and a fireplace framed by windows.

- The breakfast nook combines with the kitchen to create an everyday living area that is hidden from view. A half-bath, a laundry closet and a coat closet are nearby.
- The main-floor master suite is a real treat, with its elegant tray ceiling and private bath. The luxurious bath includes a whirlpool tub, a dual-sink vanity and a separate shower and tub area, plus a deluxe walk-in closet.
- The stairway to the upper floor is illuminated by a window at the landing. The balcony hall overlooks the family room and the foyer below.
- The two upstairs bedrooms share a compartmentalized bath.

Plan FB-1529	
Bedrooms: 3	**Baths:** 2½
Living Area:	
Upper floor	431 sq. ft.
Main floor	1,098 sq. ft.
Total Living Area:	**1,529 sq. ft.**
Daylight basement	1,098 sq. ft.
Garage	432 sq. ft.
Storage	72 sq. ft.
Exterior Wall Framing:	2x4
Foundation Options:	
Daylight basement	
Crawlspace	
Slab	
(Typical foundation & framing conversion diagram available—see order form.)	
BLUEPRINT PRICE CODE:	B

MAIN FLOOR

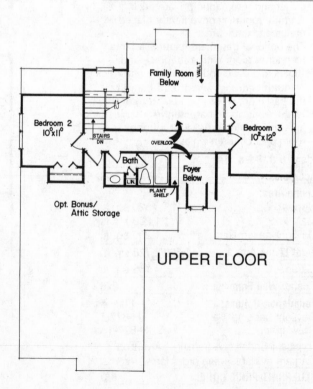

UPPER FLOOR

FRONT VIEW

REAR VIEW

Hillside Design Fits Contours

- The daylight-basement version of this popular plan is perfect for a scenic, sloping lot.
- A large, wraparound deck embraces the rear-oriented living areas, accessed through sliding glass doors.
- The spectacular living room boasts a corner fireplace, a sloped ceiling and outdoor views to the side and rear.
- The secluded master suite upstairs offers a walk-in closet, a private bath and sliders to a sun deck.
- The daylight basement (not shown) includes a fourth bedroom with private bath and walk-in closet, as well as a recreation room with fireplace and sliders to a rear patio.
- The standard basement (not shown) includes a recreation room with fireplace and a room for hobbies or child's play.
- Both basements also have a large unfinished area below the main-floor bedrooms.

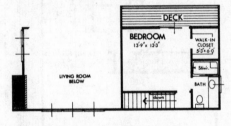

UPPER FLOOR

Plans H-877-4, -4A & -4B	
Bedrooms: 3-4	**Baths:** 2-3
Living Area:	
Upper floor	333 sq. ft.
Main floor	1,200 sq. ft.
Basement (finished portion)	591 sq. ft.
Total Living Area:	**1,533/2,124 sq. ft.**
Basement (unfinished portion)	493 sq. ft.
Garage	480 sq. ft.
Exterior Wall Framing:	2x6
Foundation Options:	**Plan #**
Daylight basement	H-877-4B
Standard basement	H-877-4
Crawlspace	H-877-4A
(Typical foundation & framing conversion diagram available—see order form.)	
BLUEPRINT PRICE CODE:	**B/C**

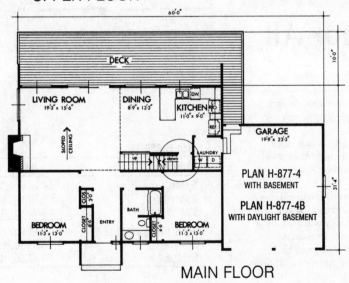

PLAN H-877-4
WITH BASEMENT

PLAN H-877-4B
WITH DAYLIGHT BASEMENT

PLAN H-877-4A
WITHOUT BASEMENT

MAIN FLOOR

Plans H-877-4, -4A & -4B

UPPER FLOOR

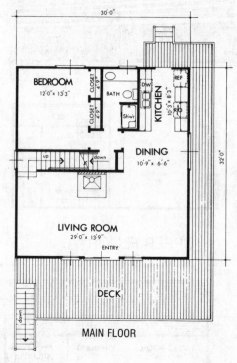

MAIN FLOOR

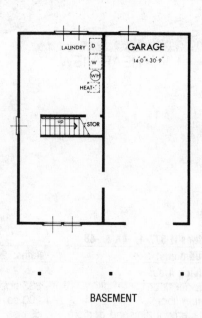

BASEMENT

Chalet for All Seasons

- Rustic exterior makes this design suitable for a lakefront, beach, or wooded setting.
- Patterned railing and wood deck edge the front and side main level, while a smaller deck assumes a balcony role.
- Designed for relaxed, leisure living, the main level features a large L-shaped Great Room warmed by a central free-standing fireplace.
- Upper level offers a second bath and added sleeping accommodations.

Plan H-858-2

Bedrooms: 3	Baths: 2
Space:	
Upper floor:	576 sq. ft.
Main floor:	960 sq. ft.
Total living area:	**1,536 sq. ft.**
Basement:	530 sq. ft.
Garage:	430 sq. ft.

Exterior Wall Framing: 2x6

Foundation options:
Daylight basement.
(Foundation & framing conversion diagram available — see order form.)

Blueprint Price Code: B

Garden Room Enhances Contemporary

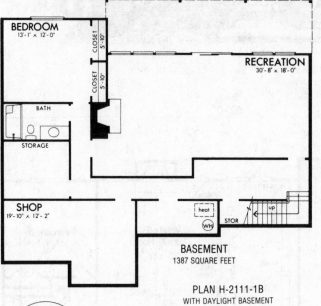

BEDROOM
13'-1" × 12'-0"

RECREATION
30'-8" × 18'-0"

CLOSET 5'-10"

CLOSET 5'-10"

BATH

STORAGE

SHOP
19'-10" × 12'-2"

heat

WH

up

STOR

BASEMENT
1387 SQUARE FEET

PLAN H-2111-1B
WITH DAYLIGHT BASEMENT

Main floor:	1,497 sq. ft.
Garden room:	92 sq. ft.
Total living area:	1,589 sq. ft.
(Not counting basement or garage)	
Airlock entry:	45 sq. ft.
Basement:	1,387 sq. ft.

FAMILY ROOM

D W heat STORAGE

WH

GARAGE

PLAN H-2111-1A
WITHOUT BASEMENT
(CRAWLSPACE FOUNDATION)

Main floor:	1,448 sq. ft.
Garden room:	92 sq. ft.
Total living area:	1,540 sq. ft.
(Not counting garage)	
Airlock entry:	45 sq. ft.

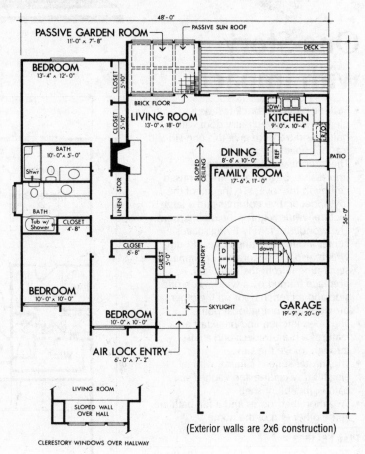

48'-0"

PASSIVE GARDEN ROOM
11'-0" × 7'-8"

PASSIVE SUN ROOF

DECK

BEDROOM
13'-4" × 12'-0"

CLOSET 5'-10"

CLOSET 5'-10"

BRICK FLOOR

LIVING ROOM
13'-0" × 18'-0"

KITCHEN
9'-0" × 10'-4"

DW

BATH
10'-0" × 5'-0"

Shwr

REF

SLOPED CEILING

DINING
8'-6" × 10'-0"

FAMILY ROOM
17'-6" × 11'-0"

PATIO

LINEN

STOR

BATH

Tub w/ Shower

CLOSET
4'-8"

56'-0"

CLOSET
6'-8"

GUEST 5'-0"

LAUNDRY

D W

down

BEDROOM
10'-0" × 10'-0"

BEDROOM
10'-0" × 10'-0"

SKYLIGHT

GARAGE
19'-9" × 20'-0"

AIR LOCK ENTRY
6'-0" × 7'-2"

LIVING ROOM

SLOPED WALL OVER HALL

CLERESTORY WINDOWS OVER HALLWAY

(Exterior walls are 2x6 construction)

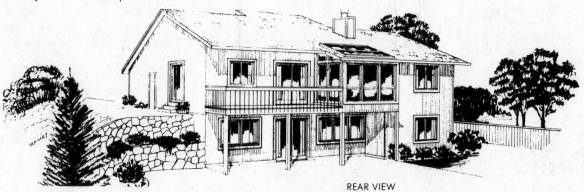

REAR VIEW

Blueprint Price Code B

One-Story with Impact

- Striking gables, a brick facade and an elegant sidelighted entry door with a half-round transom give this one-story lots of impact.
- The interior spaces are just as impressive, beginning with the raised ceiling in the foyer. To the left of the foyer, decorative columns and a large picture window grace the dining room.
- The wonderful family living spaces center around a vaulted Great Room, which also has decorative columns separating it from the main hall. A fireplace framed by a window on one side and a French door on the other provides a stunning focal point.
- The open kitchen and breakfast area features a built-in desk and a pass-through above the sink.
- The master suite is superb, with its elegant tray ceiling and vaulted spa bath with a plant shelf.
- Two more bedrooms and a full bath are at the other end of the home.

Plan FB-1553

Bedrooms: 3	Baths: 2
Living Area:	
Main floor	1,553 sq. ft.
Total Living Area:	**1,553 sq. ft.**
Daylight basement	1,553 sq. ft.
Garage	410 sq. ft.
Exterior Wall Framing:	2x4

Foundation Options:
Daylight basement
Crawlspace
Slab
(Typical foundation & framing conversion diagram available—see order form.)

BLUEPRINT PRICE CODE: B

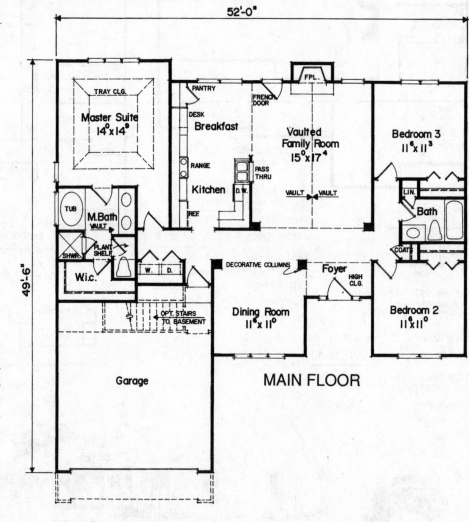

MAIN FLOOR

Plan FB-1553

Classy Design

- Brick and wood construction, combined with traditional design overtones, gives this two-story character and class.
- A covered entry porch opens to the two-story-high foyer and the formal dining room. To the left lies the full-service kitchen, which features an angled serving bar, lots of counter space and easy access to the laundry room and the two-car garage.
- The adjoining breakfast area includes a pantry closet, a built-in desk and a French door to the backyard.
- The heart of the home is the spacious Great Room, which features an inviting fireplace framed by windows.
- The upper floor is highlighted by a spectacular overlook and an equally stunning master suite. The succulent master bath includes a vaulted ceiling and a corner spa tub.

Plan FB-1563

Bedrooms: 3	Baths: 2½
Living Area:	
Upper floor	766 sq. ft.
Main floor	797 sq. ft.
Total Living Area:	**1,563 sq. ft.**
Daylight basement	766 sq. ft.
Garage	440 sq. ft.
Exterior Wall Framing:	2x4

Foundation Options:
Daylight basement
Slab
(Typical foundation & framing conversion diagram available—see order form.)

BLUEPRINT PRICE CODE: B

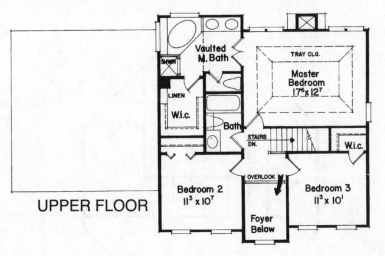

UPPER FLOOR

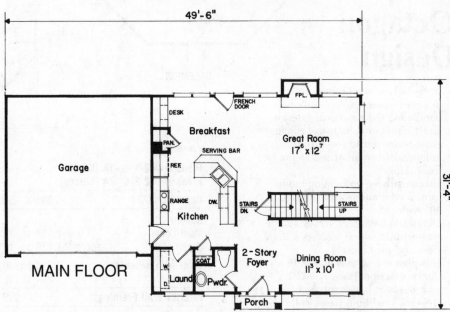

MAIN FLOOR

Unique Octagon Design

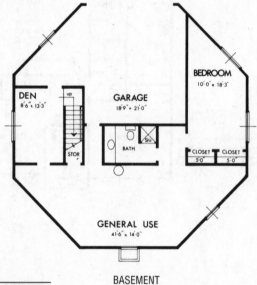

BASEMENT

DEN
8'-6" x 13'-3"

GARAGE
18'-9" x 21'-0"

BEDROOM
10'-0" x 18'-3"

up

STOR

BATH

CLOSET
5'-0"

CLOSET
5'-0"

GENERAL USE
41'-6" x 14'-0"

DECK

LIVING ROOM
24'-0" x 14'-0"

DINING
12'-3" x 11'-0"

BEDROOM
13'-3" x 18'-6"

KITCHEN
10'-6" x 9'-0"

STOR

STOR

Shower

Shower

BATH

BATH

LIN

DW

REF

CLOSET
5'-0"

CLOSET
5'-0"

BEDROOM
11'-6" x 11'-0"

LAUNDRY

D W

CLOSET
3'-0"

ENTRY

BEDROOM
11'-6" x 11'-0"

CLOSET
5'-0"

CLOSET
6'-0"

43'-6"

8'-0"

43'-6"

MAIN FLOOR

- Irregularly shaped rooms are oriented around an entrance hall paralleling the octagonal exterior.
- Short directional hallways eliminate cross-room traffic and provide independent room access to the front door.
- Spacious living and dining rooms form a continuous area more than 38' wide.
- Oversized bathroom serves a large master suite which features a deck view and dual closets.
- This plan is also available with a stucco exterior (Plans H-942-2, with daylight basement, and H-942-2A, without basement).

1/16" = 1'

0 1 2 3 4 5 6 7 8 9 10

Plans H-942-1 & -1A (Wood)
Plans H-942-2 & -2A (Stucco)

Bedrooms: 3-4	Baths: 2-3
Space:	
Main floor:	1,564 sq. ft.
Basement:	approx. 1,170 sq. ft.
Total with basement:	2,734 sq. ft.
Garage:	394 sq. ft.
Exterior Wall Framing:	2x6

Foundation options:
Daylight basement (Plans H-942-1 & -2).
Crawlspace (Plans H-942-1A & -2A).
(Foundation & framing conversion diagram available — see order form.)

Blueprint Price Code:

Without basement:	B
With basement:	D

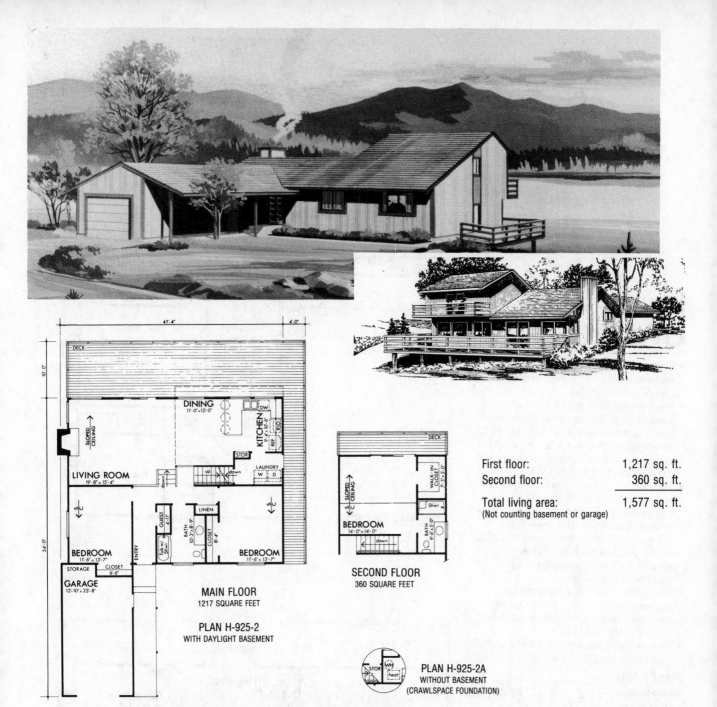

MAIN FLOOR
1217 SQUARE FEET

PLAN H-925-2
WITH DAYLIGHT BASEMENT

SECOND FLOOR
360 SQUARE FEET

PLAN H-925-2A
WITHOUT BASEMENT
(CRAWLSPACE FOUNDATION)

First floor:	1,217 sq. ft.
Second floor:	360 sq. ft.
Total living area:	1,577 sq. ft.
(Not counting basement or garage)	

Economical and Convenient

In an effort to merge the financial possibilities and the space requirements of the greatest number of families, the designers of this home restricted themselves to just over 1,200 sq. ft. of ground cover (exclusive of garage), and still managed to develop a superior three-bedroom design.

From a covered walkway, one approaches a centralized entry hall which effectively distributes traffic throughout the home without causing interruptions. Two main floor bedrooms and bath as well as the stairway to the second floor master suite are immediately accessible to the entry. Directly forward and four steps down finds one in the main living area, consisting of a large living room with vaulted ceiling and a dining-kitchen combination with conventional ceiling height. All these rooms have direct access to an outdoor living deck of over 400 sq. ft. Thus, though modest and unassuming from the street side, this home evolves into eye-popping expansion and luxury toward the rear.

To ease homemaking chores, whether this is to be a permanent or vacation home, the working equipment, including laundry space, is all on the main floor. Yet the homemaker remains part of the family scene because there is only a breakfast counter separating the work space from the living area.

Tucked away upstairs, in complete privacy, one finds a master bedroom suite equipped with separate bath, walk-in wardrobe and a romantic private deck.

The plan is available with or without a basement and is best suited to a lot that slopes gently down from the road.

Luxury and Livability

- Big on style, this modest-sized home features a quaint Colonial exerior and an open interior plan.
- The covered front porch leads to a vaulted foyer that opens to the formal living and dining rooms. A coat closet, an attractive display niche and a powder room are centrally located, as is the stairway to the upper floor.
- The kitchen, breakfast nook and family room are designed so that each room has its own definition yet also functions as part of a whole. The angled sink separates the kitchen from the breakfast nook, which is outlined by bay windows. The large family room includes a fireplace.
- The upper floor has a hard-to-miss master suite, featuring a tray ceiling in the large sleeping area and a vaulted ceiling in the spa bath.
- Two more bedrooms and a balcony hall add to this home's luxury and livability.

Plan FB-1600

Bedrooms: 3	Baths: 2½
Living Area:	
Upper floor	772 sq. ft.
Main floor	828 sq. ft.
Total Living Area:	**1,600 sq. ft.**
Daylight basement	828 sq. ft.
Garage	473 sq. ft.
Exterior Wall Framing:	2x4

Foundation Options:
Daylight basement
Crawlspace
Slab

(Typical foundation & framing conversion diagram available—see order form.)

BLUEPRINT PRICE CODE:	B

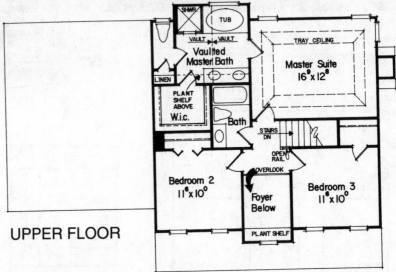

UPPER FLOOR

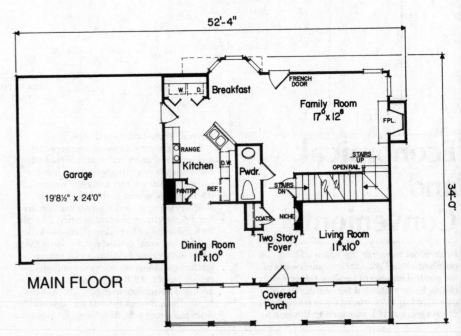

MAIN FLOOR

Lakeside Retreat Sleeps Eight

- Four bedrooms border the exterior walls of this lakeside retreat, affording a fair amount of privacy.
- A deck and a vaulted screened-in porch surround the spectacular cathedral-ceilinged Great Room and dining area. The large living space is also loaded with glass so you can enjoy your favorite scenic site.
- The adjoining kitchen features an oversized eating bar and work counter combination.
- Two full baths sit back-to-back, conveniently serving both bedroom wings. A handy main-floor laundry room is also included.

Plan PH-1600

Bedrooms: 4	Baths: 2
Space:	
Main floor	1,600 sq. ft.
Total Living Area	**1,600 sq. ft.**
Exterior Wall Framing	2x6

Foundation options:

Crawlspace
Pole
Slab
(Foundation & framing conversion diagram available—see order form.)

Blueprint Price Code	B

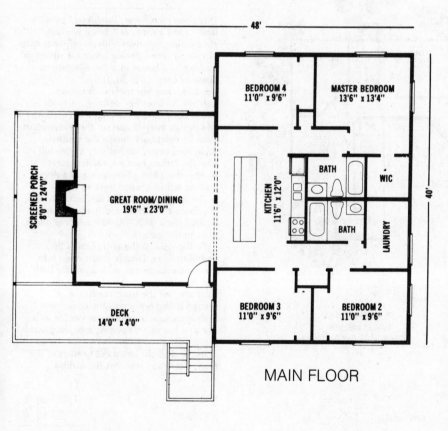

48'

40'

BEDROOM 4
11'0" x 9'6"

MASTER BEDROOM
13'6" x 13'4"

SCREENED PORCH
8'0" x 24'0"

GREAT ROOM/DINING
19'6" x 23'0"

KITCHEN
11'6" x 12'0"

BATH

WIC

BATH

LAUNDRY

DECK
14'0" x 4'0"

BEDROOM 3
11'0" x 9'6"

BEDROOM 2
11'0" x 9'6"

MAIN FLOOR

A Home for Sun Lovers

This open plan home, brightened by a landscaped atrium, also has a vaulted, glass-ceiling solarium with an optional spa, offering a sunny garden room for sitting or soaking — a bonus in a three-bedroom home of only 1,621 sq. ft.

Intersecting hip roofs with corner notches, a clerestory dormer, vertical board siding and a covered front walkway add design interest and set the house apart from its neighbors. Inside the vaulted, skylighted entry, the hallway angles left past the atrium into the vaulted great room, which has a fireplace and a door leading out to a wood deck or patio.

The spacious L-shaped kitchen also overlooks the atrium and has an adjacent vaulted nook with solarium window and a door to the garage.

To the right of the entry hall is the bedroom wing. Double doors open into the master bedroom, with a private bath and walk-in closet. Doors lead to the solarium and the front courtyard. A second bathroom serves the other two bedrooms, one of which can double as a den and has doors opening into the great room.

In the daylight basement version of the plan, a stairway replaces the atrium.

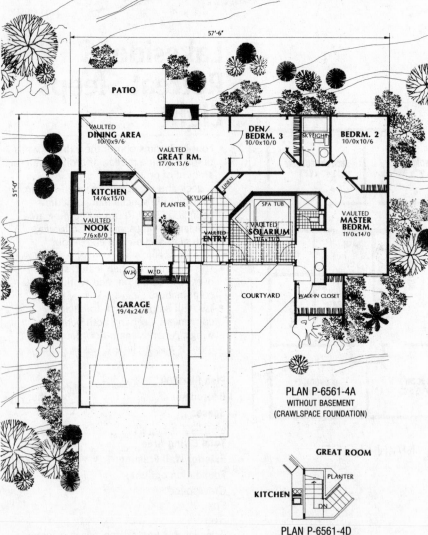

PLAN P-6561-4A
WITHOUT BASEMENT
(CRAWLSPACE FOUNDATION)

GREAT ROOM
PLANTER
KITCHEN
DN

PLAN P-6561-4D
WITH DAYLIGHT BASEMENT

Main floor:	1,497 sq. ft.
Solarium:	124 sq. ft.
Total living area:	1,621 sq. ft.
(Not counting basement or garage)	
Basement:	1,514 sq. ft.

Blueprint Price Code B

Plans P-6561-4A & -4D

Designed for Relaxed Living

Wood post and railing, shutters and covered porch give a relaxed look to this country home. A fireplace lends extra appeal to the large living room. A country kitchen with center work bar is located between the breakfast room and separate dining room.

All three bedrooms are located on one side of the house. Each bedroom has good closet space.

Total living area: 1,627 sq. ft.
(Not counting basement or garage)

Specify daylight basement, crawlspace or slab foundation.

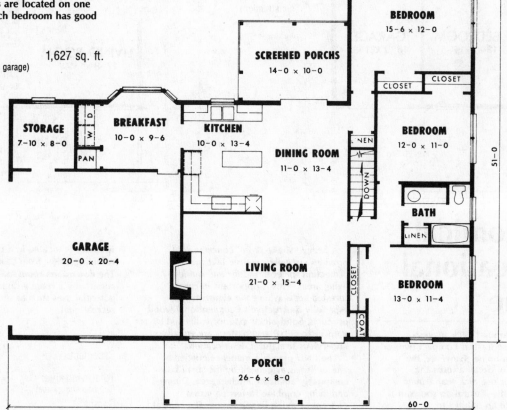

Blueprint Price Code B

Plan C-7549

TO ORDER THIS BLUEPRINT,
CALL TOLL-FREE 1-800-547-5570

PRICES AND DETAILS
ON PAGES 12-15

69

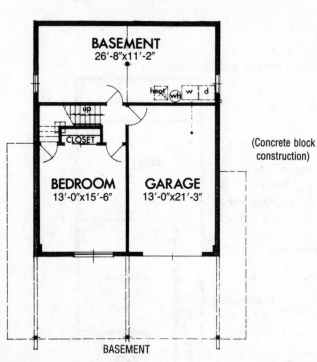

BASEMENT
26'-8"x11'-2"

heat wh w d

up

CLOSET

BEDROOM
13'-0"x15'-6"

GARAGE
13'-0"x21'-3"

BASEMENT

(Concrete block construction)

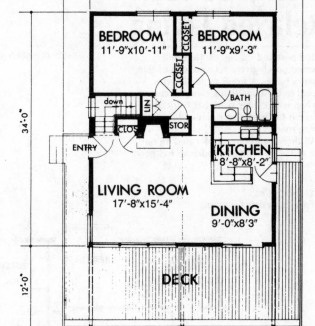

4'-0"   28'-0"   4'-0"

BEDROOM
11'-9"x10'-11"

BEDROOM
11'-9"x9'-3"

CLOSET

CLOSET

down

LIN

BATH

34'-0"

CLOS   STOR

ENTRY

KITCHEN
8'-8"x8'-2"

LIVING ROOM
17'-8"x15'-4"

DINING
9'-0"x8'3"

12'-0"

DECK

MAIN FLOOR

Economical Recreational Home

A huge wrap-around deck suggests recreational use for this compact two- or three-bedroom home. However, the completeness of detail affords the opportunity for use as a year around residence. As the illustration shows, it is best adapted to an uphill site.

A heavy "shake-style" concrete roof provides virtually carefree lifetime protection for both indoor and outdoor living areas. This is important in rural forested areas where the elements are especially destructive to conventional wood products. Solid block exterior walls laid in a distinctive 8x8 grid pattern are equally impervious to natural deterioration.

The floor plan is a model of efficiency and utility as evidenced by the small but completely adequate kitchen area. Dining and living combine to form a visual concept of much larger rooms. The central

fireplace is located in a convenient spot for refueling either from basement or outdoors. The downstairs room marked "bedroom" is admittedly a room with many other potential uses such as shop, hobby or recreational.

Main floor:	952 sq. ft.
Basement:	676 sq. ft.
Total living area: (Not counting garage)	1,628 sq. ft.
Garage:	276 sq. ft.

Blueprint Price Code B
Plan H-806-M3

PRICES AND DETAILS ON PAGES 12-15

Spectacular Sloping Design

- For the lake or mountain-view sloping lot, this spectacular design hugs the hill and takes full advantage of the views.
- A three-sided wrap-around deck makes indoor-outdoor living a pleasure.

- The sunken living room, with cathedral ceiling, skylight, fireplace, and glass galore, is the heart of the plan.
- The formal dining room and the kitchen/breakfast room both overlook the living room and deck

views beyond.
- The main-floor master bedroom has private access to the deck and the bath.
- Two more bedrooms upstairs share a skylit bath and flank a dramatic balcony sitting area overlooking the living room below.

Plan AX-98607

Bedrooms: 3	Baths: 2
Space:	
Upper floor:	531 sq. ft.
Main floor:	1,098 sq. ft.
Total living area:	**1,629 sq. ft.**
Basement:	894 sq. ft.
Garage:	327 sq. ft.
Exterior Wall Framing:	2x4

Foundation options:
Standard basement.
Slab.
(Foundation & framing conversion diagram available — see order form.)

Blueprint Price Code:	B

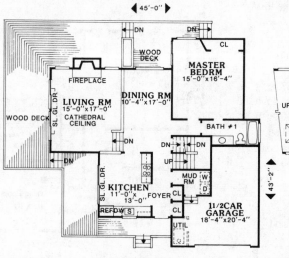

MAIN FLOOR

UPPER FLOOR

Expandable Living Spaces!

- Expandable spaces make this attractive two-story a great choice for growing families. The formal dining room or the living room could be easily converted into a library or den, while the optional bonus room above the garage provides a host of possible uses.

- The nice-sized family room offers an inviting fireplace and access to the backyard. The sunny breakfast room is just a few steps away and adjoins an efficient L-shaped kitchen.

- The upper floor features a balcony hall that overlooks the two-story-high foyer. The master suite is dignified by a tray ceiling in the sleeping area and a vaulted ceiling in the private bath with a corner spa tub. The large walk-in closet includes a handy linen closet and sports a decorative plant shelf.

- A convenient laundry closet, two bedrooms and a full bath complete the upper floor.

Plan FB-1631

Bedrooms: 3+	Baths: 2½
Living Area:	
Upper floor	787 sq. ft.
Main floor	844 sq. ft.
Bonus room	340 sq. ft.
Total Living Area:	**1,971 sq. ft.**
Daylight basement	844 sq. ft.
Garage	460 sq. ft.
Exterior Wall Framing:	**2x4**

Foundation Options:
Daylight basement
(Typical foundation & framing conversion diagram available—see order form.)

BLUEPRINT PRICE CODE: **B**

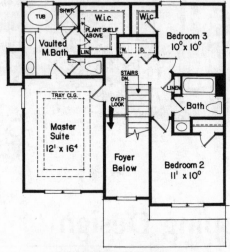

UPPER FLOOR

ALTERNATE UPPER FLOOR

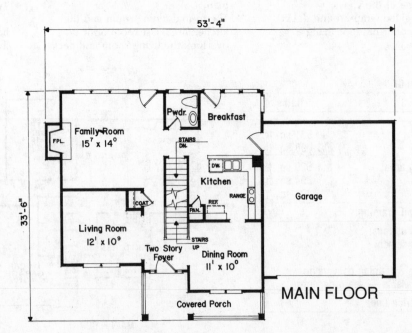

MAIN FLOOR

Plan FB-1631

PRICES AND DETAILS ON PAGES 12-15

Contemporary Retreat

- Main floor plan revolves around an open, centrally located stairway.
- Spaciousness prevails throughout entire home with open kitchen and combination dining/living room.
- Living room features a great-sized fireplace and access to two-sided deck.
- Separate baths accommodate each bedroom.
- Upstairs hallway reveals an open balcony railing to oversee activities below.

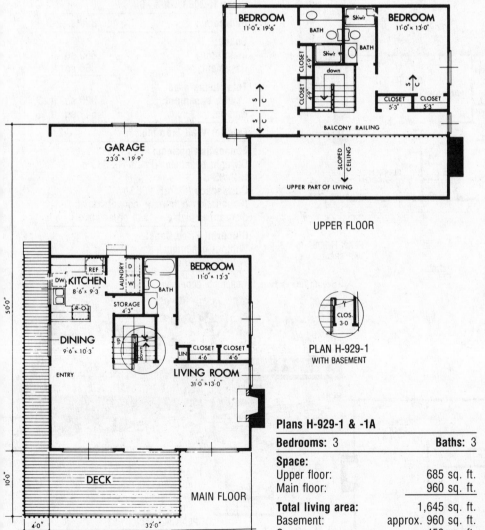

UPPER FLOOR

PLAN H-929-1
WITH BASEMENT

MAIN FLOOR

Plans H-929-1 & -1A

Bedrooms: 3	Baths: 3	Exterior Wall Framing:	2x6
Space:		**Foundation options:**	
Upper floor:	685 sq. ft.	Daylight basement (Plan H-929-1).	
Main floor:	960 sq. ft.	Crawlspace (Plan H-929-1A).	
Total living area:	1,645 sq. ft.	(Foundation & framing conversion	
Basement:	approx. 960 sq. ft.	diagram available — see order form.)	
Garage:	459 sq. ft.	**Blueprint Price Code:**	B

Surrounded by Decks

- Wrap-around deck offers a panoramic view of the surroundings as well as space for outdoor living and relaxation.
- Angular arrangement of garage, breezeway, and home provides front-yard privacy and a visual barrier to front bedrooms from street traffic.
- Exciting L-shaped dining room, attached sunken living room, and deck create a perfect atmosphere for entertaining.
- Basement is available with either a concrete floor (Plan H-2083), a framed floor for steep sloping sites (Plan H-2083-B), or on a crawlspace (Plan H-2083-A).

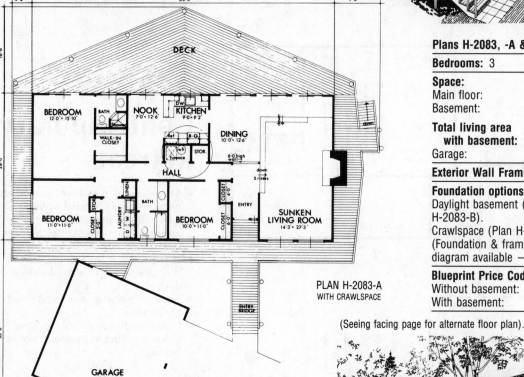

PLAN H-2083-A
WITH CRAWLSPACE

MAIN FLOOR

BASEMENT

Plans H-2083, -A & -B

Bedrooms: 3	Baths: 2-3

Space:

Main floor:	1,660 sq. ft.
Basement:	1,660 sq. ft.

Total living area with basement:	3,320 sq. ft.
Garage:	541 sq. ft.

Exterior Wall Framing:	2x4

Foundation options:
Daylight basement (Plans H-2083 & H-2083-B).
Crawlspace (Plan H-2083-A).
(Foundation & framing conversion diagram available — see order form.)

Blueprint Price Code:

Without basement:	B
With basement:	E

(Seeing facing page for alternate floor plan).

PLAN H-2083-B
WITH BASEMENT
WOOD-FRAMED
LOWER LEVEL

PLAN H-2083
WITH CONCRETE BASEMENT

FRONT VIEW

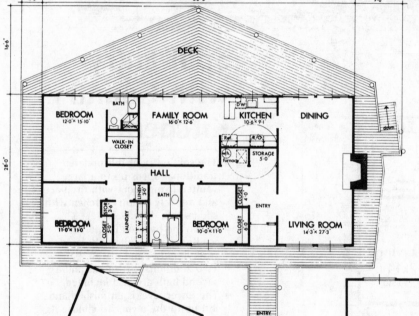

DECK

BEDROOM
12-0 × 15-10

BATH

WALK-IN
CLOSET

FAMILY ROOM
16-0 × 12-6

D/W

KITCHEN
10-6 × 9-1

Ref.   R/O

w.h.   STORAGE
furnace   5-0

HALL

DINING

down

BEDROOM
11-0 × 11-0

CLOSET
5-0

STOR
2-6

LINEN
3-0

LAUNDRY

D/W

BATH

BEDROOM
10-0 × 11-0

CLOSET
6-0

ENTRY

CLOSET
4-0

LIVING ROOM
14-3 × 27-3

ENTRY
BRIDGE

GARAGE
23-3 × 23-3

MAIN FLOOR

Gracious Indoor/ Outdoor Living

- A clean design makes this plan adaptable to almost any climate or setting.
- Perfect for a scenic, hillside lot, the structure and wrap-around deck offers a spanning view.
- Kitchen is flanked by family and dining rooms, allowing easy entrance from both.
- Foundation options include a daylight basement on concrete slab (H-2083-1), a wood-framed lower level (H-2083-1B), and a crawlspace (H-2083-1A).

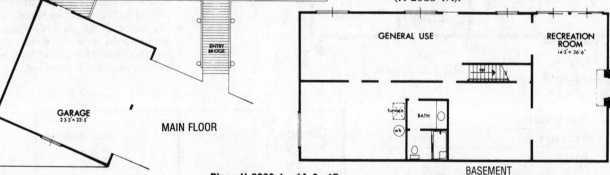

GENERAL USE

RECREATION
ROOM
14-3 × 26-6

furnace

BATH

w.h.

BASEMENT

PLAN H-2083-1
WITH DAYLIGHT BASEMENT
(ON CONCRETE SLAB)

PLAN H-2083-1B
(WITH WOOD-FRAMED LOWER LEVEL)

(See facing page for both rear view and alternate floor plan.)

Plans H-2083-1, -1A & -1B

Bedrooms: 3	Baths: 2-3

Space:

Main floor:	1,660 sq. ft.
Basement:	1,660 sq. ft.

Total living area:

with basement:	3,320 sq. ft.
Garage:	541 sq. ft.

Exterior Wall Framing: 2x4

Foundation options:
Daylight basement (Plan H-2083-1 or -1B).
Crawlspace (Plan H-2083-1A).
(Foundation & framing conversion diagram available — see order form.)

Blueprint Price Code:

Without basement:	B
With basement:	E

TO ORDER THIS BLUEPRINT,
CALL TOLL-FREE 1-800-547-5570

Plans H-2083-1, -1A & -1B

PRICES AND DETAILS
ON PAGES 12-15

75

Split Entry with Country Kitchen

- The split entry of this updated traditional opens up to a large vaulted living room with fireplace and a lovely country kitchen with sliders to a deck.
- Down the hall you'll find the vaulted master suite with large walk-in closet and private bath.
- Two additional bedrooms and a second bath are also included.
- The lower level is unfinished and left up to the owner to choose its function; room for a third bath and laundry facilities is provided.

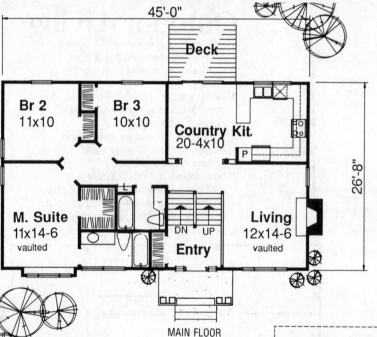

45'-0"

Deck

Br 2 11x10

Br 3 10x10

Country Kit. 20-4x10

P

26'-8"

M. Suite 11x14-6 vaulted

DN UP

Living 12x14-6 vaulted

Entry

MAIN FLOOR

Plan B-90012

Bedrooms: 3	Baths: 2-3

Space:

Main/upper level:	1,203 sq. ft.
Basement:	460 sq. ft.

Total living area:	1,663 sq. ft.
Garage:	509 sq. ft.

Exterior Wall Framing:	2x4

Foundation options:
Daylight basement.
(Foundation & framing conversion diagram available — see order form.)

Blueprint Price Code:	B

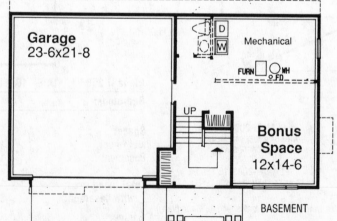

Garage 23-6x21-8

D W Mechanical

FURN WH FD

UP

Bonus Space 12x14-6

BASEMENT

Plan B-90012

PRICES AND DETAILS ON PAGES 12-15

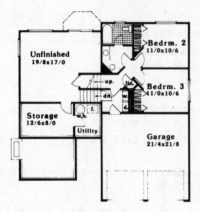

UPPER FLOOR

Plan R-4033

Bedrooms: 3	Baths: 2

Space:	
Upper two levels:	1,185 sq. ft.
Lower level:	480 sq. ft.

Total living area:	1,665 sq. ft.
Bonus area:	334 sq. ft.
Garage:	462 sq. ft.
Storage:	100 sq. ft.

Exterior Wall Framing:	2x6

Foundation options:
Daylight basement only.
(Foundation & framing conversion
diagram available — see order form.)

Blueprint Price Code:	B

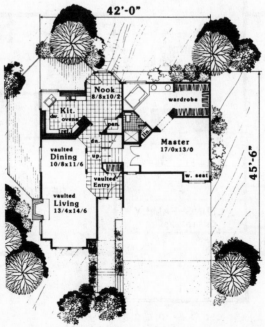

MAIN FLOOR

Exciting Design for Sloping Lot

- This design offers an exciting floor plan for a side-sloping lot.
- The vaulted foyer opens to the living room which is highlighted by a cheerful fireplace and is also vaulted.
- A half-wall with overhead arch separates the foyer and hallway from the dining room without interrupting the flow of space.
- The kitchen offers plenty of counter and cabinet space, and adjoins a brightly lit vaulted nook with a pantry in the corner.
- Separated from the rest of the household, the upper level master suite is a true haven from the day's worries, with its relaxing whirlpool tub, dual vanities and roomy closet.
- The lower level includes two bedrooms, a bath plus a large area which can be finished as a recreation room, plus a utility and storage area.

Comfortable, Open Plan

- A central Great Room features a cathedral ceiling and is visually separated from the dining area by a huge fireplace.
- A wing on the left includes two secondary bedrooms which share a bath.
- In the right wing, you'll find a spacious master bedroom with private bath and walk-in closet.
- The kitchen is roomy and well-planned,

with a utility room in the garage entry area.
- A house-spanning front deck adds an extra welcoming touch to the plan.

Plan C-8160	
Bedrooms: 3	**Baths:** 2
Space:	
Main floor	1,669 sq. ft.
Total Living Area	**1,669 sq. ft.**
Daylight basement (approx.)	1,660 sq. ft.
Carport	413 sq. ft.
Storage (approx.)	85 sq. ft.
Exterior Wall Framing:	2x4

Foundation Options:
Daylight basement
Crawlspace
Slab
(Foundation & framing conversion diagram available—see order form.)

Blueprint Price Code	B

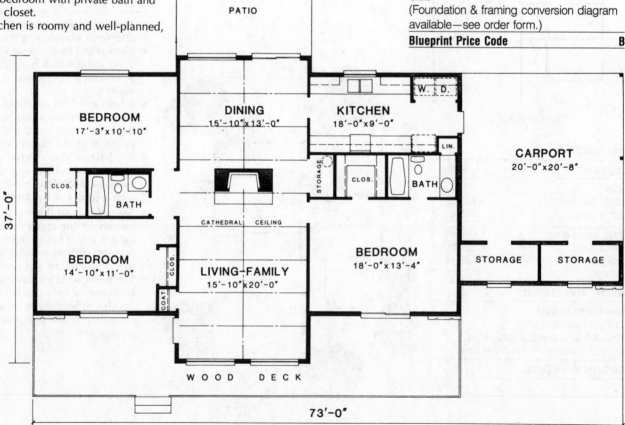

Plan C-8160

Rustic Welcome

- This rustic design boasts an appealing exterior with a covered front porch that offers guests a friendly welcome.
- The side-entry garage gives the front of the home an extra-appealing and uncluttered look.
- Inside, the centrally located Great Room features a cathedral ceiling with exposed wood beams. A massive fireplace separates the living area from the large dining area, which offers access to a nice backyard patio.

- The master suite features a walk-in closet and a compartmentalized bath.
- The galley kitchen lies between the formal dining room and the breakfast room, which features a bay window and a convenient pantry.
- A large utility room and a storage room complete the garage area.
- On the opposite side of the Great Room are two additional bedrooms with oversized closets and a second full bath.
- The optional daylight basement offers expanded living space. The stairway (not shown) would be located along the wall between the dining room and the back bedroom.

Plan C-8460	
Bedrooms: 3	**Baths:** 2
Living Area:	
Main floor	1,670 sq. ft.
Total Living Area:	**1,670 sq. ft.**
Daylight basement	1,600 sq. ft.
Garage	427 sq. ft.
Exterior Wall Framing:	2x4
Foundation Options:	
Daylight basement	
Crawlspace	
Slab	
(Typical foundation & framing conversion diagram available—see order form.)	
BLUEPRINT PRICE CODE:	B

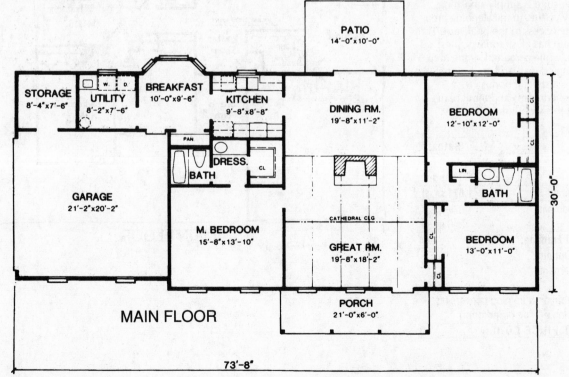

MAIN FLOOR

Smashing Master Suite!

- Corniced gables accented with arched louvers and a covered front porch with striking columns take this one-story design beyond the ordinary.
- The vaulted foyer leads directly into the family room, which also has a vaulted ceiling, plus a central fireplace framed by a window and a French door.
- The angled serving bar/snack counter connects the family room to the sunny dining room and kitchen. The adjoining breakfast room has easy access to the garage, the optional basement and the laundry room with a plant shelf.
- The master suite is simply smashing, with a tray ceiling in the sleeping area and private access to the backyard. The vaulted bath has all of today's finest amenities, while a vaulted sitting area with an angled wall and an optional fireplace is a special bonus.
- Two more bedrooms and a full bath round out this wonderful one-story.

Plan FB-1671

Bedrooms: 3	Baths: 2
Living Area:	
Main floor	1,671 sq. ft.
Total Living Area:	**1,671 sq. ft.**
Daylight basement	1,671 sq. ft.
Garage	240 sq. ft.
Exterior Wall Framing:	2x4

Foundation Options:

Daylight basement
Crawlspace
(Typical foundation & framing conversion diagram available—see order form.)

BLUEPRINT PRICE CODE:	**B**

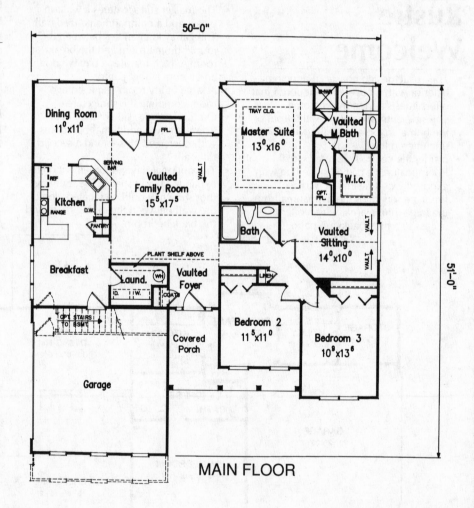

MAIN FLOOR

TO ORDER THIS BLUEPRINT,
CALL TOLL-FREE 1-800-547-5570

Plan FB-1671

PRICES AND DETAILS
ON PAGES 12-15

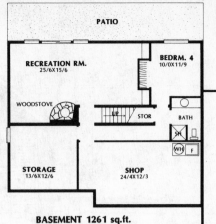

BASEMENT 1261 sq.ft.

Multi-Level Contemporary Design

Offset angles of multi-leveled gables and crisp, contemporary walls of vertical board siding enclose this economically arranged home featuring a secluded master bedroom in a second-level loft with a vaulted ceiling. The main-floor living areas are neatly laid out in 1,261 sq. ft. around a central hallway. The loft adds 412 sq. ft.

Adding curb appeal to the house are an eyebrow ridge with clerestory windows, an open-rafter arbor over a bedroom window, a window seat bumpout, and a circular cutout in the entry wing wall, echoing a round window in the bathroom. Sliding glass doors from the great room open to a wood deck.

Main floor:	1,261 sq. ft.
Second floor:	412 sq. ft.
Total living area: (Not counting basement or garage)	1,673 sq. ft.
Basement level:	1,261 sq. ft.
Total living area with basement:	2,934 sq. ft.

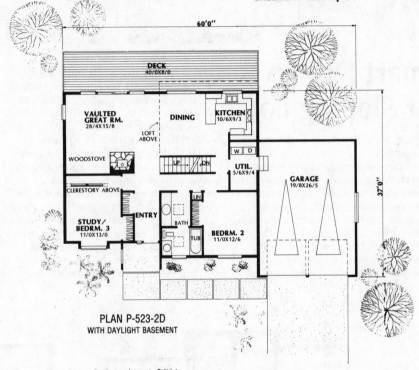

PLAN P-523-2D
WITH DAYLIGHT BASEMENT

REAR VIEW

PLAN P-523-2A
WITHOUT BASEMENT

Blueprint Price Code B Without Basement
Blueprint Price Code D With Daylight Basement

Smart Design for Sloping Lot

- This design is perfect for a narrow, sloping lot.
- The main entry opens to a spacious, vaulted living area. A comfortable Great Room and a sunny dining area merge with corner windows that create a dramatic boxed bay. Another attention-getter is the cozy woodstove in the corner of the beautiful Great Room.
- The dining area offers sliding glass doors that extend family activities or

entertaining to the adjoining deck.
- The dining area flows into the kitchen, which features a vaulted ceiling and a windowed sink that overlooks the deck.
- Two bedrooms are located at the back of the home, each with a private, skylighted bath. The master bedroom also has a walk-in wardrobe, a lovely window seat and deck access.
- A vaulted, skylighted hall leads to the stairway to the basement, where there are a third bedroom and another full bathroom. A very large shop/storage area and a two-car garage are also included. An extra bonus is the carport/storage area below the deck.

Plan P-529-2D	
Bedrooms: 3	**Baths:** 3
Living Area:	
Main floor	1,076 sq. ft.
Daylight basement	597 sq. ft.
Total Living Area:	**1,673 sq. ft.**
Tuck-under garage	425 sq. ft.
Exterior Wall Framing:	2x6
Foundation Options:	
Daylight basement	
BLUEPRINT PRICE CODE:	B

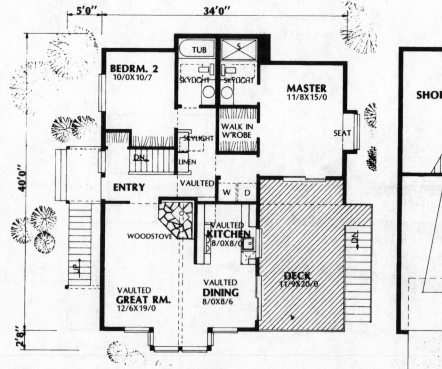

MAIN FLOOR

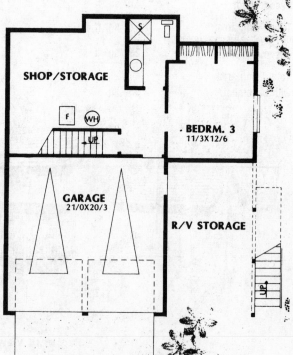

DAYLIGHT BASEMENT

Plan P-529-2D

Sun Room Adds Warmth to "Switched-Level" Contemporary

Solar warmth abounds in this dining area sun room, bolstered by a nearby free-standing wood fireplace and heat-storing masonry. An unusual feature of this design is that the active areas are on the second floor for a better view, and the sleeping rooms on the lower floor.

The spacious entry hall, with a door in from the double garage, has stairs with an open balcony railing leading up to the living-dining-kitchen floor, or down to the bedrooms, for complete traffic separation.

The open-plan upper floor, with vaulted ceiling, has an eight-foot wall screening the dining area from the stairway and the half-bath that is adjacent to the kitchen.

The glass roof and windows over and around the dining area are passive solar collectors and a brick or slate floor provides a storage mass.

A sliding glass door in the living room window wall opens onto the large wood deck, enhancing the view orientation of the house. Another small deck is reached by a French door next to the woodstove.

Downstairs, a hallway from the stairs leads to the master bedroom, with its own bath and large closets, and to the other two bedrooms, second bath and utility room.

The upper floor has 886 sq. ft., and there are 790 sq. ft. downstairs. Ceilings have R-30 insulation and the 2x6 stud walls hold R-19 batts.

Upper floor:	886 sq. ft.
Lower floor:	790 sq. ft.
Total living area: (Not counting garage)	1,676 sq. ft.

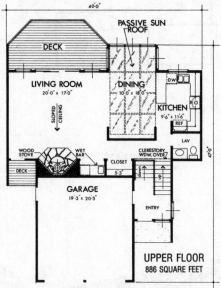

UPPER FLOOR
886 SQUARE FEET

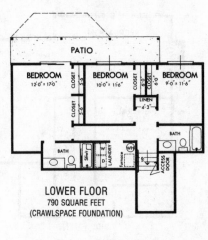

LOWER FLOOR
790 SQUARE FEET
(CRAWLSPACE FOUNDATION)

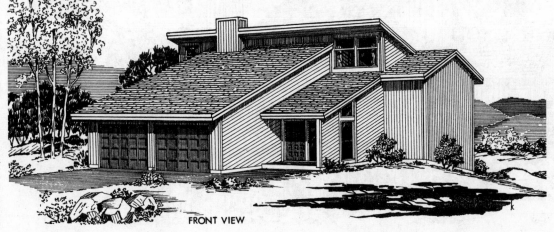

FRONT VIEW

Blueprint Price Code B
Plan H-945-1A

TO ORDER THIS BLUEPRINT,
CALL TOLL-FREE 1-800-547-5570

PRICES AND DETAILS
ON PAGES 12-15

83

FRONT VIEW

Sunny Family Living

- Pleasant-looking and unassuming from the front, this plan breaks into striking, sun-catching angles at the rear.
- The living room sun roof gathers passive solar heat, which is stored in the tile floor and the two-story high masonry backdrop to the wood stove.
- A 516-square-foot master suite with private bath and balcony makes up the second floor.
- The main floor offers two more bedrooms and a full bath.

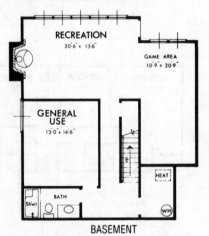

BASEMENT

PASSIVE SUN ROOM BELOW

BALCONY RAILING

BEDROOM
17'3" x 13'3"

SLOPED CEILING

WALK-IN CLOSET
10'9" x 6'6"

BATH

UPPER FLOOR

STOR

WITHOUT BASEMENT
(CRAWLSPACE FOUNDATION)

40'-0"

PASSIVE SUN ROOM

THERMAL STORAGE FLOOR

DINING
10'3" x 12'0"

DECK

WOOD STOVE

LIVING ROOM
20'9" x 13'6"

SLOPED CEILING

KITCHEN
9'0" x 10'0"

BEDROOM
11'0" x 10'0"

CLOSET
5'0"

CLOSET
4'0"

STOR
4'0"

REF

STOR

HEAT WH

BATH

LIN

GARAGE
11'9" x 23'9"

ENTRY

LAUNDRY
W D

CLOSET
6'0"

BEDROOM
11'0" x 10'0"

50'-0"

MAIN FLOOR

Plans H-947-1A & -1B

Bedrooms: 3	Baths: 2-3
Space:	
Upper floor:	516 sq. ft.
Main floor:	1,162 sq. ft.
Total without basement:	1,678 sq. ft.
Daylight basement:	966 sq. ft.
Total with basement:	2,644 sq. ft.
Garage:	279 sq. ft.
Exterior Wall Framing:	2x6

Foundation options:
Daylight basement (H-947-1B).
Crawlspace (H-947-1A).
(Foundation & framing conversion diagram available — see order form.)

Blueprint Price Code:

Without basement:	B
With basement:	D

RECREATION
20'6" x 13'6"

GAME AREA
10'9" x 20'9"

GENERAL USE
13'0" x 14'6"

HEAT

BATH

Shwr

WH

REAR VIEW

Plans H-947-1A & -1B

PRICES AND DETAILS ON PAGES 12-15

Compact Three-Bedroom Home

- A stylish blend of traditional and contemporary architecture emanates from this compact, three-bedroom home.
- Two bedrooms and an adjoining bath occupy one corner of the main level, segregated from the living areas by a central hallway.
- Large living and dining area has sloped ceilings, wood stove, and access to side deck.
- Master suite occupies entire 516 sq. ft. second floor, features sloped ceilings, and overlooks the living room below.

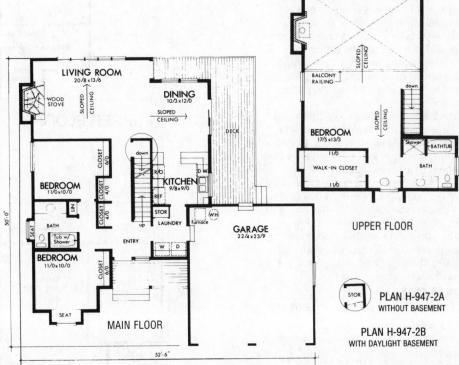

UPPER FLOOR

PLAN H-947-2A
WITHOUT BASEMENT

PLAN H-947-2B
WITH DAYLIGHT BASEMENT

MAIN FLOOR

Plans H-947-2A & -2B	
Bedrooms: 3	**Baths:** 2

Space:	
Upper floor:	516 sq. ft.
Main floor:	1,162 sq. ft.
Total living area:	**1,678 sq. ft.**
Basement:	approx. 1,162 sq. ft.
Garage:	530 sq. ft.

Exterior Wall Framing: 2x6

Foundation options:
Daylight basement (Plan H-947-2B).
Crawlspace (Plan H-947-2A).
(Foundation & framing conversion diagram available — see order form.)

Blueprint Price Code: B

Plenty of Presence

- A stucco facade complemented by fieldstone, handsome keystones accenting the interesting window treatments and an imposing roofline give this home lots of presence.

- Inside, a two-story foyer an open stairway with a balcony overlook above provides an impressive welcome. Straight ahead, the huge family room is expanded by a vaulted ceiling, plus a tall window and a French door that frame the fireplace.

- The adjoining dining room flows into the kitchen and breakfast room, which feature an angled serving bar, lots of sunny windows and a French door that opens to a covered patio.

- The main-floor master suite is the pride of the floor plan, offering a tray ceiling, a vaulted spa bath and a spacious walk-in closet brightened by a window.

- The upper floor has two bedrooms, each with a walk-in closet, and a full bath. Abundant attic storage space is easily accessible.

Plan FB-1681

Bedrooms: 3	Baths: 2½
Living Area:	
Upper floor	449 sq. ft.
Main floor	1,232 sq. ft.
Total Living Area:	**1,681 sq. ft.**
Daylight basement	1,232 sq. ft.
Garage	420 sq. ft.
Storage	15 sq. ft.
Exterior Wall Framing:	2x4

Foundation Options:
Daylight basement
Slab
(Typical foundation & framing conversion diagram available—see order form.)

BLUEPRINT PRICE CODE: B

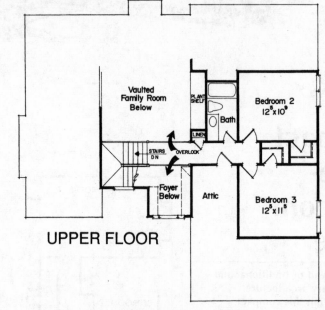

UPPER FLOOR

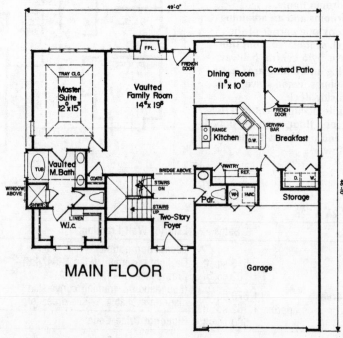

MAIN FLOOR

Rustic Home
With Porches
Means Relaxation

A spacious screened porch serves as a great place to eat out during warm summer days and nights, while the front porch is ideal for relaxed rocking or a swing. The Great Room to the left of the entry has a fireplace and connects to the dining area and country kitchen. The large master bedroom features a private bath and ample closets.

For entertaining large groups, the combined dining area, living room and screened porch provide lots of space. Also note the large kitchen/utility and pantry area.

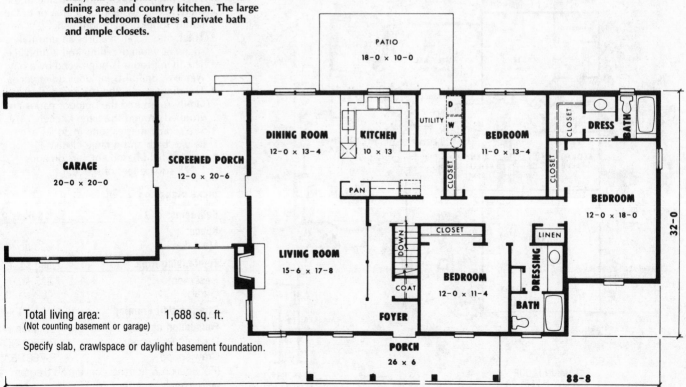

Total living area: 1,688 sq. ft.
(Not counting basement or garage)

Specify slab, crawlspace or daylight basement foundation.

Blueprint Price Code B
Plan C-7557

TO ORDER THIS BLUEPRINT,
CALL TOLL-FREE 1-800-547-5570

PRICES AND DETAILS
ON PAGES 12-15   **87**

Exciting Interior Angles

- A relatively modest-looking exterior encloses an exciting interior design that's loaded with surprises.
- The Y-shaped entry directs traffic to the more formal living/dining area or to the family room or bedroom wing.
- The family room features an unusual shape, a vaulted ceiling and a fireplace.
- The living room is brightened by a bay window, and also includes a fireplace.
- The dining area, the sun room, the family room and the outdoor patios are grouped around the large kitchen.
- The roomy master suite includes a deluxe bath and a large closet.
- The daylight-basement version adds 1,275 square feet of space.

Plans P-7661-3A & -3D

Bedrooms: 2-3	**Baths:** 2

Space:	
Main floor	1,693 sq. ft.
Total Living Area	**1,693 sq. ft.**
Basement	1,275 sq. ft.
Garage	462 sq. ft.
Exterior Wall Framing	2x4

Foundation options:	**Plan #**
Daylight Basement	P-7661-3D
Crawlspace	P-7661-3A

(Foundation & framing conversion diagram available—see order form.)

Blueprint Price Code	**B**

MAIN FLOOR PLAN P-7661-3A
WITH CRAWLSPACE

Floor plan labels: 55'-0", 54'-0", WARDROBE, MASTER 13/0x15/6, PATIO, VAULTED FAMILY RM. 17/0x13/6, KITCHEN 13/0x10/0, LINEN, LIN, WOODSTOVE, VAULTED SUN RM., EXP. BM., PATIO, PANTRY, ENTRY, DINING AREA, BEDRM. 2 10/0x10/0, DEN/BEDRM. 3 10/0x11/6, W, D, F, WH, LIVING RM. 18/4x18/4, GARAGE 21/4x21/8

PLAN P-7661-3D
WITH DAYLIGHT BASEMENT

Labels: BAR, MASTER, DN

Plans P-7661-3A & -3D

PRICES AND DETAILS ON PAGES 12-15

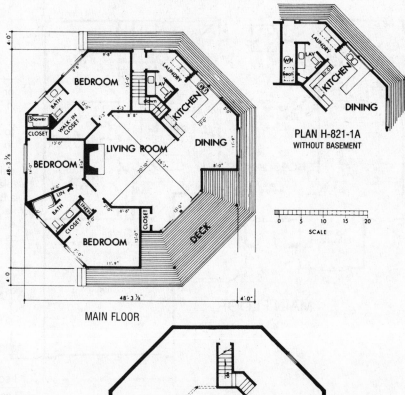

MAIN FLOOR

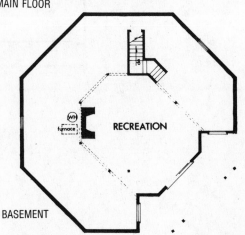

BASEMENT

PLAN H-821-1A
WITHOUT BASEMENT

SCALE
0   5   10   15   20

Versatile Octagon

- **Popular octagonal design features a secondary raised roof to allow light into the 500 sq. ft. living room.**
- **Unique framing design allows you to divide the living space any way you choose: left open, with 3 or more bedrooms, a den, library or other options.**
- **Large, winding deck can accommodate outdoor parties and guests.**
- **Optional basement expands recreational opportunities.**

Plans H-821-1 & -1A

Bedrooms: 3	Baths: 2½
Space:	
Main floor:	1,699 sq. ft.
Total living area:	1,699 sq. ft.
Basement:	approx. 1,699 sq. ft.
Exterior Wall Framing:	2x4

Foundation options:
Daylight basement (Plan H-821-1).
Crawlspace (Plan H-821-1A).
(Foundation & framing conversion
diagram available — see order form.)

Blueprint Price Code:
Without basement	B
With basement	E

Dramatic Dining Room

- The highlight of this lovely one-story design is its dramatic dining room, which boasts a high ceiling and a tall wall of windows.
- The soaring foyer ushers guests through an arched opening and into the vaulted Great Room, which is warmed by a showy fireplace.
- The kitchen features a large pantry, a serving bar and a handy pass-through to the family room. The bright breakfast area offers outdoor access and a convenient laundry closet.
- The two secondary bedrooms share a compartmentalized bath.
- The master suite is unsurpassed, with its sitting room, plant shelves and volume ceilings. A gorgeous corner tub is found in the luxurious master bath.

Plan FB-5008-ALLE

Bedrooms: 3	Baths: 2
Living Area:	
Main floor	1,715 sq. ft.
Total Living Area:	**1,715 sq. ft.**
Daylight basement	1,715 sq. ft.
Garage	400 sq. ft.
Exterior Wall Framing:	2x4

Foundation Options:

Daylight basement

Crawlspace

Slab

(All plans can be built with your choice of foundation and framing. A generic conversion diagram is available. See order form.)

BLUEPRINT PRICE CODE:	**B**

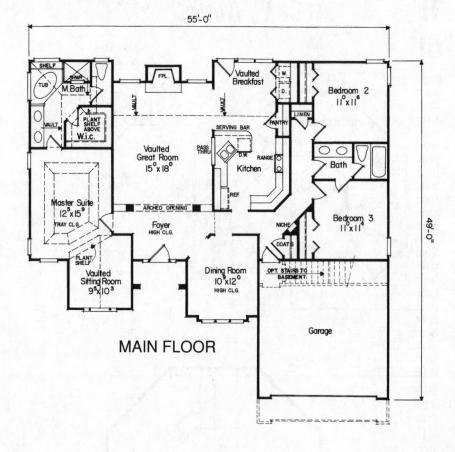

MAIN FLOOR

High, Dramatic Interior Spaces

- High ceilings and dramatic window treatments are the keynotes of this light-filled one-story home.
- A covered porch with elegant columns leads to the foyer and the living room beyond, with views of the backyard through French doors and windows.
- The living room flows into the bayed breakfast area and the gourmet kitchen. An angled serving bar is convenient to both the breakfast area and the family room, which features a fireplace and access to the outdoors.
- A half-round window and a tray ceiling make the master suite airy and cozy at the same time. The master bath features a garden tub, a double-sink vanity with knee space and a separate shower. A plant shelf adorns the walk-in closet.
- Two secondary bedrooms, one with a vaulted ceiling, share a hall bath.

Plan FB-5024-BRYS

Bedrooms: 3	Baths: 2
Living Area:	
Main floor	1,715 sq. ft.
Total Living Area:	**1,715 sq. ft.**
Daylight basement	1,715 sq. ft.
Garage	427 sq. ft.
Exterior Wall Framing:	2x4

Foundation Options:

Daylight basement

Crawlspace

(Typical foundation & framing conversion diagram available—see order form.)

BLUEPRINT PRICE CODE: B

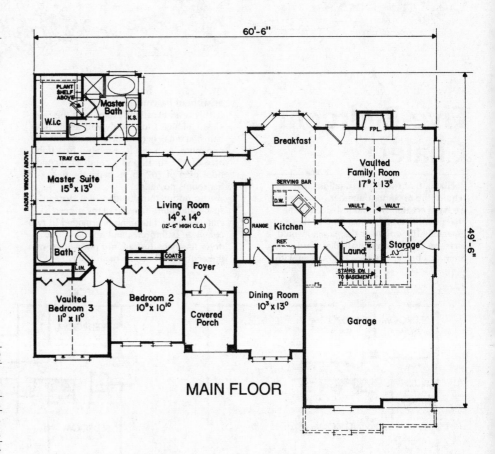

MAIN FLOOR

Five-Bedroom Chalet

Realizing that there are situations that require the maximum number of bedrooms, we have created this modest-sized home containing five bedrooms. One of these, especially the one over the garage, would serve very well as a private den, card room or library. The plan is available with or without basement.

This is an excellent example of the classic chalet. Close study will reveal how hall space has been kept at an absolute minimum. As a result, a modest first floor area of 952 sq. ft. and a compact second floor plan of 767 sq. ft. make the five bedrooms possible.

Also notice the abundance of storage space and built-ins with many other conveniences. Plumbing is provided in two complete bathrooms, and a washer and dryer has been tucked into one corner of the central hall on the main floor.

A clever technique has been used in the design of the staircase as it progresses halfway up to a landing midway between the two floors. From here it branches in two directions to a bedroom over the garage and to a hallway common to other rooms.

First floor:	952 sq. ft.
Second floor:	767 sq. ft.
Total living area:	1,719 sq. ft.

(Not counting basement or garage)

FIRST FLOOR
952 SQUARE FEET

SECOND FLOOR
767 SQUARE FEET

PLAN H-804-2
WITH BASEMENT
PLAN H-804-2A
WITHOUT BASEMENT
(CRAWLSPACE FOUNDATION)

Blueprint Price Code B

Plans H-804-2 & -2A

92   *TO ORDER THIS BLUEPRINT,*
CALL TOLL-FREE 1-800-547-5570

PRICES AND DETAILS
ON PAGES 12-15

Panoramic View Embraces Outdoors

- This geometric design takes full advantage of scenic sites.
- Living area faces a glass-filled wall and wrap-around deck.
- Open dining/living room arrangement is complemented by vaulted ceilings, an overhead balcony, and a 5-ft-wide fireplace.
- 12' deep main deck offers generous space for outdoor dining and entertaining.

PLAN H-855-1A
WITHOUT BASEMENT

SCALE

BEDROOM
11'-4" x 13'-6"

Sh'w'r

BEDROOM
10'-0" x 15'-0"

BATH
8'-6" x 7'-6"

CLOSET
5'-2"

down

CLOSET
4'-6"

CLOSET
4'-6"

LINEN

BALCONY

UPPER FLOOR

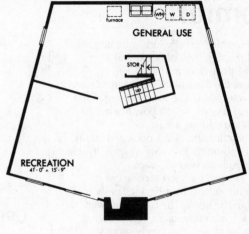

furnace

WH W D

GENERAL USE

STOR

UP

RECREATION
41'-0" x 15'-9"

BASEMENT

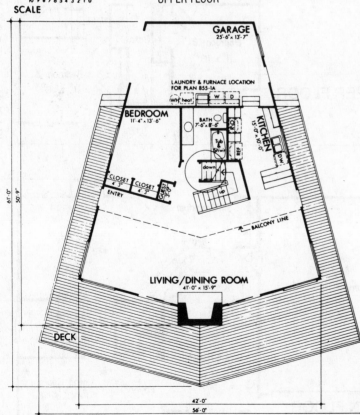

GARAGE
25'-6" x 13'-7"

LAUNDRY & FURNACE LOCATION
FOR PLAN 855-1A

WH heat W D

BEDROOM
11'-4" x 13'-6"

BATH
7'-6" x 8'-6"

KITCHEN
15'-0" x 10'-0"

DW

REF

down

CLOSET
4'-3"

CLOSET
4'-3"

GUEST
3'-0"

ENTRY

up

BALCONY LINE

LIVING/DINING ROOM
41'-0" x 15'-9"

DECK

42'-0"

56'-0"

61'-0"

50'-9"

MAIN FLOOR

Plans H-855-1 & -1A

Bedrooms: 3	Baths: 2

Space:	
Upper floor:	625 sq. ft.
Main floor:	1,108 sq. ft.

Total living area:	1,733 sq. ft.
Basement:	approx. 1,108 sq. ft.
Garage:	346 sq. ft.

Exterior Wall Framing:	2x6

Foundation options:
Daylight basement (Plan H-855-1).
Crawlspace (Plan H-855-1A).
(Foundation & framing conversion diagram available — see order form.)

Blueprint Price Code:	
Without basement	B
With basement	D

Class with Comfort

- Twin gables, great window treatments and the rich look of brick lend a sophisticated air to this design.
- Inside, the floor plan is comfortable and unpretentious. The foyer is open to the formal spaces, which flow freely into the casual living areas.
- The kitchen, breakfast nook and family room combine to create a highly livable area with no wasted space.
- The kitchen's angled serving bar accommodates those in the family room and in the nook. The bay-windowed nook has a convenient, space-saving laundry closet. The family room's fireplace warms the entire area.
- The upper floor is highlighted by an irresistible master suite featuring his-and-hers walk-in closets and a vaulted bath with a garden tub.

Plan FB-1744-L

Bedrooms: 4	Baths: 2½
Living Area:	
Upper floor	860 sq. ft.
Main floor	884 sq. ft.
Total Living Area:	**1,744 sq. ft.**
Daylight basement	884 sq. ft.
Garage	456 sq. ft.
Exterior Wall Framing:	2x4

Foundation Options:

Daylight basement
Crawlspace
Slab
(Typical foundation & framing conversion diagram available—see order form.)

BLUEPRINT PRICE CODE:	B

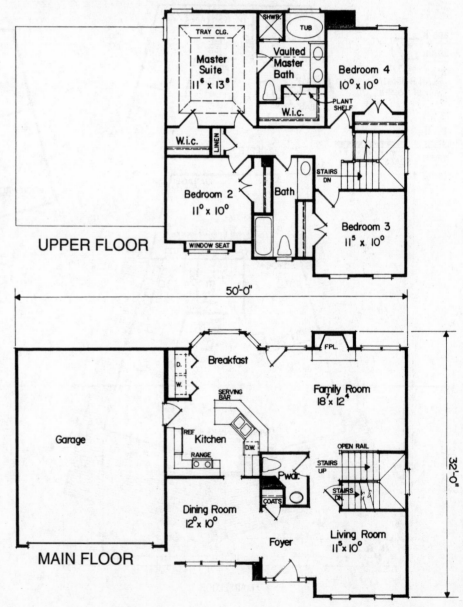

UPPER FLOOR

MAIN FLOOR

50'-0"

32'-0"

Plan FB-1744-L

PRICES AND DETAILS ON PAGES 12-15

REAR VIEW

Solar Flair

- Full window walls and a sun room with glass roof act as passive energy collectors in this popular floor plan.
- Expansive living room features wood stove and vaulted ceilings.
- Dining room shares a breakfast counter with the merging kitchen.
- Convenient laundry room is positioned near kitchen and garage entrance.
- Second level is devoted entirely to the private master suite, featuring vaulted ceiling and a balcony view to the living room below.

Plans H-877-5A & -5B

Bedrooms: 3-4	**Baths:** 2-3

Space:

Upper floor:	382 sq. ft.
Main floor:	1,200 sq. ft.
Sun room:	162 sq. ft.
Total living area:	**1,744 sq. ft.**
Basement:	approx. 1,200 sq. ft.
Garage:	457 sq. ft.

Exterior Wall Framing: 2x6

Foundation options:
Daylight basement (Plan H-877-5B).
Crawlspace (Plan H-877-5A).
(Foundation & framing conversion diagram available — see order form.)

Blueprint Price Code:

Without basement:	B
With basement:	D

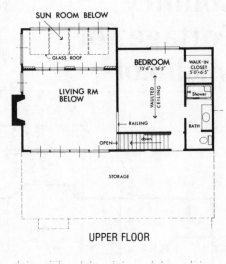

UPPER FLOOR

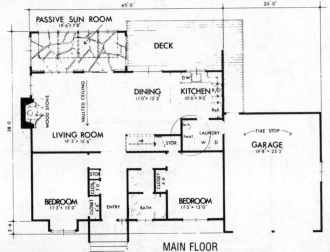

MAIN FLOOR

PLAN H-877-5B
WITH BASEMENT

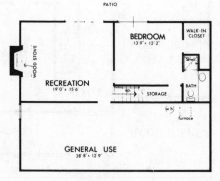

BASEMENT

FRONT VIEW

Modern Country Cottage for Small Lot

This drive-under garage design is great for smaller lots. But even though the home is relatively compact, it's still loaded with modern features. The deluxe master bedroom has a large bath with garden tub and shower. The country kitchen/dining room combination has access to a deck out back. The large living room with fireplace is accessible from the two story foyer.

The upper floor has two large bedrooms and a full bath, and the large basement has room for two cars and expandable living areas.

This plan is available with daylight basement foundation only.

Main floor:	1,100 sq. ft.
Second floor:	664 sq. ft.
Total living area: (Not counting basement or garage)	1,764 sq. ft.
Basement:	1,100 sq. ft.

PLAN C-8870
WITH DAYLIGHT BASEMENT

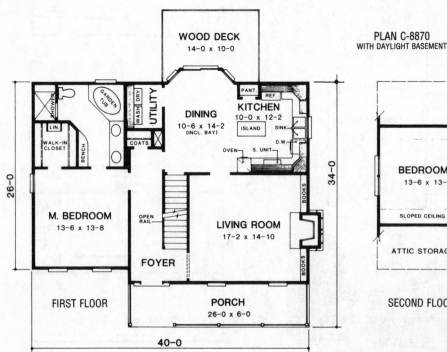

Blueprint Price Code B
Plan C-8870

PRICES AND DETAILS ON PAGES 12-15

FRONT VIEW

Sun Lovers' Hideaway

- Attractive, cozy and sunny are only three adjectives that come immediately to mind as one looks at this plan. Energy efficiency is also a major element.
- An air-lock entry helps seal heated or cooled air inside, and the home is well-insulated in walls, ceilings and floors for tight control of energy bills.
- The major portion of the main floor is devoted to a spacious living/dining/kitchen area with easy access to the large sun room.
- Two downstairs bedrooms share a full bath and include large double-glazed windows.
- Upstairs, the master suite features a private bath and large closet, plus a balcony overlook into the living room.
- An optional daylight basement offers potential for an additional bedroom as well as a large recreation room and general use area. In this version, the sun room is on the lower level, and a dramatic spiral staircase ascends to the main floor.

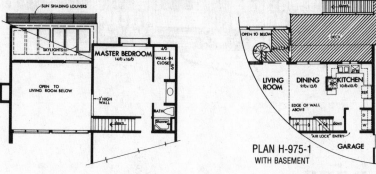

UPPER FLOOR

PLAN H-975-1
WITH BASEMENT

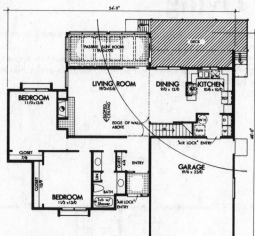

MAIN FLOOR
PLAN H-975-1A
WITHOUT BASEMENT

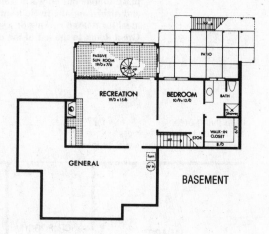

BASEMENT

Plans H-975-1 & -1A

Bedrooms: 3	**Baths:** 2

Space:

Upper floor	370 sq. ft.
Main floor	
(including sun room)	1,394 sq. ft.
Optional daylight basement	1,394 sq. ft.
Finished (including sun room)	782 sq. ft.
Unfinished	612 sq. ft.
Total Living Area	**1,764/2,546 sq. ft.**
Garage	448 sq. ft.
Exterior Wall Framing	2x6

Foundation options:	**Plan #**
Daylight Basement	H-975-1
Crawlspace	H-975-1A

(Foundation & framing conversion diagram available—see order form.)

Blueprint Price Code	B/D

REAR VIEW

Rustic Home for Relaxed Living

A screened-in breezeway provides a cool place to dine out on warm summer days and nights, and the rustic front porch is ideal for relaxed rocking or a swing. A Great Room to the left of the entry has a fireplace and connects the dining area to the country kitchen.

The large master suite contains separate shower, garden tub, vanities and walk-in closets.

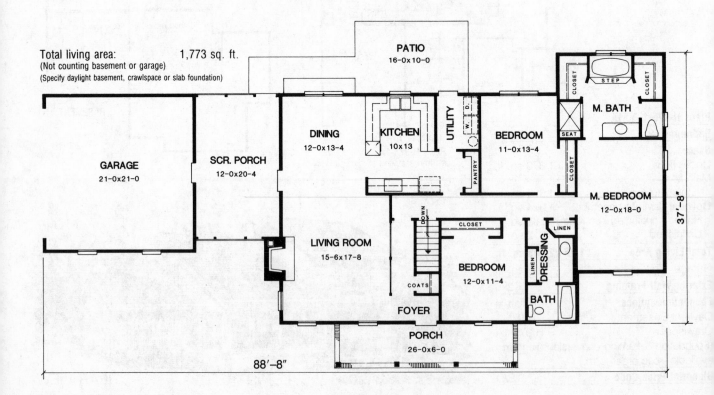

Total living area: 1,773 sq. ft.
(Not counting basement or garage)
(Specify daylight basement, crawlspace or slab foundation)

PATIO
16-0 x 10-0

GARAGE
21-0 x 21-0

SCR. PORCH
12-0 x 20-4

DINING
12-0 x 13-4

KITCHEN
10 x 13

UTILITY

W. D.

PANTRY

BEDROOM
11-0 x 13-4

CLOSET

STEP

CLOSET

M. BATH

SEAT

CLOSET

M. BEDROOM
12-0 x 18-0

37'-8"

LIVING ROOM
15-6 x 17-8

DOWN

CLOSET

LINEN

LINEN

DRESSING

BATH

BEDROOM
12-0 x 11-4

COATS

FOYER

PORCH
26-0 x 6-0

88'-8"

Blueprint Price Code B
Plan C-8650

PRICES AND DETAILS
ON PAGES 12-15

FRONT VIEW

Popular Plan for Any Setting

- City, country, or casual living is possible in this versatile two-story design.
- A spa room and sunning area lie between the master suite and Great Room, all encased in an extended eating and viewing deck.
- U-shaped kitchen, nook, and dining area fulfill your entertaining and dining needs.
- Two additional bedrooms and a balcony hall are located on the second level.
- Daylight basement option provides a fourth bedroom, shop, and recreation area.

REAR VIEW

UPPER FLOOR

- OPEN TO GREAT ROOM
- FIXED SKYLIGHTS
- OPENABLE SKYLIGHTS
- OPEN RAILING
- BALCONY HALL
- SLOPED CEILING
- BEDROOM 12'-0" x 10'-0"
- CLOSET / BATH / CLOSET
- BEDROOM 11'-0" x 13'-4"
- PULL DOWN STAIR
- STORAGE 9'-3" x 10'-0"

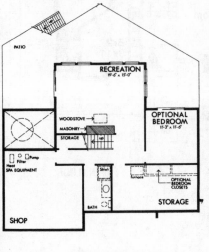

BASEMENT

- PATIO
- RECREATION 19'-6" x 15'-0"
- WOODSTOVE
- OPTIONAL BEDROOM 17'-3" x 11'-6"
- MASONRY
- STORAGE
- up
- Heat SPA EQUIPMENT
- Filter Pump
- Furnace
- OPTIONAL BEDROOM CLOSETS
- STORAGE
- BATH
- SHOP

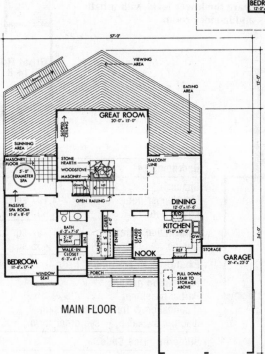

MAIN FLOOR

- 57'-0"
- VIEWING AREA
- SUNNING AREA
- GREAT ROOM 20'-0" x 15'-0"
- SLOPED CEILING
- EATING AREA
- MASONRY FLOOR
- 5'-0" DIAMETER SPA
- STONE HEARTH
- WOODSTOVE
- MASONRY
- BALCONY LINE
- PASSIVE SPA ROOM 11'-6" x 8'-0"
- OPEN RAILING
- DINING 12'-0" x 11'-5"
- BATH 6'-3" x 7'-6"
- GUEST
- LEADED GLASS
- KITCHEN 15'-0" x 10'-0"
- BEDROOM 11'-6" x 17'-4"
- 5'-0" Shwr
- WALK-IN CLOSET 6'-3" x 6'-1"
- LAUNDRY W D
- ENTRY
- NOOK
- REF
- STORAGE
- GARAGE 21'-4" x 23'-3"
- WINDOW SEAT
- PORCH
- PULL DOWN STAIR TO STORAGE ABOVE

Plans H-952-1A &-1B

Bedrooms: 3-4	Baths: 2-3

Space:	
Upper floor:	470 sq. ft.
Main floor:	1,207 sq. ft.
Passive spa room:	102 sq. ft.
Total living area:	**1,779 sq. ft.**
Basement:	1,105 sq. ft.
Garage:	496 sq. ft.

Exterior Wall Framing:	2x6

Foundation options:
Daylight Basement (Plan H-952-1B).
Crawlspace (Plan H-952-1A).
(Foundation & framing conversion diagram available — see order form.)

Blueprint Price Code:

H-952-1A:	B
H-952-1B:	D

New Yet Familiar

- You'll find style and value in this newly planned split entry home.
- Ground-hugging front roof lines cover the vaulted Great Room, dining room, kitchen and master bedroom.
- The front-facing Great Room features a lovely fireplace flanked by windows and entrance to a deck; it is overlooked by a balcony dining room above.

- The breakfast room off the kitchen also offers an exciting adjoining deck, which may be entered through the master bedroom as well.
- Two additional bedrooms are found on the upper level; a fourth bedroom and generous family room share the lower level with a bath and laundry room.

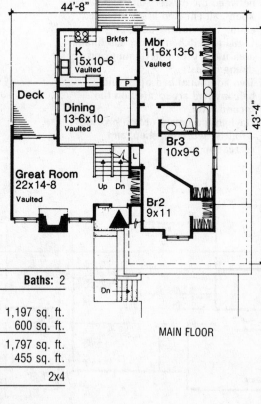

MAIN FLOOR

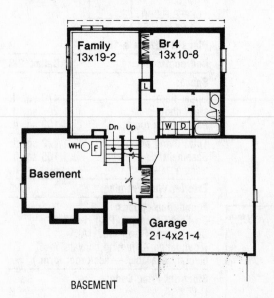

BASEMENT

Plan B-903

Bedrooms: 4	Baths: 2
Space:	
Main/upper floor:	1,197 sq. ft.
Lower floor:	600 sq. ft.
Total living area:	1,797 sq. ft.
Garage:	455 sq. ft.
Exterior Wall Framing:	2x4

Foundation options:
Partial basement.
(Foundation & framing conversion diagram available — see order form.)

| **Blueprint Price Code:** | B |

FRONT VIEW

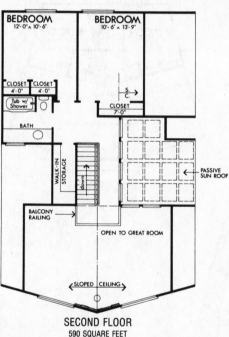

BEDROOM
12'-0" x 10'-6"

BEDROOM
10'-6" x 13'-9"

CLOSET
4'-0"

CLOSET
4'-0"

S.C.

CLOSET
7'-0"

Tub w/ Shower

BATH

WALK-IN STORAGE

down

PASSIVE SUN ROOF

BALCONY RAILING

OPEN TO GREAT ROOM

SLOPED CEILING

SECOND FLOOR
590 SQUARE FEET

First floor:	1,074 sq. ft.
Passive sun room:	136 sq. ft.
Second floor:	590 sq. ft.
Total living area:	**1,800 sq. ft.**
(Not counting basement or garage)	

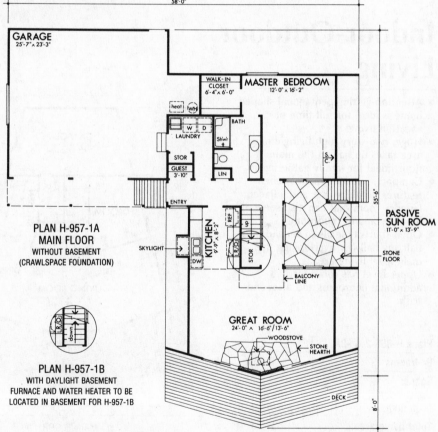

58'-0"

GARAGE
25'-7" x 23'-3"

WALK-IN CLOSET
6'-4" x 6'-0"

MASTER BEDROOM
12'-0" x 16'-2"

heat   WH

W D

LAUNDRY

BATH

Sh/wr

STOR

GUEST
3'-10"

LIN

S.C.

ENTRY

PLAN H-957-1A
MAIN FLOOR
WITHOUT BASEMENT
(CRAWLSPACE FOUNDATION)

SKYLIGHT

REF

KITCHEN
9'-9" x 8'-2"

R/O

UP

STOR

DW

BALCONY LINE

PASSIVE SUN ROOM
11'-0" x 13'-9"

STONE FLOOR

55'-6"

R/O

down

PLAN H-957-1B
WITH DAYLIGHT BASEMENT
FURNACE AND WATER HEATER TO BE
LOCATED IN BASEMENT FOR H-957-1B

GREAT ROOM
24'-0" x 16'-6"/13'-6"

WOODSTOVE

STONE HEARTH

DECK

8'-0"

A Truly Livable Retreat

For a number of years the A-Frame idea has enjoyed great acceptance and popularity, especially in recreational areas. Too often, however, hopeful expectations have led to disappointment because

economic necessity resulted in small and restricted buildings. Not so with this plan. Without ignoring the need for economy, the designers allowed themselves enough freedom to create a truly livable and practical home with a main floor of 1,210 sq. ft., exclusive of the garage area. The second floor has 590 sq. ft., and includes two bedrooms, a bath and ample storage space.

Take special note of the multi-use passive sun room. Its primary purpose is to collect, store and redistribute the sun's heat, not only saving a considerable

amount of money but contributing an important function of keeping out dampness and cold when the owners are elsewhere. Otherwise the room might serve as a delightful breakfast room, a lovely arboretum, an indoor exercise room or any of many other functions limited only by the occupants' ingenuity.

A truly livable retreat, whether for weekend relaxation or on a daily basis as a primary residence, this passive solar A-Frame is completely equipped for the requirements of today's active living. Exterior walls are framed with 2x6 studs.

Blueprint Price Code B

Plans H-957-1A & -1B

PRICES AND DETAILS
ON PAGES 12-15

Indoor-Outdoor Living

- Attention-getting pentagonal-shaped home is ideal for full-time or vacation living.
- Huge, two-story high living/dining area takes up half of the main floor, ideal for family gatherings.
- Compact, but functional kitchen features breakfast bar and adjacent laundry room that can also serve as a pantry and/or mudroom.
- Open stairway leads to second-floor balcony hallway overlooking the main level living area.
- Upper level has room for two additional bedrooms and a second bath.

Plans H-855-2 & -2A

Bedrooms: 3	Baths: 2

Space:	
Upper floor:	660 sq. ft.
Main floor:	1,174 sq. ft.

Total living area:	1,834 sq. ft.
Basement:	approx. 1,174 sq. ft.
Garage:	277 sq. ft.

Exterior Wall Framing: 2x4

Foundation options:
Daylight basement (Plan H-855-2).
Crawlspace (Plan H-855-2A).
(Foundation & framing conversion diagram available — see order form.)

Blueprint Price Code:	
Without basement	B
With basement	E

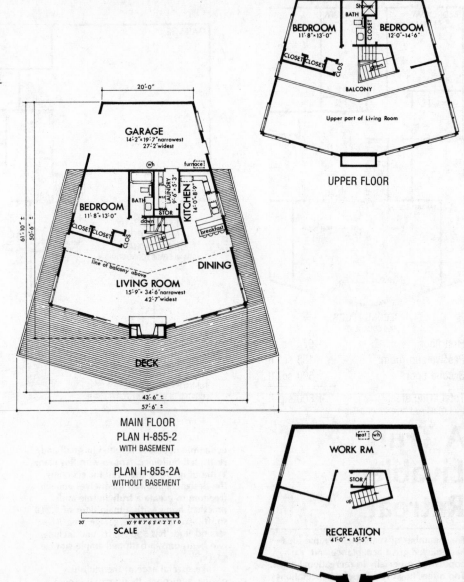

UPPER FLOOR

MAIN FLOOR
PLAN H-855-2
WITH BASEMENT

PLAN H-855-2A
WITHOUT BASEMENT

SCALE

BASEMENT

Plans H-855-2 & -2A

PRICES AND DETAILS ON PAGES 12-15

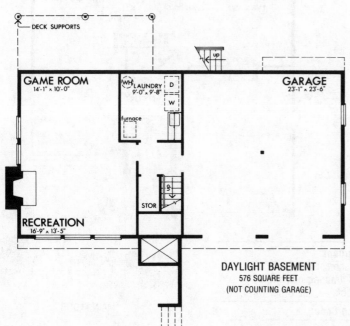

DECK

DINING
10'-0" x 9'-4"

NOOK

KITCHEN
14'-6" x 9'-0"

DW

R/O

PANTRY   REF.

GUEST
3'-0"

Tub w/
Sh'wr

BATH

BATH
12'-4" x 5'-0"

Sh'wr

LINEN

BEDROOM
11'-0" x 13'-3"

WALK-IN
CLOSET
7'-0" x 3'-0"

LIVING ROOM
17'-0" x 15'-8"

WROUGHT IRON RAILING

UP   down

ENTRY

BEDROOM
10'-0" x 10'-0"

CLOSET
4'-10"

CLOSET
4'-10"

CLOSET
4'-10"

BEDROOM
10'-4" x 10'-0"

← WROUGHT IRON
RAILING

48'-0"

8'-0"

26'-0"

12'-6"

28'-0"

MAIN FLOOR
1262 SQUARE FEET
(Exterior walls are 2x6 construction)

DECK SUPPORTS

GAME ROOM
14'-1" x 10'-0"

WH LAUNDRY
9'-0" x 9'-8"

D

W

furnace

up

GARAGE
23'-1" x 23'-6"

up

STOR

RECREATION
16'-9" x 13'-5"

DAYLIGHT BASEMENT
576 SQUARE FEET
(NOT COUNTING GARAGE)

Economical Hillside Design

The solid, expansive, well-to-do appearance of this home plan belies the fact that it contains only 1,262 sq. ft. on the main floor and 1,152 sq. ft. on the lower level, including garage space.

This plan has a simple framing pattern, rectangular shape and straight roof line, and it lacks complicated embellishments. Even the excavation, only half as deep as usual, helps make this an affordable and relatively quick and easy house to build.

A split-level entry opens onto a landing between floors, providing access up to the main living room or down to the recreation and work areas.

The living space is large and open. The dining and living rooms combine with the stairwell to form a large visual space. A large 8'x20' deck, visible through the picture window in the dining room, adds visual expansiveness to this multi-purpose space.

The L-shaped kitchen and adjoining nook are perfect for daily food preparation and family meals, and the deck is also accessible from this area through sliding glass doors. The kitchen features a 48 cubic foot pantry closet.

The master bedroom has a complete private bathroom and oversized closet. The remaining bedrooms each have a large closet and access to a full-size bathroom.

A huge rec and game room is easily accessible from the entry, making it ideal for a home office or business.

Main floor:	1,262 sq. ft.
Lower level:	576 sq. ft.
Total living area:	1,838 sq. ft.
(Not counting garage)	

**TO ORDER THIS BLUEPRINT,
CALL TOLL-FREE 1-800-547-5570**

Blueprint Price Code B
Plan H-1332-5

*PRICES AND DETAILS
ON PAGES 12-15* **103**

Three Bedrooms in Daylight Basement

- Front porch offers warm welcome to vaulted entry area.
- Main floor offers plenty of space for family living and entertaining.
- Lower level provides three bedrooms, with the master suite including a private bath and walk-in closet.

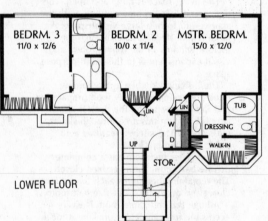

LOWER FLOOR

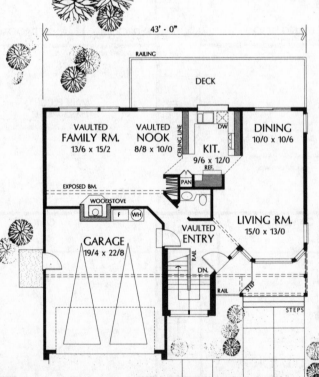

MAIN FLOOR

Plan P-7725-2D

Bedrooms: 3	Baths: 2½

Space:

Main floor:	921 sq. ft.
Lower floor:	921 sq. ft.
Total living area:	**1,842 sq. ft.**
Garage:	438 sq. ft.
Exterior Wall Framing:	2x6

Foundation options:
Daylight basement only.
(Foundation & framing conversion diagram available — see order form.)

Blueprint Price Code: B

Country Styling for Up-to-Date Living

- Nearly surrounded by a covered wood porch, this traditional 1,860 square-foot farm-styled home is modernized for today's active, up-to-date family.
- Inside, the efficient floor plan promotes easy mobility with a minimum of cross-traffic.
- The spacious living and dining area is warmed by a fireplace with a stone hearth; the U-shaped country kitchen is centrally located between these areas and the nook and family room with wood stove on the other side.
- Sliding glass doors lead out to both the rear patio and the deck that adjoins the dining and living rooms.
- The large master bedroom with corner window, dressing area and private bath and two other bedrooms with a second shared bath are found on the upper level.

Plans P-7677-2A & -2D	
Bedrooms: 3	**Baths:** 2 ½
Space:	
Upper floor	825 sq. ft.
Main floor	1,035 sq. ft.
Total Living Area	**1,860 sq. ft.**
Basement	1,014 sq. ft.
Garage	466 sq. ft.
Exterior Wall Framing	2x6
Foundation options:	Plan #
Daylight Basement	P-7677-2D
Crawlspace	P-7677-2A
(Foundation & framing conversion diagram available—see order form.)	
Blueprint Price Code	B

PLAN P-7677-2D
WITH DAYLIGHT BASEMENT

PLAN P-7677-2A
(CRAWLSPACE)

Two-Story Great Room

- An expansive two-story-high Great Room with an oversized hearth and high transom windows highlights this updated traditional design.
- The cozy front porch and bright, open foyer welcome visitors.
- The nice-sized dining room opens to the backyard and is nestled between the Great Room and the efficient island kitchen. This trio of rooms creates a large, open expanse for a dramatic setting. The spacious kitchen boasts a pantry and windows above the sink.
- The main-floor master suite is in a separate wing for privacy and features a whirlpool tub and a separate shower.
- Upstairs, a balcony joins two bedrooms and a hall bath. The balcony overlooks the Great Room and the foyer.

Plan PI-92-510

Bedrooms: 3	Baths: 2½
Living Area:	
Upper floor	574 sq. ft.
Main floor	1,298 sq. ft.
Total Living Area:	**1,872 sq. ft.**
Daylight basement	1,298 sq. ft.
Garage	660 sq. ft.
Exterior Wall Framing:	2x6

Foundation Options:

Daylight basement
(Typical foundation & framing conversion diagram available—see order form.)

BLUEPRINT PRICE CODE: B

UPPER FLOOR

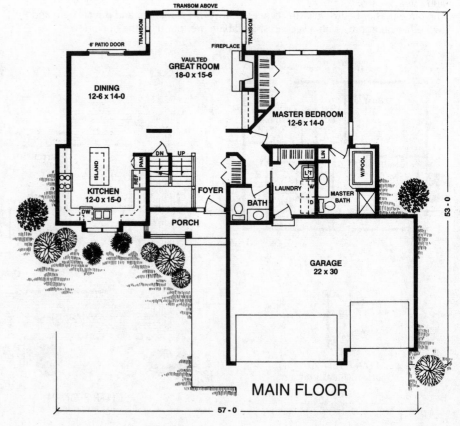

MAIN FLOOR

Customize Your Floor Plan!

- An optional bonus room and a choice between a loft or a bedroom allow you to customize the floor plan of this striking two-story traditional.
- The vaulted foyer leads guests past a handy powder room and directly into the vaulted family room straight ahead or into the formal dining room on the right. A beautiful open-railed staircase pleasantly breaks up the spaces while giving more privacy to the kitchen and the breakfast room.
- The sunny breakfast room is open to the island kitchen. A pantry closet, loads of counter space and direct access to the laundry room and the garage add to the kitchen's efficiency.
- The main-floor master suite is a treasure, with its tray ceiling and vaulted, amenity-filled master bath.
- Upstairs, two bedrooms, a full bath and an optional loft as well as a bonus room provide plenty of opportunity for expansion and customization.

Plan FB-1874

Bedrooms: 3+	Baths: 2½
Living Area:	
Upper floor	554 sq. ft.
Main floor	1,320 sq. ft.
Bonus room	155 sq. ft.
Total Living Area:	**2,029 sq. ft.**
Daylight basement	1,320 sq. ft.
Garage	240 sq. ft.
Storage	38 sq. ft.
Exterior Wall Framing:	2x4

Foundation Options:
Daylight basement
(Typical foundation & framing conversion diagram available—see order form.)

BLUEPRINT PRICE CODE:	C

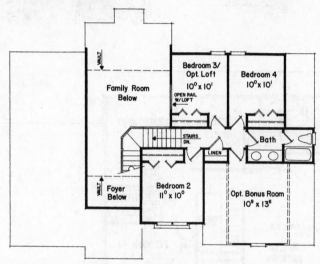

UPPER FLOOR

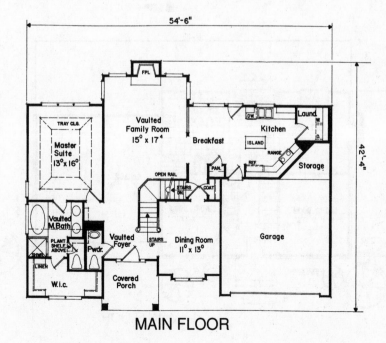

MAIN FLOOR

Exemplary Colonial

- Inside this traditionally designed home is an exciting floor plan for today's lifestyles.
- The classic center-hall arrangement of this Colonial allows easy access to all living areas.
- Plenty of views are possible from the formal rooms at the front of the home, as well as from the informal areas at the rear.
- The spacious kitchen offers lots of counter space, a handy work island, a laundry closet and a sunny bayed breakfast nook.
- The adjoining family room shows off a fireplace and elegant double doors to the rear. An optional set of double doors offers easy access to the living room.
- The beautiful master suite on the upper level boasts a vaulted ceiling, two closets, twin vanities, a garden tub and a separate shower.

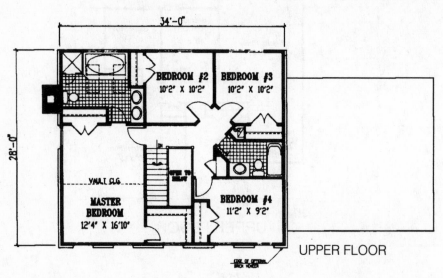

UPPER FLOOR

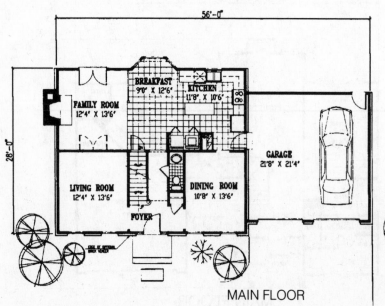

MAIN FLOOR

Plan CH-100-A

Bedrooms: 4	**Baths: 2 ½**
Space:	
Upper floor	923 sq. ft.
Main floor	965 sq. ft.
Total Living Area	**1,888 sq. ft.**
Basement	952 sq. ft.
Garage	462 sq. ft.
Exterior Wall Framing	2x4

Foundation options:

Standard Basement
Daylight Basement
Crawlspace

(Foundation & framing conversion diagram available—see order form.)

Blueprint Price Code	B

Spacious Octagon

- Highly functional main floor plan makes traffic easy and minimizes wasted hall space.
- Double-sized entry opens to spacious octagonal living room with central fireplace and access to all rooms.
- U-shaped kitchen and attached dining area allow for both informal and formal occasions.
- Contiguous bedrooms each have independent deck entrances.
- Exciting deck borders entire home.

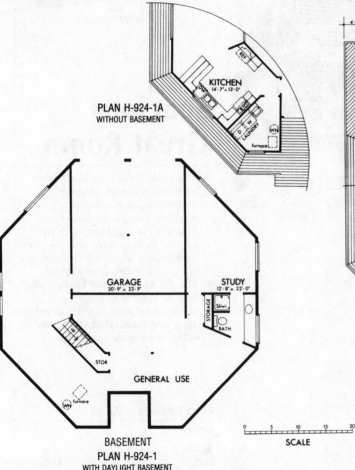

PLAN H-924-1A
WITHOUT BASEMENT

KITCHEN
14'-7" x 13'-0"

GARAGE
20'-9" x 23'-9"

STUDY
12'-8" x 22'-0"

STORAGE

STOR

BATH

GENERAL USE

furnace

BASEMENT
PLAN H-924-1
WITH DAYLIGHT BASEMENT

SCALE
0 5 10 15 20

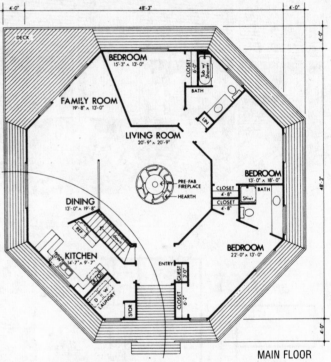

DECK

BEDROOM
15'-3" x 13'-0"

CLOSET
BATH
Tub w/ Shower

FAMILY ROOM
19'-8" x 13'-0"

LIVING ROOM
20'-9" x 20'-0"

PRE-FAB FIREPLACE
HEARTH

BEDROOM
13'-0" x 18'-0"

CLOSET 4'-8"
CLOSET 4'-8"
BATH
Shwr

DINING
13'-0" x 19'-2"

REF

KITCHEN
14'-7" x 9'-7"

BEDROOM
22'-0" x 13'-0"

ENTRY

GUEST 3'-0"
CLOSET 6'-2"

STOR

MAIN FLOOR

Plans H-924-1 & -1A

Bedrooms: 3-4	Baths: 2-3

Space:

Main floor:	1,888 sq. ft.
Total without basement:	1,888 sq. ft.
Basement:	1,395 sq. ft.
Total with basement:	3,283 sq. ft.
Garage:	493 sq. ft.
Exterior Wall Framing:	2x4

Foundation options:
Daylight basement (Plan H-924-1).
Crawlspace (Plan H-924-1A).
(Foundation & framing conversion diagram available — see order form.)

Blueprint Price Code:

Without basement:	B
With basement:	E

P-524-5D Exterior

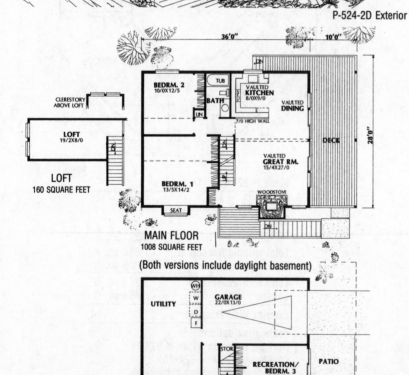

P-524-2D Exterior

Spacious Great Room

- This same floor plan is available with two different exterior treatments, as illustrated.
- In either case, a spacious Great Room is the highlight, with its vaulted ceiling, wide windows and sliding glass doors which open to a deck, and to the view beyond.
- The dining room and kitchen also feature vaulted ceilings.
- A loft room adds another sleeping area, and the daylight basement offers even more usable space.

LOFT
160 SQUARE FEET

MAIN FLOOR
1008 SQUARE FEET

(Both versions include daylight basement)

BASEMENT
FLOOR AREA 722 SQUARE FEET
(Not counting garage)

Plans P-524-2D & -5D

Bedrooms: 2+	Baths: 1

Space:	
Loft:	160 sq. ft.
Main floor:	1,008 sq. ft.
Lower level:	722 sq. ft.

Total living area:	1,890 sq. ft.
Garage:	286 sq. ft.

Exterior Wall Framing:	2x6

Foundation options:
Daylight basement.
(Foundation & framing conversion diagram available — see order form.)

Blueprint Price Code:	B

TO ORDER THIS BLUEPRINT,
CALL TOLL-FREE 1-800-547-5570

Plans P-524-2D & -5D

PRICES AND DETAILS
ON PAGES 12-15

Eye-Catching Layout in Hillside Design

Multi-paned windows and details give a very traditional feel to this contemporary design. The beautifully vaulted living room and the dining room are separated for elegant, formal entertaining.

The spacious kitchen is equipped with abundant storage and counter space. Both the nook and kitchen overlook the family room and hearth below for an eye-catching layout.

Note, too, how the upper level opens to the nook and family room to add visual height and excitement to the interior.

Upstairs, you'll find a spacious master suite with an enormous walk-in closet and private bath.

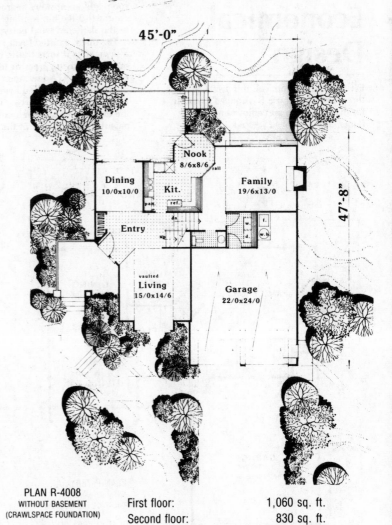

45'-0"

47'-8"

Nook
8/6x8/6

Dining
10/0x10/0

Kit.
ref.

Family
19/6x13/0

Entry

vaulted
Living
15/0x14/6

Garage
22/0x24/0

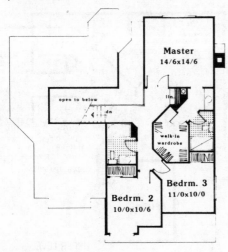

Master
14/6x14/6

open to below

dn

walk-in
wardrobe

Bedrm. 2
10/0x10/6

Bedrm. 3
11/0x10/0

PLAN R-4008
WITHOUT BASEMENT
(CRAWLSPACE FOUNDATION)

First floor: 1,060 sq. ft.

Second floor: 830 sq. ft.

Total living area: 1,890 sq. ft.
(Not counting garage)

Blueprint Price Code B

Plan R-4008

PRICES AND DETAILS
ON PAGES 12-15

Exciting, Economical Design

Exciting but economical, this 1,895 sq. ft., three-bedroom house is arranged carefully for maximum use and enjoyment on two floors, and is only 42 feet wide to minimize lot size requirements. The multi-paned bay windows of the living room and an upstairs bedroom add contrast to the hip rooflines and lead you to the sheltered front entry porch.

The open, vaulted foyer is brightened by a skylight as it sorts traffic to the downstairs living areas or to the upper bedroom level. A few steps to the right puts you in the vaulted living room and the adjoining dining area. Sliding doors in the dining area and the nook, and a pass-through window in the U-shaped kitchen, make the patio a perfect place for outdoor activities and meals.

A large fireplace warms the spacious family room, which has a corner wet bar for efficient entertaining. A utility room leading to the garage and a powder room complete the 1,020 sq. ft. main floor.

An open stairway in the foyer leads to the 875 sq. ft. upper level. The master bedroom has a large walk-in wardrobe, twin vanity, shower and bathroom. The front bedroom has a seat in the bay window and the third bedroom has a built-in seat overlooking the vaulted living room. A full bath with twin vanity serves these bedrooms.

The daylight basement version of the plan adds 925 sq. ft. of living space.

Main floor:	1,020 sq. ft.
Upper floor:	875 sq. ft.
Total living area:	1,895 sq. ft.
(Not counting basement or garage)	

PLAN P-7681-3D
BASEMENT LEVEL: 925 sq. ft.

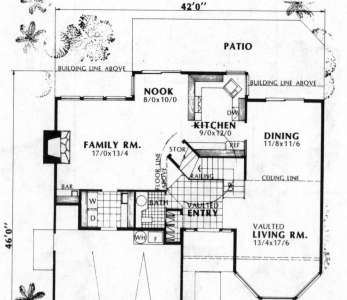

PLAN P-7681-3A
WITHOUT BASEMENT
(CRAWLSPACE FOUNDATION)

PLAN P-7681-3D
WITH DAYLIGHT BASEMENT

MAIN LEVEL

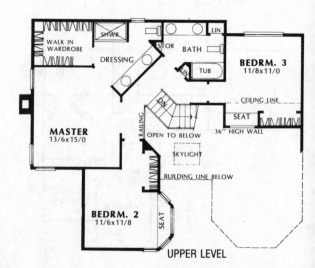

UPPER LEVEL

TO ORDER THIS BLUEPRINT, CALL TOLL-FREE 1-800-547-5570

Blueprint Price Code B
Plans P-7681-3A & 3D

PRICES AND DETAILS ON PAGES 12-15

Playful Floor Plan

- High, hipped roofs and a recessed entry give this home a smart-looking exterior. A dynamic floor plan – punctuated with angled walls, high ceilings and playful window treatments – gives the home an exciting interior.
- The sunken and vaulted Great Room, the circular dining room and the angled island kitchen are the heartbeat of the home. The Great Room offers a fireplace, a built-in corner entertainment center and tall arched windows overlooking the backyard.

- An angled railing separates the Great Room from the open kitchen and dining room. An atrium door next to the glassed-in dining area opens to the backyard. The kitchen includes an island snack bar and a garden window.
- The master bedroom is nestled into one corner for quiet and privacy. This deluxe suite features two walk-in closets and a whirlpool bath. The two smaller bedrooms share another full bath.
- An extra-large laundry area, complete with a clothes-folding counter and a coat closet, is accessible from the three-car garage.
- The home is visually expanded by 9-ft. ceilings throughout, with the exception of the vaulted Great Room.

Plan PI-90-435

Bedrooms: 3	Baths: 2
Living Area:	
Main floor	1,896 sq. ft.
Total Living Area:	**1,896 sq. ft.**
Basement	1,889 sq. ft.
Garage	667 sq. ft.
Exterior Wall Framing:	2x6

Foundation Options:
Daylight basement
Standard basement
(Typical foundation & framing conversion diagram available—see order form.)

BLUEPRINT PRICE CODE:	B

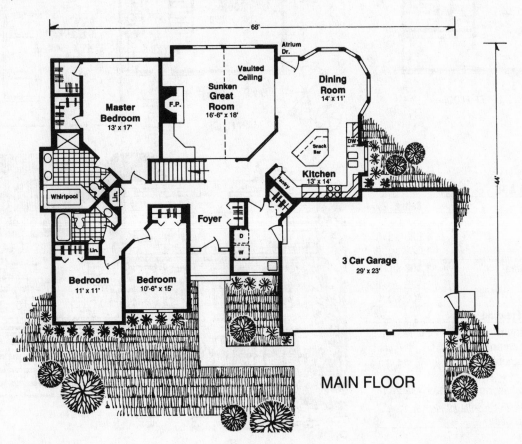

MAIN FLOOR

CH-210-B

Alternate Exteriors

- Timeless exterior detailing and a functional, cost-effective interior are found in this traditional home.
- The kitchen, bayed breakfast room and vaulted family room with skylights and fireplace flow together to form the heart of the home.
- Lots of light filters into the front-facing formal living room.
- Upstairs, the master suite boasts a vaulted ceiling, large walk-in closet and private luxury bath.
- For the flavor of a full, covered front porch, Plan CH-210-B should be your choice.

BEDROOM 2
10'0" X 11'4"

BEDROOM 3
10'0" X 11'4"

MASTER BEDROOM
13'0" X 17'8"

DN

VAULT CLG.

EDGE OF OPTIONAL BRICK VENEER

UPPER FLOOR

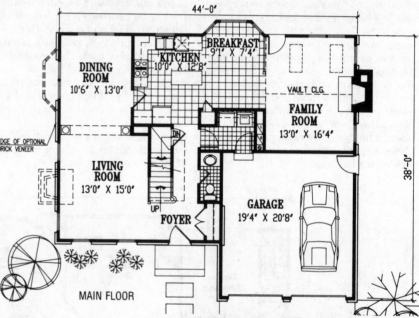

44'-0"

DINING ROOM
10'6" X 13'0"

KITCHEN
10'0" X 12'8"

BREAKFAST
9'1" X 7'4"

VAULT CLG.

FAMILY ROOM
13'0" X 16'4"

EDGE OF OPTIONAL BRICK VENEER

LIVING ROOM
13'0" X 15'0"

DN

UP

FOYER

GARAGE
19'4" X 20'8"

38'-0"

MAIN FLOOR

CH-210-A

Plan CH-210-A & -B

Bedrooms: 3	**Baths:** 2½

Space:

Upper floor	823 sq. ft.
Main floor	1,079 sq. ft.
Total Living Area	**1,902 sq. ft.**
Basement	978 sq. ft.
Garage	400 sq. ft.
Exterior Wall Framing	2x4

Foundation options:

Standard Basement
Daylight Basement
Crawlspace
(Foundation & framing conversion diagram available—see order form.)

Blueprint Price Code	**B**

A Blend of Extras

- A sophisticated blend of country and contemporary design flows through this exceptional home.
- Specially designed for a side sloping lot, the home has a tuck-under garage and an open, economical interior.
- Attractive features include vaulted ceilings, a front wrapping deck, a rear deck off the family room, skylights, interior plant shelves in the kitchen and master bath, and an optional fourth bedroom, guest room or study.
- The vaulted family room is uniquely set below the main level, separated from the nook by a handrail.
- Three bedrooms and two full baths are found on the upper floor.

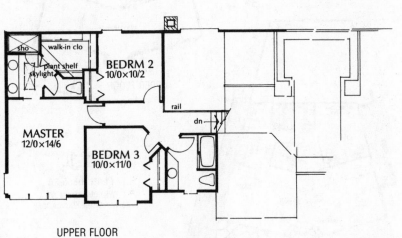

UPPER FLOOR

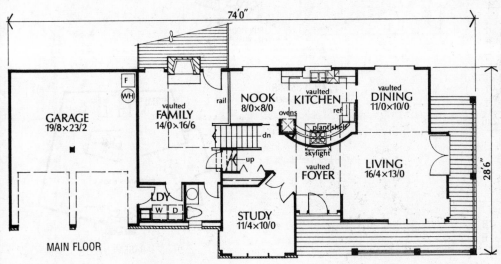

MAIN FLOOR

Plan CDG-4005	
Bedrooms: 3-4	**Baths:** 2½
Space:	
Upper floor:	732 sq. ft.
Main floor:	1,178 sq. ft.
Total living area:	**1,910 sq. ft.**
Garage:	456 sq. ft.
Exterior Wall Framing:	2x4
Foundation options: Crawlspace. (Foundation & framing conversion diagram available — see order form.)	
Blueprint Price Code:	B

Proven Plan Features Passive Sun Room

- A passive sun room, energy-efficient wood stove, and a panorama of windows make this design highly economical.
- Open living/dining room features attractive balcony railing, stone hearth, and adjoining sun room with durable stone floor.
- Well-equipped kitchen is separated from dining area by a convenient breakfast bar.
- Second level sleeping areas border a hallway and balcony.
- Optional basement plan provides extra space for entertaining or work.

Plans H-855-3A & -3B

Bedrooms: 3	Baths: 2-3

Space:	
Upper floor:	586 sq. ft.
Main floor:	1,192 sq. ft.
Sun room:	132 sq. ft.
Total living area:	**1,910 sq. ft.**
Basement:	approx. 1,192 sq. ft.
Garage:	520 sq. ft.

Exterior Wall Framing:	2x6

Foundation options:
Daylight basement (Plan H-855-3B).
Crawlspace (Plan H-855-3A).
(Foundation & framing conversion diagram available — see order form.)

Blueprint Price Code:	
Without basement	B
With basement	E

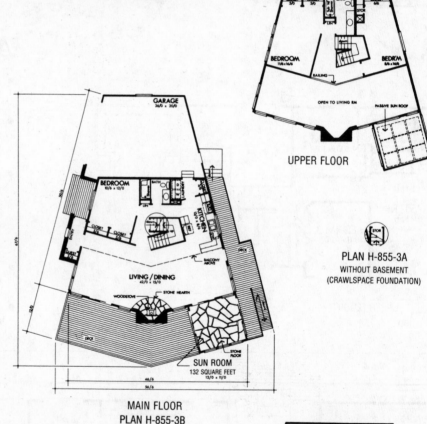

UPPER FLOOR

PLAN H-855-3A
WITHOUT BASEMENT
(CRAWLSPACE FOUNDATION)

MAIN FLOOR
PLAN H-855-3B
WITH DAYLIGHT BASEMENT

BASEMENT

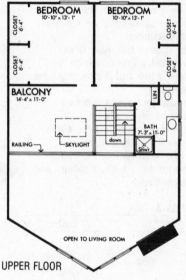

UPPER FLOOR

Soaring Design
Lifts the Human Spirit

- Suitable for level or sloping lots, this versatile design can be expanded or finished as time and budget allow.
- Surrounding deck accessible from all main living areas.
- Great living room enhanced by vaulted ceilings, second-floor

balcony, skylights and dramatic window wall.
- Rear entrance has convenient access to full bath and laundry room.
- Two additional bedrooms on upper level share second bath and balcony room.

Plans H-930-1 & -1A

Bedrooms: 3	Baths: 2
Space:	
Upper floor:	710 sq. ft.
Main floor:	1,210 sq. ft.
Total living area:	**1,920 sq. ft.**
Basement:	605 sq. ft.
Garage/shop:	605 sq. ft.
Exterior Wall Framing:	2x6

Foundation options:
Daylight basement (Plan H-930-1).
Crawlspace (Plan H-930-1A).
(Foundation & framing conversion diagram available — see order form.)

Blueprint Price Code:
| Without basement: | B |
| With basement: | D |

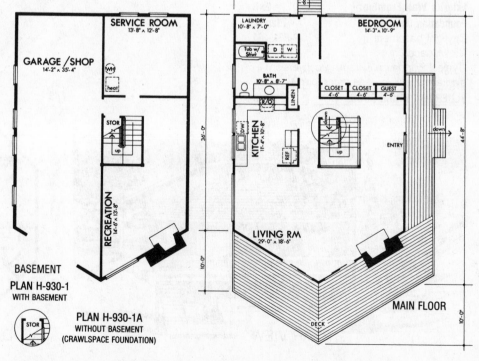

BASEMENT
PLAN H-930-1
WITH BASEMENT

PLAN H-930-1A
WITHOUT BASEMENT
(CRAWLSPACE FOUNDATION)

MAIN FLOOR

Octagonal Home with Lofty View

- There's no better way to avoid the ordinary than by building an octagonal home and escaping from square corners and rigid rooms.
- The roomy main floor offers plenty of space for full-time family living or for a comfortable second-home retreat.
- The vaulted entry hall leads to the bedrooms on the right or down the hall to the Great Room.
- Warmed by a woodstove, the Great Room offers a panoramic view of the surrounding scenery.
- The center core of the main floor houses two baths, one of which contains a spa tub and is private to the master bedroom.
- This plan also includes a roomy kitchen and handy utility area.
- A large loft is planned as a recreation room, also with a woodstove.
- The daylight basement version adds another bedroom, a bath, a garage and a large storage area.

Plans P-532-3A & -3D

Bedrooms: 3-4	Baths: 2-3
Living Area:	
Upper floor	355 sq. ft.
Main floor	1,567 sq. ft.
Daylight basement	430 sq. ft.
Total Living Area:	**1,922/2,352 sq. ft.**
Garage and storage	1,137 sq. ft.
Exterior Wall Framing:	2x6
Foundation Options:	**Plan #**
Daylight basement	P-532-3D
Crawlspace	P-532-3A

(Typical foundation & framing conversion diagram available—see order form.)

BLUEPRINT PRICE CODE:	**B/C**

FRONT VIEW

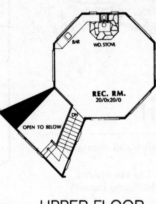

UPPER FLOOR

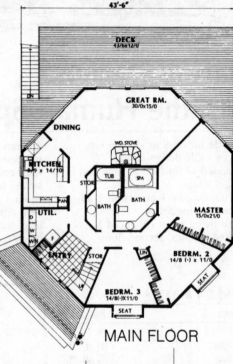

MAIN FLOOR

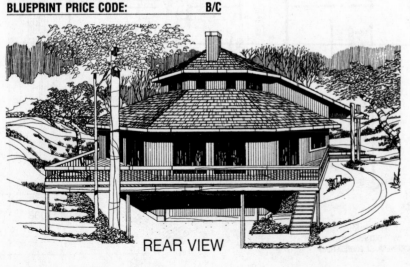

REAR VIEW

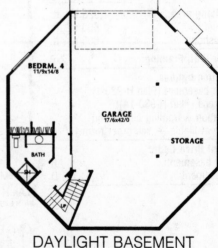

DAYLIGHT BASEMENT

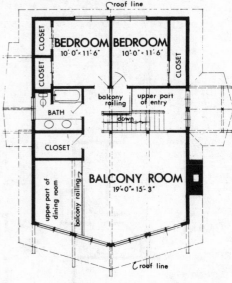

UPPER FLOOR

Decked Out for Fun

- Spacious deck surrounds this comfortable cabin/chalet.
- Sliding glass doors and windows blanket the living-dining area, indulged with raised hearth and a breathtaking view.
- Dining area and compact kitchen

separated by breakfast bar.
- Master bedroom, laundry room and bath complete first floor; two additional bedrooms located on second floor.
- Upper level also features impressive balcony room with exposed beams.

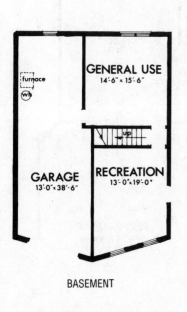

BASEMENT

MAIN FLOOR

Plans H-919-1 & -1A	
Bedrooms: 3	**Baths:** 2

Space:

Upper floor:	869 sq. ft.
Main floor:	1,064 sq. ft.
Total living area:	**1,933 sq. ft.**
Basement:	475 sq. ft.
Garage:	501 sq. ft.

Exterior Wall Framing:	2x6

Foundation options:
Daylight basement (Plan H-919-1).
Crawlspace (Plan H-919-1A).
(Foundation & framing conversion diagram available — see order form.)

Blueprint Price Code:

Without basement:	B
With basement:	C

UPPER FLOOR

MASTER
11/10x15/0

SHWR

DRESSING

WALK IN
WARDROBE

LIN

BATH

TUB

BEDRM. 2
10/0x11/0

OPEN TO KITCHEN
BELOW

DN

OPEN TO
ENTRY BELOW

KITCHEN

DN

ENTRY

PLAN P-7689-3D
WITH DAYLIGHT BASEMENT

61'0''

DECK

SKYLIGHTS

DECK

Vaulted
NOOK
11/0x11/0

BAR

Vaulted
KITCHEN
10/6x13/9

REF

OPEN TO
FAMILY RM.

FAMILY RM.
17/4x13/6

Vaulted
DINING
9/10x12/0

36" HIGH
WALL

BATH

SH

UTILITY

W D

GARAGE
23/2x23/2

SKYLIGHT

ENTRY

DEN/
BEDRM. 3
11/4x10/6

F

WH

Vaulted
LIVING RM.
16/0x13/0

PLANTER

41'0''

MAIN FLOOR

PLAN P-7689-3A
WITHOUT BASEMENT
(CRAWLSPACE FOUNDATION)

Main floor:	1,358 sq. ft.
Upper floor:	576 sq. ft.
Total living area:	1,934 sq. ft.
(Not counting basement or garage)	
Basement level:	1,358 sq. ft.

Blueprint Price Code B

FRONT VIEW

Octagonal Sunshine Special

- Octagon homes offer the ultimate for taking advantage of a view, and are fascinating designs even for more ordinary settings.
- This plan offers a huge, house-spanning living/dining area with loads of glass and a masonry collector wall to store solar heat.
- The 700-square-foot upper level is devoted entirely to an enormous master suite, with a balcony overlooking the living room below, a roomy private bath and a large closet/dressing area.
- Scissor-trusses allow vaulted ceilings over the two-story-high living room and the master suite.
- A second roomy bedroom and full bath are offered downstairs, along with an efficient kitchen, a laundry area and inviting foyer.
- A daylight basement option offers the potential for more bedrooms, hobbies, work rooms or recreational space.

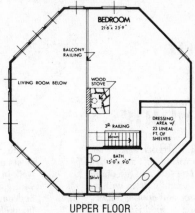

UPPER FLOOR

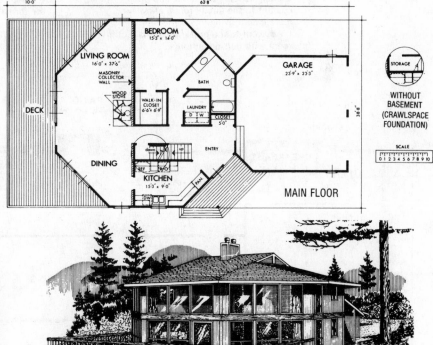

MAIN FLOOR

WITHOUT BASEMENT (CRAWLSPACE FOUNDATION)

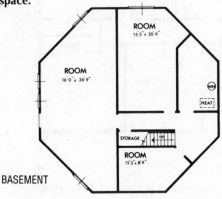

BASEMENT

Plans H-948-1A & -1B	
Bedrooms: 2-4	Baths: 2

Space:

Upper floor:	700 sq. ft.
Main floor:	1,236 sq. ft.
Total without basement:	1,936 sq. ft.
Daylight basement:	1,236 sq. ft.
Total with basement:	3,172 sq. ft.
Garage:	550 sq. ft.

Exterior Wall Framing:	2x6

Foundation options:
Daylight basement (H-948-1B).
Crawlspace (H-948-1A).
(Foundation & framing conversion diagram available — see order form.)

Blueprint Price Code:

Without basement:	B
With basement:	E

REAR VIEW

Ideal for Formal Entertaining

This lovely 1,940 sq. ft. French Provincial design features a formal foyer flanked by the living room on one side and the dining room on the other. A family room with a raised-hearth fireplace and double doors to the patio, and the L-shaped island kitchen with breakfast bay and open counter to the family room, allow for more casual living.

Adjacent to the breakfast bay is a utility room with outside entrance.

The master suite includes one double closet and a compartmentalized bath with walk-in closet, step-up garden tub, double vanity and linen closet. Two front bedrooms and a second full bath with linen closet complete the design. A recessed entry and circular porch add to the formal exterior.

Total living area: 1,940 sq. ft.
(Not counting basement or garage)

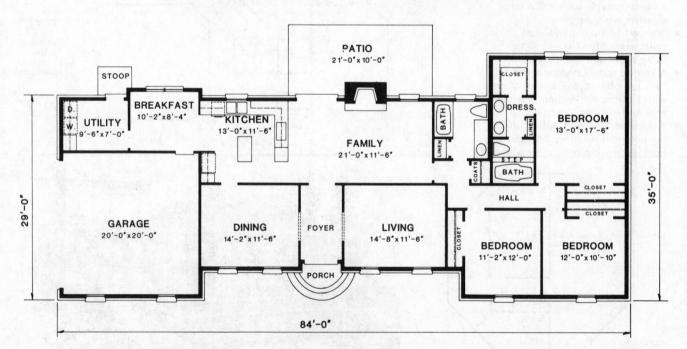

Specify daylight basement, crawlspace or slab foundation when ordering.

Blueprint Price Code B

Plan C-8103

Cozy L-Shaped Bungalow

This pleasing L-shaped design packs a smooth-flowing floor plan into 1,950 sq. ft. The master suite includes garden tub, shower, his and her vanities and separate walk-in closets. Two other bedrooms and a full bath complete the sleeping wing.

A large family room, foyer and separate living-dining room combine to form the center section. U-shaped kitchen, breakfast nook with bay window and separate utility complete the plan.

Total living area: 1,950 sq. ft.
(Not counting basement or garage)

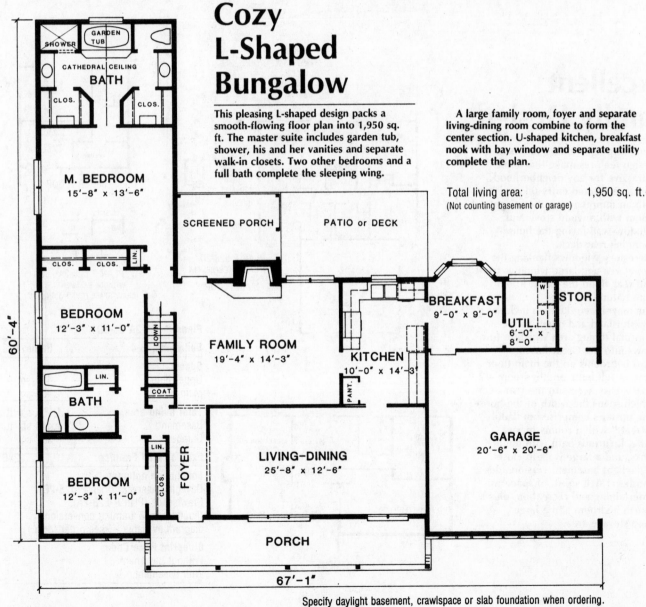

BATH — CATHEDRAL CEILING
SHOWER / GARDEN TUB / CLOS.

M. BEDROOM 15'-8" x 13'-6"

CLOS. CLOS. LIN.

BEDROOM 12'-3" x 11'-0"

BATH / LIN.

BEDROOM 12'-3" x 11'-0"

CLOS. LIN.

FOYER

DOWN / COAT

SCREENED PORCH — **PATIO or DECK**

FAMILY ROOM 19'-4" x 14'-3"

KITCHEN 10'-0" x 14'-3" / PANT.

BREAKFAST 9'-0" x 9'-0"

UTIL. 6'-0" x 8'-0" / W D / **STOR.**

LIVING-DINING 25'-8" x 12'-6"

GARAGE 20'-6" x 20'-6"

PORCH

60'-4"

67'-1"

Specify daylight basement, crawlspace or slab foundation when ordering.

Blueprint Price Code B
Plan C-8620

Excellent Family Design

- Long sloping rooflines and bold design features make this home attractive for any neighborhood.
- Inside, a vaulted entry takes visitors into an impressive vaulted Great Room with a wood stove and window-wall facing the house-spanning rear deck.
- Clerestory windows flanking the stove area and large windows front and rear flood the Great Room with natural light.
- The magnificent kitchen includes a stylish island and opens to the informal dining area which in turn flows into the Great Room.
- Two bedrooms on the main floor share a full bath, and bedroom #2 boasts easy access to the rear deck which spans the width of the house.
- The upstairs comprises an "adult retreat," with a roomy master suite, luxurious bath with double sinks, and a large walk-in closet.
- A daylight basement version adds another 1,410 sq. ft. of space for entertaining and recreation, plus a fourth bedroom and a large shop/storage area.

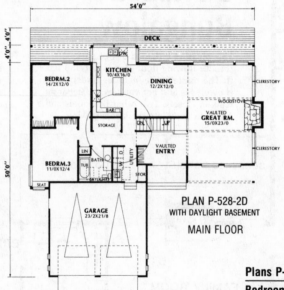

PLAN P-528-2D
WITH DAYLIGHT BASEMENT
MAIN FLOOR

UPPER FLOOR

PLAN P-528-2A
WITHOUT BASEMENT
(CRAWLSPACE FOUNDATION)

BASEMENT

Plans P-528-2A & -2D

Bedrooms: 3-4	Baths: 2-3

Space:	
Upper floor:	498 sq. ft.
Main floor:	1,456 sq. ft.

Total living area:	1,954 sq. ft.
Basement:	1,410 sq. ft.
Garage:	502 sq. ft.

Exterior Wall Framing:	2x6

Foundation options:
Daylight basement (Plan P-528-2D).
Crawlspace (Plan P-528-2A).
(Foundation & framing conversion diagram available — see order form.)

Blueprint Price Code:

Without basement:	B
With basement:	E

Indoor/Outdoor Living on A Sloping Lot

- The wood siding, the front deck, and the multi-paned exterior of this Northwest contemporary will beckon you up to the entry stairs and inside.
- The two-story entry opens up to a vaulted living room with tall windows, exposed beam ceiling and adjoining dining area which accesses the hand-railed deck.
- An updated kitchen offers a walk-in

pantry, eating bar and breakfast nook with sliders to a rear deck.
- A fireplace and rear patio highlight the attached family room.
- A washer/dryer in the upper level bath is convenient to all three bedrooms, making laundry a breeze.

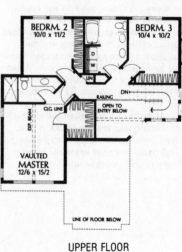

UPPER FLOOR

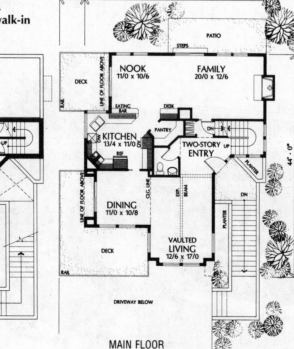

BASEMENT

MAIN FLOOR

Plan P-7737-4D

Bedrooms: 3	Baths: 2½

Space:	
Upper floor:	802 sq. ft.
Main floor:	1,158 sq. ft.

Total living area:	1,960 sq. ft.
Garage/basement:	736 sq. ft.

Exterior Wall Framing:	2x6

Foundation options:
Crawlspace.
(Foundation & framing conversion diagram available — see order form.)

Blueprint Price Code:	B

TO ORDER THIS BLUEPRINT,
CALL TOLL-FREE 1-800-547-5570

Plan P-7737-4D

PRICES AND DETAILS
ON PAGES 12-15

125

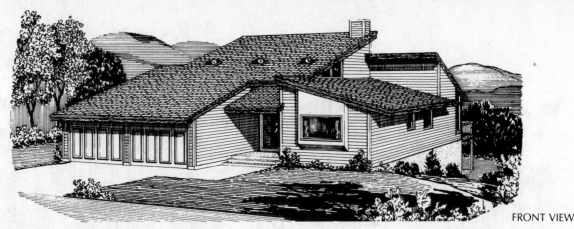

FRONT VIEW

Sun Chaser

A passive sun room with two fully glazed walls and an all-glass roof offers leeway when siting this comfortable, contemporary leisure home. Orientation is towards the south to capture maximum solar warmth. The window wall in the living room and a bank of clerestory windows high on the master bedroom wall soak up the winter rays for direct heat gain, yet are shaded with overhangs to block out the higher sun in the summer.

The 165 sq. ft. sun room is a focal point from the living and family rooms, through windows and sliding glass doors between these rooms. A dining table in the family room would command a sweeping view, or meals could be enjoyed in the sun room.

Sloping ceilings in the living and sun rooms allow balcony railings to open the master bedroom partially for a view down to these rooms, and let warm air flow up from the masonry storage floor of the sun room.

Accent walls of solid board paneling add visual warmth and texture to the rooms. Western cedar bevel siding adds beauty and individuality to the exterior. Exterior walls are of 2x6 construction.

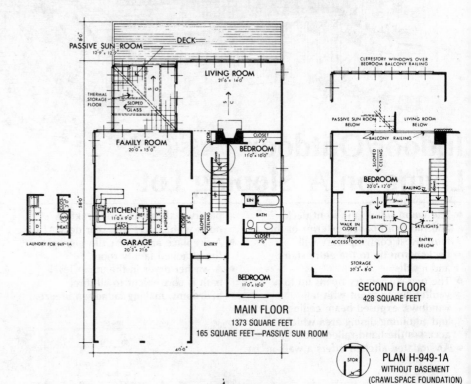

MAIN FLOOR
1373 SQUARE FEET
165 SQUARE FEET—PASSIVE SUN ROOM

SECOND FLOOR
428 SQUARE FEET

PLAN H-949-1A
WITHOUT BASEMENT
(CRAWLSPACE FOUNDATION)

PLAN H-949-1B
DAYLIGHT BASEMENT

PLAN H-949-1
STANDARD BASEMENT

First floor:	1,373 sq. ft.
Passive sun room:	165 sq. ft.
Second floor:	428 sq. ft.
Total living area:	1,966 sq. ft.

(Not counting basement or garage)

Blueprint Price Code B

Plans H-949-1, -1A & -1B

PRICES AND DETAILS
ON PAGES 12-15

Spacious Vaulted Great Room

- Behind an unpretentious facade lies an exciting and highly livable floor plan.
- A vaulted entry leads visitors to an impressive vaulted Great Room with exposed-beam ceiling.
- The roomy kitchen also boasts a vaulted ceiling, and skylights as well.
- The sunny nook looks out onto a large patio, and includes a built-in desk.
- A first-class master suite includes a large dressing area, enormous walk-in closet and sumptuous bath.
- Bedroom 2 also contains a walk-in closet.
- Also note other details such as the pantry, linen storage and convenient washer/dryer area in the garage entry.

Plans P-6577-3A & -3D

Bedrooms: 3	Baths: 2

Space:

Main floor (crawlspace version):	1,978 sq. ft.
Main floor (basement version):	2,047 sq. ft.
Basement:	1,982 sq. ft.
Garage:	438 sq. ft.

Exterior Wall Framing:	2x4

Foundation options:
Daylight basement (Plan P-6577-3D).
Crawlspace (Plan P-6577-3A).
(Foundation & framing conversion diagram available — see order form.)

Blueprint Price Code:

Without basement:	B
With basement:	C

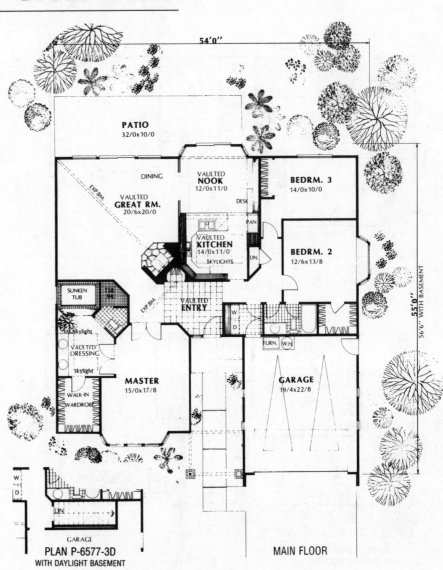

PLAN P-6577-3D
WITH DAYLIGHT BASEMENT

MAIN FLOOR

Old Homestead

Almost everyone has a soft place in his heart for a certain home in his childhood. A home like this one, with understated farmhouse styling and wrap-around porch, may be the image of "Home" that your children remember.

Two versions of the first floor plan provide a choice between a country kitchen and a more formal dining room.

All versions feature 2x6 exterior wall framing.

Upper floor:	626 sq. ft.
Main floor:	1,359 sq. ft.
Total living area:	1,985 sq. ft.

(Not counting basement or garage)
(Non-basement versions designed with crawlspace)

Garage:	528 sq. ft.

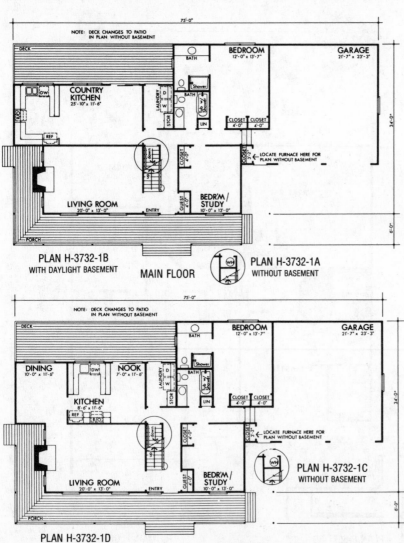

PLAN H-3732-1B
WITH DAYLIGHT BASEMENT

MAIN FLOOR

PLAN H-3732-1A
WITHOUT BASEMENT

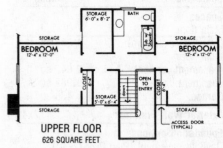

UPPER FLOOR
626 SQUARE FEET

PLAN H-3732-1D
WITH DAYLIGHT BASEMENT

MAIN FLOOR

PLAN H-3732-1C
WITHOUT BASEMENT

Blueprint Price Code B

Practical Perfection

- This practical split-foyer home is perfect for a growing family, offering a huge lower area for a future recreation room.
- The vaulted foyer is brightened by transom and sidelight windows.
- A few steps up from the foyer, the living room boasts a cathedral ceiling and a fireplace flanked by angled window walls, one viewing to a large rear patio and the other to a wraparound deck.
- Sliding glass doors in the adjoining dining room open to the deck. The nearby eat-in kitchen also accesses the deck and has views of the front yard.
- The large master bedroom boasts a walk-in closet and a private bathroom with glass-block walls framing the designer shower. Two more main-floor bedrooms share a full bath.
- Downstairs, the future recreation room has space set aside for a wet bar and another fireplace. Laundry facilities and garage access are also convenient.

Plan AX-97511

Bedrooms: 3	Baths: 2
Living Area:	
Main floor	1,286 sq. ft.
Daylight basement (finished)	565 sq. ft.
Total Living Area:	**1,851 sq. ft.**
Utility room	140 sq. ft.
Tuck-under garage	400 sq. ft.
Exterior Wall Framing:	2x4

Foundation Options:

Daylight basement
(All plans can be built with your choice of foundation and framing. A generic conversion diagram is available. See order form.)

BLUEPRINT PRICE CODE:	**B**

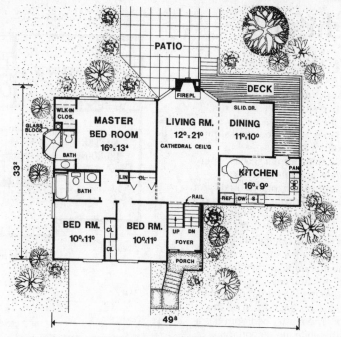

MAIN FLOOR

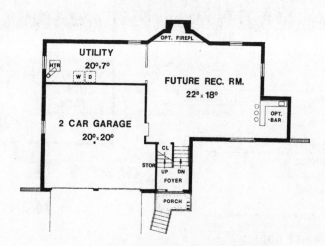

DAYLIGHT BASEMENT

Delightful Choices

- Its simple structure makes this four-bedroom, two-story home the perfect choice for the economical family. This versatile plan is available with a siding or brick exterior finish.
- Comfortably sized formal spaces, open informal areas and lots of windows make the floor plan light and bright. An optional bay window in the living room and fireplace in the family room can add further ambience.
- The breakfast nook's delightful boxed bay provides a sunny site for casual dining. The adjoining kitchen has a windowed sink and easy access to the garage and to the formal dining room.
- All four bedrooms are housed on the upper floor. The master bedroom has a private bath, while the secondary bedrooms share another.

Plan CH-110-A

Bedrooms: 4	Baths: 2½
Living Area:	
Upper floor	860 sq. ft.
Main floor	846 sq. ft.
Total Living Area:	**1,706 sq. ft.**
Basement	834 sq. ft.
Garage	380 sq. ft.
Exterior Wall Framing:	2x4

Foundation Options:

Daylight basement

Standard basement

Crawlspace

(All plans can be built with your choice of foundation and framing. A generic conversion diagram is available. See order form.)

BLUEPRINT PRICE CODE: B

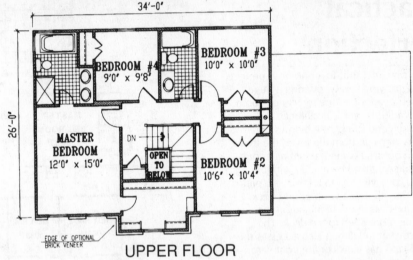

UPPER FLOOR

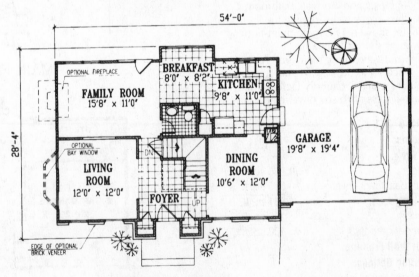

MAIN FLOOR

TO ORDER THIS BLUEPRINT, CALL TOLL-FREE 1-800-547-5570   Plan CH-110-A   **PRICES AND DETAILS ON PAGES 12-15**

Charming Choices

- This charming farmhouse design has a simple and economical structure that can be finished with siding or brick. With four bedrooms, the home is ideal for a large or growing family.
- Comfortably sized formal spaces, open informal areas and lots of windows make the floor plan light and bright. An optional bay window in the living room and fireplace in the family room can add further ambience.
- The breakfast nook's delightful boxed bay provides a sunny site for casual dining. The adjoining kitchen has a windowed sink and easy access to the garage and to the formal dining room.
- All four bedrooms are housed on the upper floor. The master bedroom has a private bath, while the secondary bedrooms share another.

Plan CH-110-B

Bedrooms: 4	Baths: 2½
Living Area:	
Upper floor	860 sq. ft.
Main floor	846 sq. ft.
Total Living Area:	**1,706 sq. ft.**
Basement	834 sq. ft.
Garage	380 sq. ft.
Exterior Wall Framing:	2x4

Foundation Options:
Daylight basement
Standard basement
Crawlspace
(All plans can be built with your choice of foundation and framing. A generic conversion diagram is available. See order form.)

BLUEPRINT PRICE CODE: B

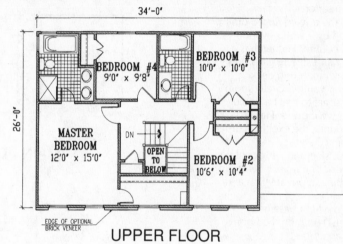

UPPER FLOOR

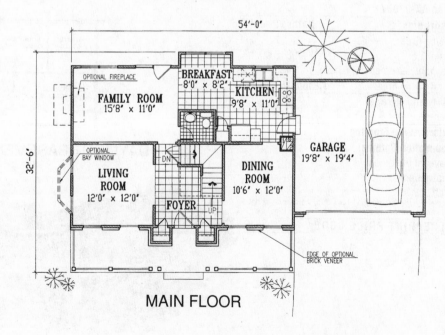

MAIN FLOOR

Graceful Wings

- Past the inviting entrance to this graceful contemporary home, the skylighted foyer welcomes guests into the dramatic interior.
- Off the foyer, the tray-ceilinged dining room is graced by a wall of windows. The spacious country kitchen has a bright skylight and sliding glass doors to an enormous wraparound deck.
- The spectacular vaulted Great Room's 17-ft. ceiling soars to greet a row of large clerestory windows. Flanked by sliding glass doors, the exciting corner fireplace warms the area.
- The main-floor sleeping wing contains three bedrooms. The master bedroom has a tray ceiling, a private bath and two closets.
- The optional daylight basement includes a den, two more bedrooms, a family room and more!

Plan AX-97837

Bedrooms: 3+	Baths: 2½-3½

Living Area:

Main floor	1,816 sq. ft.
Daylight basement (finished)	1,435 sq. ft.
Total Living Area:	**1,816/3,251 sq. ft.**
Utility and storage	381 sq. ft.
Garage	400 sq. ft.
Exterior Wall Framing:	**2x4**

Foundation Options:

Daylight basement

Crawlspace

Slab

(All plans can be built with your choice of foundation and framing. A generic conversion diagram is available. See order form.)

BLUEPRINT PRICE CODE:	**B/E**

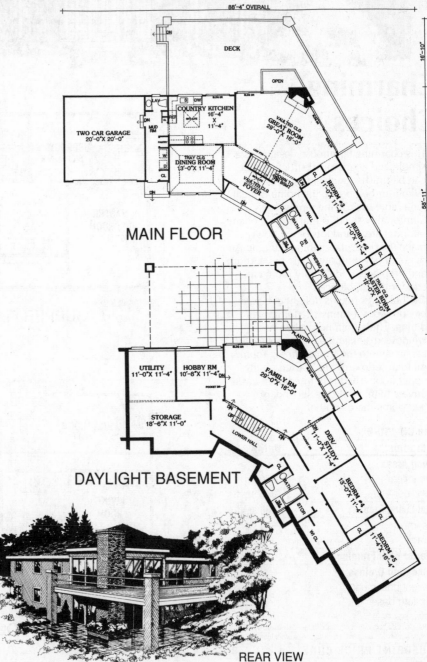

MAIN FLOOR

DAYLIGHT BASEMENT

REAR VIEW

Four-Season Appeal

- Fantastic easy-living spaces clustered around a delightful four-season porch take center stage in this unique home.
- An intriguing trapezoid window brightens the vaulted foyer, which views into the sunken, vaulted Great Room. Here, an even larger trapezoid window fills the wall overlooking the backyard. A built-in TV cabinet handsomely complements the fireplace.

- French doors in the adjoining dinette and island kitchen open to the inviting four-season porch. This bright, cheerful haven features a vaulted ceiling and three walls of glass.
- A garden sink, a built-in desk and a pocket door to a deluxe laundry room highlight the kitchen. The dinette spreads into a formal dining room, framed by an angled wall and columns.
- A 12-ft. tray-vaulted ceiling embellishes the master bedroom. A whirlpool bath and a walk-in closet are also included.
- The remaining bedroom offers a cozy window seat and easy access to a bath.

Plan PI-92-203	
Bedrooms: 2	**Baths: 2**
Living Area:	
Main floor	1,762 sq. ft.
Four-season porch	224 sq. ft.
Total Living Area:	**1,986 sq. ft.**
Daylight basement	1,744 sq. ft.
Garage	744 sq. ft.
Exterior Wall Framing:	2x6
Foundation Options:	

Daylight basement
(All plans can be built with your choice of foundation and framing. A generic conversion diagram is available. See order form.)

BLUEPRINT PRICE CODE:	B

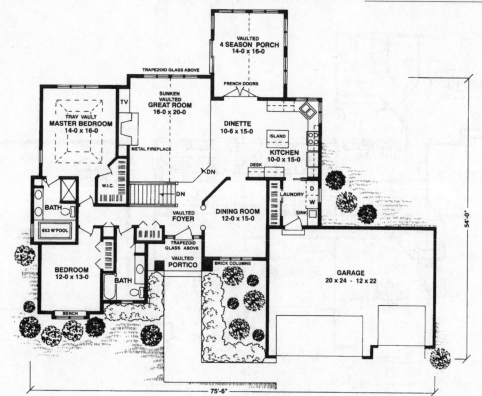

MAIN FLOOR

Plan PI-92-203

Alluring Design

- Hipped roofs and brick accents artfully adorn this alluring design, which is well suited to a side-sloping lot.
- The covered porch opens to a tiled entry hall, where angled walls point to the main living areas straight ahead and to the bedrooms on the left.
- A column ushers guests into the sunken living room, which features an 11-ft. vaulted ceiling, an elegant boxed-out window and an inviting fireplace.
- A railing provides voluminous views into the dining room and the family room, which are up four steps from the hall. The dining room boasts a 15-ft. vaulted ceiling, and the family room has an 11-ft. coffered ceiling.
- The adjoining kitchen offers a 9-ft. ceiling, an island cooktop and a corner sink set beneath windows. The neighboring nook has an 11-ft. vaulted ceiling and access to the backyard. A pantry and a laundry are close by.
- Sequestered at the opposite corner of the home, the master bedroom opens to the backyard and features a walk-in closet and a private bath.
- A central bath serves the remainder of the household. All three bedrooms are enhanced by 9-ft. ceilings.

Plan LMB-9827-W

Bedrooms: 3	**Baths:** 2
Living Area:	
Main floor	1,997 sq. ft.
Total Living Area:	**1,997 sq. ft.**
Tuck-under garage	732 sq. ft.
Exterior Wall Framing:	2x6

Foundation Options:

Crawlspace
(All plans can be built with your choice of foundation and framing. A generic conversion diagram is available. See order form.)

BLUEPRINT PRICE CODE:	**B**

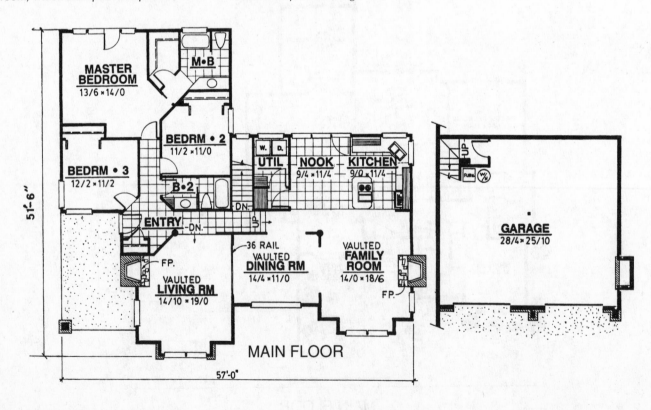

MAIN FLOOR

TO ORDER THIS BLUEPRINT, CALL TOLL-FREE 1-800-547-5570 Plan LMB-9827-W **PRICES AND DETAILS ON PAGES 12-15**

REAR VIEW

Three Levels of Fun

- Contemporary styling is found throughout this exciting and rustic three-level home.
- Double doors on the main level open to a dramatic two-story foyer that soars to the upper balcony. A huge activity area combining the living room, dining room and kitchen unfolds from the foyer for a spacious and spectacular effect!
- A handsome brick fireplace is the focal point of the living room, which also features a 15-ft. vaulted ceiling.
- The airy kitchen offers an oversized snack or serving bar, which comes in handy for quick meals or entertaining. Parties can be extended to the adjoining deck through sliding glass doors.
- Two bedrooms, one with a private deck, are located near a full bath. The loft areas off the upper-level balcony provide space for more sleeping rooms.
- Still another bedroom with its own sitting area is offered in the daylight basement. Generous storage space and a relaxing lounge complete with a wet bar are also included.

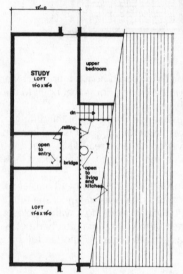

UPPER FLOOR

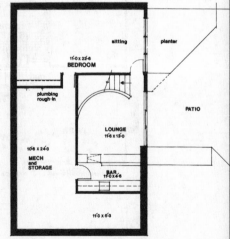

FRONT VIEW

Plan CPS-1136-D

Bedrooms: 3+	Baths: 1
Living Area:	
Upper floor	480 sq. ft.
Main floor	945 sq. ft.
Daylight basement (finished)	576 sq. ft.
Total Living Area:	**2,001 sq. ft.**
Daylight basement (unfinished)	384 sq. ft.
Exterior Wall Framing:	2x6

Foundation Options:
Daylight basement
(All plans can be built with your choice of foundation and framing. A generic conversion diagram is available. See order form.)

BLUEPRINT PRICE CODE: C

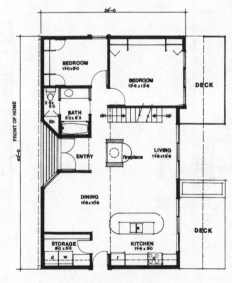

MAIN FLOOR

DAYLIGHT BASEMENT

European Eye-Catcher

- The quaint exterior of this European traditional features an eye-catching entry, a front balcony and a unique assortment of windows.
- The foyer, brightened by paned sidelight and transom windows, has elegant columns that divide it from the living room.

- The living room boasts a fireplace and double French doors that open to the charming front balcony.
- Beyond the living room, the dining room and the adjacent island kitchen overlook a large rear deck, which is accessed through a French door in the bayed breakfast area.
- Upstairs, the tray-ceilinged master suite boasts a dual-sink vanity, a spa tub, a separate shower and a walk-in closet.
- Each of the two remaining bedrooms has private access to another full bath.

Plan APS-2005	
Bedrooms: 3	**Baths: 2½**
Living Area:	
Upper floor	937 sq. ft.
Main floor	936 sq. ft.
Daylight basement	132 sq. ft.
Total Living Area:	**2,005 sq. ft.**
Tuck-under garage and storage	760 sq. ft.
Exterior Wall Framing:	2x4

Foundation Options:

Daylight basement
(All plans can be built with your choice of foundation and framing. A generic conversion diagram is available. See order form.)

BLUEPRINT PRICE CODE:	C

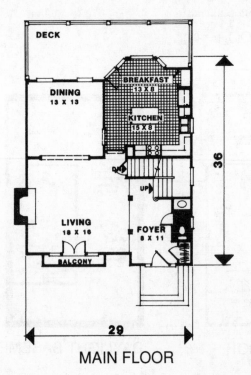

MAIN FLOOR

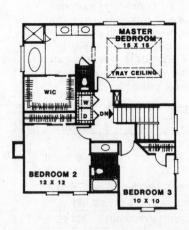

UPPER FLOOR

TO ORDER THIS BLUEPRINT, CALL TOLL-FREE 1-800-547-5570

Plan APS-2005

PRICES AND DETAILS ON PAGES 12-15

Striking Look, Vaulted Spaces

- An arched entryway with half-round windows above the front door and in the living room give this handsome hillside home a striking look.
- The living room and dining room flow together beneath a vaulted ceiling, creating an impressive entertainment area. The living room offers a fireplace, while the dining room has French doors that open to a rear patio.
- The kitchen is also vaulted and features a garden window above the sink. An optional bayed nook and an alternate kitchen layout are included with the blueprints.
- The enticing master suite incorporates a roomy sitting area and a plush bath with a whirlpool tub, a corner shower and a walk-in closet.
- A hall bath serves the two other main-floor bedrooms.
- In addition to a large family room, the daylight basement hosts a fourth bedroom, a half-bath and a utility room.

Plan LMB-9826-W

Bedrooms: 4	Baths: 2½
Living Area:	
Main floor	1,380 sq. ft.
Daylight basement	632 sq. ft.
Total Living Area:	**2,012 sq. ft.**
Garage	495 sq. ft.
Exterior Wall Framing:	2x6

Foundation Options:

Daylight basement

(All plans can be built with your choice of foundation and framing. A generic conversion diagram is available. See order form.)

BLUEPRINT PRICE CODE:	**C**

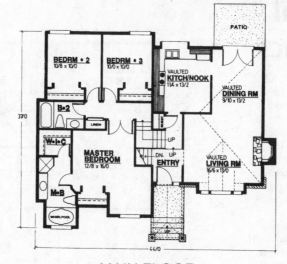

MAIN FLOOR

ALTERNATE KITCHEN AND NOOK

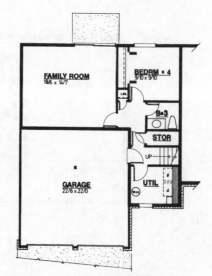

DAYLIGHT BASEMENT

New Colonial in Classic Brick

- With its detailed masonry, big, bright windows and classic entry, this brick Colonial is a neighborhood standout.
- The living room, which can be enhanced with an optional fireplace, features a bright front window. The adjoining dining room, which includes plans for a sunny bay window area, is convenient to the kitchen. Both rooms are enhanced by a shared 12-ft.-high vaulted ceiling.
- The kitchen/breakfast area has a pantry and sliding glass doors to the backyard.
- The master bedroom, which boasts a roomy walk-in closet, can be extended with an optional boxed-out bay window. The private master bath features a dual-sink vanity.
- Two other bedrooms share a full bath and a hallway linen closet.
- The daylight basement has enough space for another bedroom, another bath and a spacious family room.

Plan CH-830-A

Bedrooms: 3	Baths: 2
Living Area:	
Main floor	1,344 sq. ft.
Total Living Area:	**1,344 sq. ft.**
Daylight basement	670 sq. ft.
Tuck-under garage	550 sq. ft.
Exterior Wall Framing:	2x4

Foundation Options:

Daylight basement

(All plans can be built with your choice of foundation and framing. A generic conversion diagram is available. See order form.)

BLUEPRINT PRICE CODE: **A**

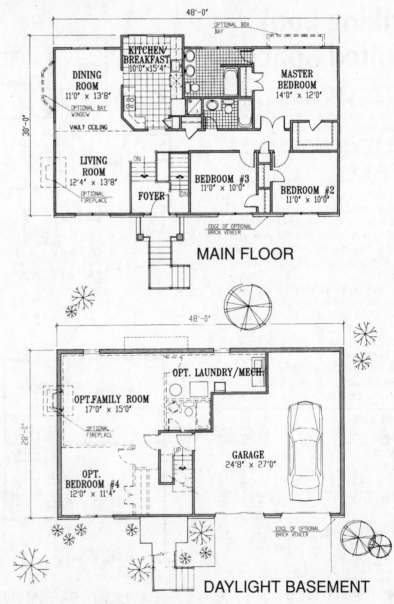

MAIN FLOOR

DAYLIGHT BASEMENT

Plan CH-830-A

PRICES AND DETAILS ON PAGES 12-15

Flexible Floor Plan

- This split-entry's flexible floor plan is easily adaptable to serve the needs of a growing family.
- The living room, which can be enhanced with a fireplace, features a bright front window. The adjoining dining room, which includes plans for a sunny bay window area, is convenient to the kitchen. Both rooms are enhanced by a shared 12-ft.-high vaulted ceiling.
- The kitchen/breakfast area has a pantry and sliding glass doors to the backyard.
- The master bedroom, which boasts a roomy walk-in closet, can be extended with a boxed-out bay window. The private master bath features a dual-sink vanity.
- Two other bedrooms share a full bath and a hallway linen closet.
- The daylight basement has enough space for another bedroom, another bath and a spacious family room.

Plan CH-830-B	
Bedrooms: 3	**Baths:** 2
Living Area:	
Main floor	1,344 sq. ft.
Total Living Area:	**1,344 sq. ft.**
Daylight basement	670 sq. ft.
Tuck-under garage	550 sq. ft.
Exterior Wall Framing:	2x4

Foundation Options:

Daylight basement

(All plans can be built with your choice of foundation and framing. A generic conversion diagram is available. See order form.)

BLUEPRINT PRICE CODE: A

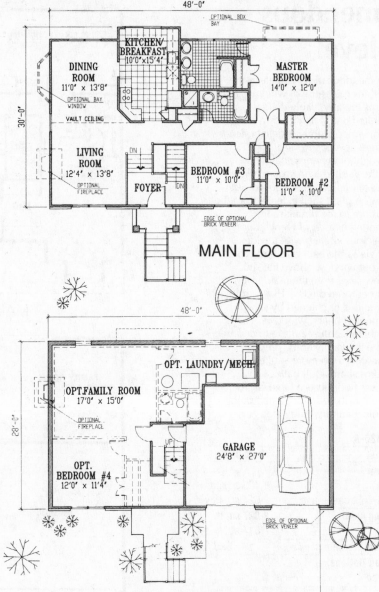

MAIN FLOOR

DAYLIGHT BASEMENT

Tremendous Tri-level

- This tremendous tri-level pleases the eye with its multitude of windows that brightens the airy, vaulted areas.
- The vaulted entry, lighted by a huge transom window and a sidelight, leads to all three levels.
- To the right of the entry, half-walls frame the vaulted living room, which features a fireplace and a boxed-out window. A plant shelf extends from the living room to the dining room, culminating in a set of French doors.
- The spacious kitchen with a wide pantry views the backyard through a boxed-out window above the sink.
- Up a few steps from the main level, the master bedroom offers a 10-ft. vaulted ceiling and is brightened by an assortment of paned windows. The master bath features a makeup counter opposite the vanity and a private shower area. Two more vaulted bedrooms share a full bath.
- The lower floor hosts a large family room, a fourth bedroom, a half-bath and a nice laundry/utility area.

Plan I-2026-A

Bedrooms: 4	Baths: 2½
Living Area:	
Main floor	1,403 sq. ft.
Partial daylight basement	624 sq. ft.
Total Living Area:	**2,027 sq. ft.**
Garage	517 sq. ft.
Exterior Wall Framing:	2x6

Foundation Options:

Crawlspace
(All plans can be built with your choice of foundation and framing. A generic conversion diagram is available. See order form.)

BLUEPRINT PRICE CODE:	**C**

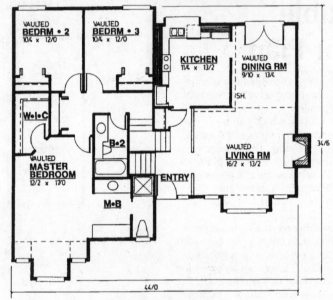

MAIN FLOOR

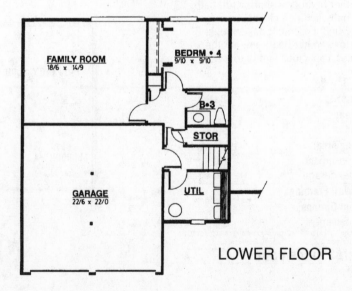

LOWER FLOOR

TO ORDER THIS BLUEPRINT, CALL TOLL-FREE 1-800-547-5570

Plan I-2026-A

PRICES AND DETAILS ON PAGES 12-15

Inviting Entry Deck

- The inviting entry deck of this side-sloping design serves as a distinctive bridge to the interior's angled foyer.
- The vaulted foyer is flanked by a nice guest room and the central stairs as it opens to the living areas of the home.
- The living room boasts an oversized bay window, a soaring 14-ft. vaulted ceiling and a handsome fireplace. In the adjoining dining room, sliding glass doors open to a rear deck, bathing the entire area in light.
- The adjacent kitchen features a windowed sink and an angled breakfast bar that serves the dining room. A hallway leads to a handy pantry, a laundry room and a bath, in addition to a two-car garage.
- Corner windows brighten the master bedroom on the lower floor. An optional deck and a private bath with a dual-sink vanity, a whirlpool tub and a separate shower are other amenities. A second bedroom and a versatile bonus room are also included.

Plan LMB-9640

Bedrooms: 3+	Baths: 3
Living Area:	
Main floor	1,099 sq. ft.
Lower floor	983 sq. ft.
Total Living Area:	**2,082 sq. ft.**
Garage	548 sq. ft.
Exterior Wall Framing:	2x6

Foundation Options:

Crawlspace
(All plans can be built with your choice of foundation and framing. A generic conversion diagram is available. See order form.)

BLUEPRINT PRICE CODE:	C

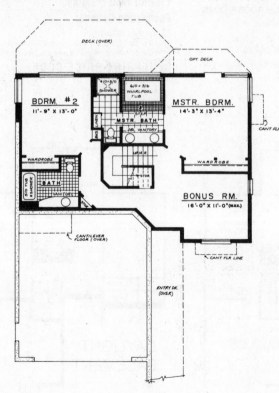

LOWER FLOOR

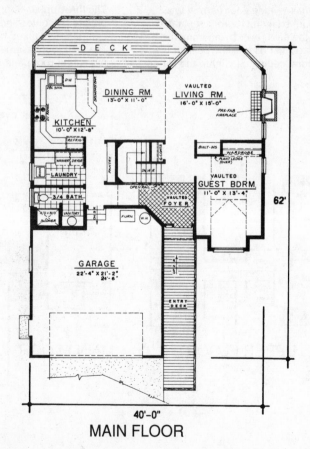

MAIN FLOOR

Dominant and Deluxe Styling

- Vertical cedar siding, a dominant roofline and clerestory windows give this home an exciting facade.
- The interior spaces are just as inspiring, fully intended to take advantage of scenic views. The home's modest width also makes it ideal for narrow lots.
- The sunken living room is separated from the tiled foyer by an immense fireplace that rises to the peak of the cathedral ceiling. Skylights and sliding glass doors line the rear half of the room, which is surrounded by a deck.
- The adjacent dining room also has access to the deck. Extra eating space is provided by a roomy snack bar facing the efficient U-shaped kitchen.
- The oversized master suite has a large walk-in closet, a private bath and sliding glass doors to the deck.
- Upstairs, a balcony hall overlooks the living room and a portion of the foyer. The three upper-floor bedrooms boast private balconies and share a compartmentalized bath.
- The walk-out basement offers a recreation room and expansion space.

Plan AX-98597

Bedrooms: 4	Baths: 3
Living Area:	
Upper floor	685 sq. ft.
Main floor	1,056 sq. ft.
Daylight basement (finished)	465 sq. ft.
Total Living Area:	**2,206 sq. ft.**
Daylight basement (unfinished)	585 sq. ft.
Garage	337 sq. ft.
Exterior Wall Framing:	2x4
Foundation Options:	

Daylight basement
(All plans can be built with your choice of foundation and framing. A generic conversion diagram is available. See order form.)

BLUEPRINT PRICE CODE: C

UPPER FLOOR

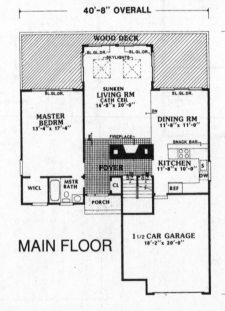

MAIN FLOOR

DAYLIGHT BASEMENT

New England Cottage

- Unique styling characterizes this rustic split-entry home, perfectly suited for a sloping lot. A prominent turret and an exterior of cedar shakes give it the look of a New England cottage.
- The living areas unfold from the skylighted entry, which has a convenient powder room nearby.
- Up a half flight of stairs, the spacious living and dining rooms merge for an open, airy atmosphere that extends to an outdoor deck.
- French doors close off the dining room from the central kitchen. A lazy Susan, a windowed sink and generous counter space make the kitchen more delightful.
- The main hallway leads to the sleeping wing, which houses three bedrooms, two baths and an easily accessible laundry closet. Each bedroom has a walk-in wardrobe. The master suite also features a 17-ft. vaulted ceiling, a private balcony and its own bath.
- A two-car garage and shop space are located in the daylight basement, as are a wine cellar, a storage area and a large bonus room.

Plan LMB-9810-E

Bedrooms: 3	Baths: 2½
Living Area:	
Main floor	1,700 sq. ft.
Daylight basement	768 sq. ft.
Total Living Area:	**2,468 sq. ft.**
Tuck-under garage/shop space	811 sq. ft.
Exterior Wall Framing:	2x6
Foundation Options:	
Daylight basement	

(All plans can be built with your choice of foundation and framing. A generic conversion diagram is available. See order form.)

BLUEPRINT PRICE CODE:	C

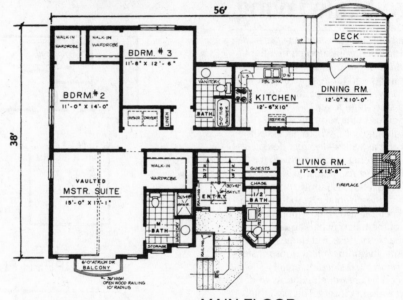

MAIN FLOOR

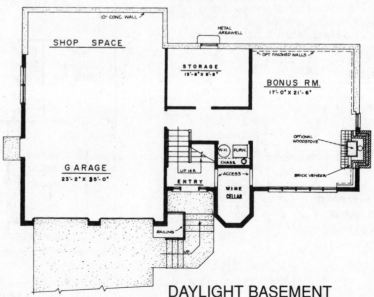

DAYLIGHT BASEMENT

Large-Scale Living

- Eye-catching windows and an appealing wraparound porch highlight the exterior of this outstanding home.
- High ceilings and large-scale living spaces prevail inside, beginning with the two-story-high foyer.
- The spacious living room flows into the formal dining room, which accesses the front porch as well as the rear deck.
- The island kitchen combines with a bright breakfast room, also with deck access. The fabulous family room offers a warm corner fireplace, a soaring 18-ft. vaulted ceiling, a wall of windows and a view of the balcony hall above.
- The upper floor hosts four large bedrooms, including a luxurious master suite. The vaulted sleeping area is brightened by an arched window and has two walk-in closets. The skylighted master bath features a spa tub, a separate shower and a dual-sink vanity.
- The three remaining bedrooms are reached via a balcony hall, which offers stunning views of the family room.

Plan AX-93309

Bedrooms: 4	Baths: 2½
Living Area:	
Upper floor	1,180 sq. ft.
Main floor	1,290 sq. ft.
Total Living Area:	**2,470 sq. ft.**
Basement	1,290 sq. ft.
Garage	421 sq. ft.
Exterior Wall Framing:	2x4

Foundation Options:

Daylight basement

Standard basement

Slab

(All plans can be built with your choice of foundation and framing. A generic conversion diagram is available. See order form.)

BLUEPRINT PRICE CODE:	C

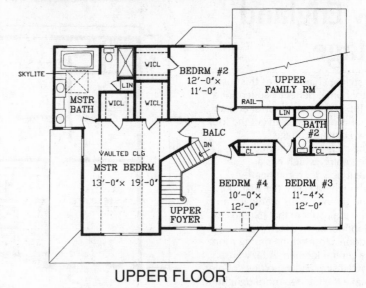

UPPER FLOOR

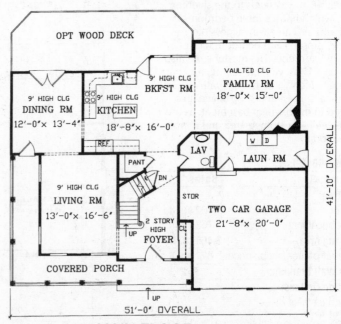

MAIN FLOOR

TO ORDER THIS BLUEPRINT,
CALL TOLL-FREE 1-800-547-5570

Plan AX-93309

PRICES AND DETAILS
ON PAGES 12-15

Modern Class

- This modern traditional defines class with its brick columns, double-door entry and stylish windows.
- The vaulted entry is brightened by a transom and flows into the living room.
- The formal areas are highlighted by 13-ft. vaulted ceilings with an arched window in the living room and a bay window in the adjoining dining room.
- The island kitchen features a roomy desk, a handy snackbar and and a unique room-width bay window over the sink area.
- French doors open from the adjacent breakfast nook to a covered porch that merges with a larger backyard deck. A large fireplace warms both the bayed family room and the breakfast nook.
- Upstairs, double doors introduce the vaulted master bedroom, boasting a walk-in closet and a posh bath that includes a spa tub and a separate shower. Two more vaulted bedrooms share a skylighted bath with an angled dual-sink vanity.

Plan I-2619-A

Bedrooms: 3+	Baths: 2½
Living Area:	
Upper floor	1,042 sq. ft.
Main floor	1,577 sq. ft.
Total Living Area:	**2,619 sq. ft.**
Partial daylight basement	941 sq. ft.
Garage	832 sq. ft.
Exterior Wall Framing:	2x6

Foundation Options:

Partial daylight basement

(All plans can be built with your choice of foundation and framing. A generic conversion diagram is available. See order form.)

BLUEPRINT PRICE CODE: D

UPPER FLOOR

MAIN FLOOR

Split-Level Suits Sloping Lot

- Attractive terraced planters and winding stairs climb to the entry of this contemporary split-level home.
- The entry offers an exciting view of the spacious living/dining room and the expansive deck that extends along the back of the home. Access to the deck is possible from the living room, the breakfast room and the master suite!
- The floor plan's big kitchen rewards the cook with a pantry and a functional

work island that includes a vegetable sink. A windowed sink and a sunny breakfast bay are also featured.
- A half-bath and an oversized laundry room are handily located between the kitchen and the garage.
- A private bath serves the homeowners in the secluded master suite at the opposite end of the home. An isolated toilet and separate vanities allow for privacy and convenience.
- Two more bedrooms, another bath, a huge family room and a versatile home office occupy the daylight basement, along with a utility room and extra storage space.

Plan CPS-1139-S

Bedrooms: 3+	Baths: 2½
Living Area:	
Main floor	1,342 sq. ft.
Daylight basement	1,342 sq. ft.
Total Living Area:	**2,684 sq. ft.**
Garage	576 sq. ft.
Exterior Wall Framing:	2x6

Foundation Options:

Daylight basement
(All plans can be built with your choice of foundation and framing. A generic conversion diagram is available. See order form.)

BLUEPRINT PRICE CODE:	**D**

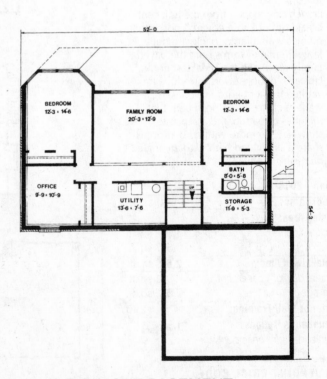

MAIN FLOOR

DAYLIGHT BASEMENT

TO ORDER THIS BLUEPRINT, CALL TOLL-FREE 1-800-547-5570

Plan CPS-1139-S

PRICES AND DETAILS ON PAGES 12-15

Bright Ideal

- Highlighted by skylights and sunny bay windows, this modern home offers a bright, inventive floor plan.
- Past the inviting covered entry, the skylighted foyer flows into the sunken living room, which features a fireplace.
- The adjoining dining room is enhanced by overhead plant shelves and a large bayed window area. The nearby kitchen offers a pantry and a boxed-out window over the sink. The sunny breakfast area accesses an attractive backyard deck through French doors.
- The luxurious master bedroom also extends to to a private deck. A designer shower, a dual-sink vanity and a walk-in closet are featured in the skylighted master bath.
- Two additional main-floor bedrooms share another skylighted bath.
- The daylight basement features a walk-out family room and game room combination. A fourth bedroom found here can function as a den, a playroom or a library.

Plan LMB-9559-CD

Bedrooms: 3+	Baths: 3
Living Area:	
Main floor	1,527 sq. ft.
Daylight basement	1,206 sq. ft.
Total Living Area:	**2,733 sq. ft.**
Garage	588 sq. ft.
Exterior Wall Framing:	2x6

Foundation Options:

Daylight basement

(All plans can be built with your choice of foundation and framing. A generic conversion diagram is available. See order form.)

BLUEPRINT PRICE CODE:	D

MAIN FLOOR

DAYLIGHT BASEMENT

ELEVATION A

Spectacular Family Room

- Available with either a traditional or a contemporary exterior, this handsome home's floor plan is designed for living.
- The inviting skylighted entry flows into the comfortable living room, which is brightened by a boxed-out window.
- The spectacular family room boasts a 14-ft. vaulted ceiling, bright boxed-out windows and a warm fireplace flanked by French doors to a backyard deck.

- The modern U-shaped kitchen services the family room via a handy pass-through. The adjoining nook is ideal for informal meals. A laundry room and a half-bath are nearby.
- Three nice-sized bedrooms are upstairs. The master bedroom has a private, compartmentalized master bath that features a designer shower and a dual-sink vanity.
- A tuck-under garage and a big multi-purpose area make up the daylight basement.
- When ordering blueprints, please specify Elevation A or Elevation B.

Plan LMB-9611-E	
Bedrooms: 3	**Baths: 2½**
Living Area:	
Upper floor	826 sq. ft.
Main floor	1,332 sq. ft.
Total Living Area:	**2,158 sq. ft.**
Daylight basement	669 sq. ft.
Tuck-under garage	484 sq. ft.
Exterior Wall Framing:	2x6
Foundation Options:	
Daylight basement	

(All plans can be built with your choice of foundation and framing. A generic conversion diagram is available. See order form.)

BLUEPRINT PRICE CODE:	**C**

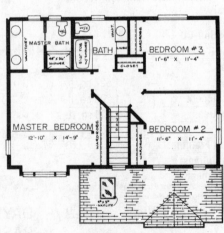

ELEVATION B

WOOD DECK
24'-0" X 12'-0"

FAMILY ROOM
13'-6" X 23'-0"

KITCHEN
9'-0" X 9'-6"

UTILITY
6'-0"X9'-0"

BATH

DINING ROOM
12'-0" X 13'-9"

NOOK
9'-2" X 9'-4"

LIVING ROOM
14'-0" X 17'-0"

ENTRY

COVERED PORCH

MAIN FLOOR

33'

49'

MASTER BATH

BATH

BEDROOM #3
11'-6" X 11'-4"

MASTER BEDROOM
12'-10" X 14'-9"

BEDROOM #2
11'-6" X 11'-4"

UPPER FLOOR

TO ORDER THIS BLUEPRINT,
CALL TOLL-FREE 1-800-547-5570

Plan LMB-9611-E

PRICES AND DETAILS
ON PAGES 12-15

Life of Leisure

- This modern home lends itself to leisure with a large activity room, a shop area and a recreational vehicle garage.
- The vaulted entry is brightened by sidelights and a high half-round window as it flows by an open-railed central stairway into the living room.
- The vaulted living room shows off an attractive bay and adjoins the formal dining room with a stunning arched opening. The dining room has convenient access to the kitchen.
- The family room merges with the breakfast nook and accesses a large backyard deck. A handsome fireplace warms the entire area.
- The roomy island kitchen features a built-in planning desk and a handy pantry. An oversized laundry room and a convenient half-bath are nearby.
- The removed master bedroom boasts a 12-ft. vaulted ceiling and French doors to a private deck. The master bath offers a dual-sink vanity, a large walk-in closet and a whirlpool tub.
- Two more bedrooms and an exciting activity room with a fireplace and a wet bar are housed in the daylight basement. A big shop area and a full bath are also included.

Plan LMB-9816

Bedrooms: 3	Baths: 2½
Living Area:	
Main floor	1,531 sq. ft.
Daylight basement	1,426 sq. ft.
Total Living Area:	**2,957 sq. ft.**
Garage	500 sq. ft.
Exterior Wall Framing:	2x6

Foundation Options:

Daylight basement

(All plans can be built with your choice of foundation and framing. A generic conversion diagram is available. See order form.)

BLUEPRINT PRICE CODE:	**D**

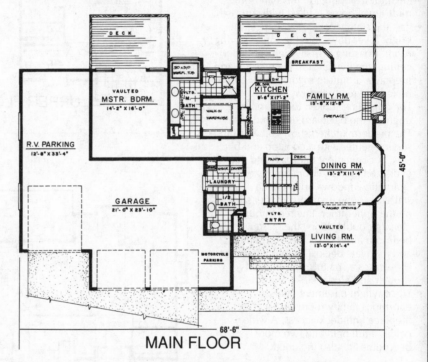

MAIN FLOOR

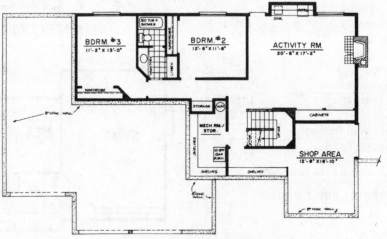

DAYLIGHT BASEMENT

Hillside Heaven

- Ideal for a sloping lot, this handsome multi-level home is filled with surprises.
- Past the stately covered entrance, the bright foyer flows into the sunken living room. Boasting a 14-ft.-high vaulted ceiling, the living room features a warm fireplace, a built-in media center and a boxed-out rear window.
- The adjoining sunken dining room opens to the backyard deck and spa.
- The modern kitchen shows off an island service center with a cooktop and bar sink. A convenient half-bath and an oversized laundry room are nearby.
- Dramatic windows brighten the stairway to the luxurious master suite on the upper floor. Entered through elegant double doors, the master bedroom also boasts a coved ceiling and a private deck. The master bath showcases a spa tub, a skylighted shower and a dual-sink vanity.
- The daylight basement offers an enormous family room with a cozy fireplace and deck access. A wine cellar, a full bath and two more bedrooms are also included.

UPPER FLOOR

REAR VIEW

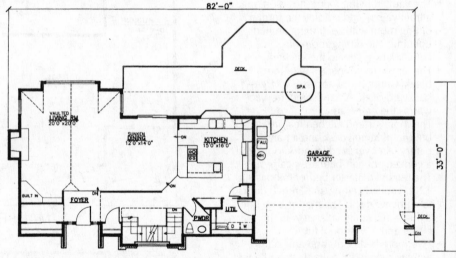

MAIN FLOOR

Plan I-3153-A

Bedrooms: 3	**Baths:** 2½

Living Area:	
Upper floor	579 sq. ft.
Main floor	1,307 sq. ft.
Daylight basement	1,267 sq. ft.
Total Living Area:	**3,153 sq. ft.**
Garage	808 sq. ft.
Exterior Wall Framing:	2x6

Foundation Options:

Daylight basement

(All plans can be built with your choice of foundation and framing. A generic conversion diagram is available. See order form.)

BLUEPRINT PRICE CODE:	E

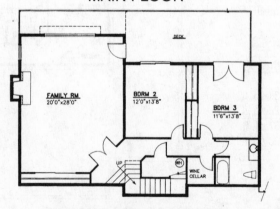

DAYLIGHT BASEMENT

TO ORDER THIS BLUEPRINT,
CALL TOLL-FREE 1-800-547-5570

Plan I-3153-A

PRICES AND DETAILS
ON PAGES 12-15

Sprawling Plan Sleeps Several

- Decorative gables, elaborate window treatments and beautiful bays adorn this sprawling traditional home.
- Covered porches wind along the front of the home while expansive decks are attached at the rear.
- With six bedrooms and more than four baths, the interior comfortably accommodates a large or extended family. Four bedrooms located on the upper floor are connected by an open-railed balcony that overlooks the foyer and living room. The stunning master bedroom is secluded on the main floor and is embellished with a bayed sitting area, a romantic fireplace, a private bath and access to a deck.
- The spacious living room sits at the center of the floor plan, while the gourmet kitchen and the family room adjoin to the left. The kitchen features a walk-in pantry and an oversized eating bar that seats seven!
- A computer room and a three-car garage are other exciting extras.

Plan LMB-9694-M

Bedrooms: 6	**Baths:** 4½

Living Area:	
Upper floor	1,048 sq. ft.
Main floor	2,376 sq. ft.
Total Living Area:	**3,424 sq. ft.**
Partial daylight basement	1,260 sq. ft.
Garage	691 sq. ft.

Exterior Wall Framing:	2x6

Foundation Options:

Partial daylight basement
(All plans can be built with your choice of foundation and framing. A generic conversion diagram is available. See order form.)

BLUEPRINT PRICE CODE:	E

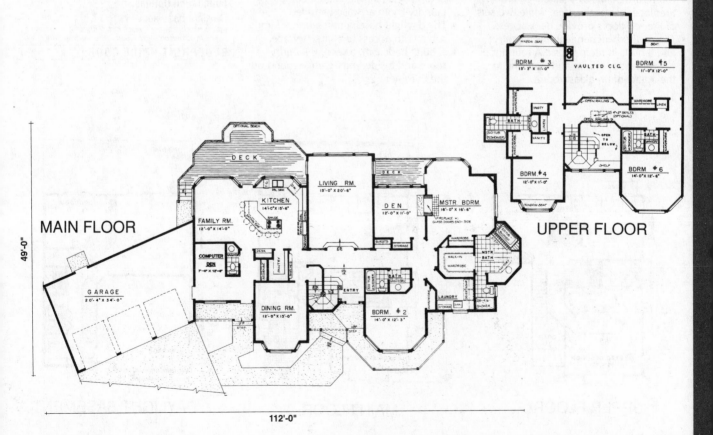

MAIN FLOOR

49'-0"

112'-0"

UPPER FLOOR

Scenic Slope

- This French country design is perfect for a narrow lot with a side-to-side slope. A rear-facing terrace, deck and balcony take advantage of scenic views.
- Transom and sidelight windows surround the gorgeous front door and brighten the two-story-high foyer.
- Straight ahead, the living and dining rooms are defined by stately columns. A fireplace warms the area, while two sets of French doors provide deck access.
- The vaulted kitchen features a pantry and a built-in recipe desk. A round-top window adds charm and sunshine to the adjacent breakfast room.

- A large guest room with private bath access completes the main floor.
- Upstairs, the smart master suite boasts a soaring vaulted ceiling and a half-round transom window. The vaulted master bath has a step-up garden tub, a glass shower, a walk-in closet, a private toilet and a dual-sink vanity.
- The vaulted second bedroom offers a fireplace and a private balcony. A third bedroom, a hall bath and a compact laundry room are also included.
- The daylight basement features a family room with access to a large terrace.
- A quiet bedroom, a second laundry room and a side-entry garage round out the basement level.

Plan APS-3501

Bedrooms: 5	Baths: 4
Living Area:	
Upper floor	1,215 sq. ft.
Main floor	1,455 sq. ft.
Daylight basement	916 sq. ft.
Total Living Area:	**3,586 sq. ft.**
Tuck-under garage	484 sq. ft.
Exterior Wall Framing:	2x4

Foundation Options:

Daylight basement
(All plans can be built with your choice of foundation and framing.
A generic conversion diagram is available. See order form.)

BLUEPRINT PRICE CODE: F

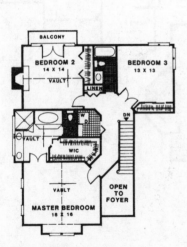

UPPER FLOOR

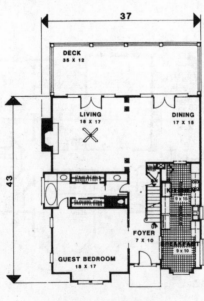

MAIN FLOOR

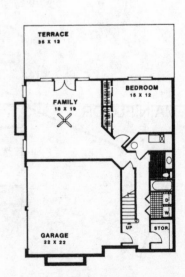

DAYLIGHT BASEMENT

Creative Charm

- This creative home is charming, with its oversized master suite, deluxe island kitchen and nifty shop off the garage.
- A two-story-high split entry, lighted by generous windows, leads up to the foyer and down to the family room.
- The foyer opens to the adjoining formal spaces that look to a rear deck. The bayed living room is warmed by a fireplace and accesses the deck through sliding glass doors.
- The huge island kitchen features double ovens, a corner pantry, a bayed breakfast area with deck access and a raised bar that services the dining room.
- Upstairs, double doors open to the coffered master suite from a loft area, which offers a window seat and bookshelves. The master bath boasts a step-up whirlpool tub, a separate tiled shower and dual vanities.
- Halfway upstairs a large multi-purpose room with a half-bath has views of the backyard.
- Downstairs, the bayed family room with a second fireplace opens to a rear patio. Two more bedrooms share a full bath.

Plan LMB-9613

Bedrooms: 3	Baths: 2 full, 2 half
Living Area:	
Upper floor	1,210 sq. ft.
Main floor	1,288 sq. ft.
Daylight basement	1,116 sq. ft.
Total Living Area:	**3,614 sq. ft.**
Garage	917 sq. ft.
Exterior Wall Framing:	2x6

Foundation Options:

Daylight basement

(All plans can be built with your choice of foundation and framing. A generic conversion diagram is available. See order form.)

BLUEPRINT PRICE CODE:	F

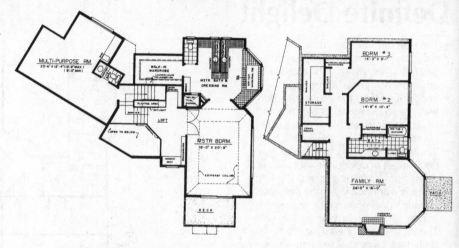

UPPER FLOOR

DAYLIGHT BASEMENT

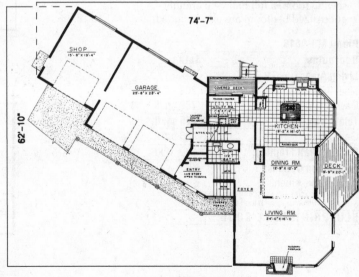

MAIN FLOOR

Definite Delight

- The covered front porch of this delightful contemporary opens into the vaulted foyer, which is brightened by an assortment of windows.
- Just off the foyer, the vaulted kitchen features an octagonal cooktop island, a bayed, vaulted nook and a stylish counter that services the dining room.
- Vaulted formal areas look to the rear deck areas, accessed through sliding doors from the dining room. The living room is warmed by a stone fireplace.
- Double doors open to the impressive master suite with private deck access. The luxurious vaulted master bath has a skylighted Jacuzzi, a separate shower and a dual-sink vanity.
- Downstairs, the large recreation room boasts a deluxe wet bar, a woodstove and backyard access. An office, a sewing room, a full bath and another good-sized bedroom are also included.

Plan LMB-9618

Bedrooms: 2	Baths: 2½
Living Area:	
Main floor	1,866 sq. ft.
Daylight basement	1,789 sq. ft.
Total Living Area:	**3,655 sq. ft.**
Garage	498 sq. ft.
Exterior Wall Framing:	2x6

Foundation Options:

Daylight basement

(All plans can be built with your choice of foundation and framing. A generic conversion diagram is available. See order form.)

BLUEPRINT PRICE CODE: F

MAIN FLOOR

DAYLIGHT BASEMENT

TO ORDER THIS BLUEPRINT, CALL TOLL-FREE 1-800-547-5570   Plan LMB-9618   **PRICES AND DETAILS ON PAGES 12-15**

Dynamic
Two-Story

- This exciting two-story home is handsomely adorned with brick piers, arched windows and a French-door entry with striking sidelights.
- The airy foyer boasts a vaulted ceiling that rises to 18 ft., while it also shows off an open-railed stairway and a view into the living and dining rooms.
- A dramatic corner fireplace and a high 11-ft. ceiling emphasize the living room, while lovely French doors with bright transoms enhance the dining room. The French doors open to a winding deck that is also accessible from the breakfast nook and the adjoining family room.
- Double doors close off the kitchen from the foyer area. A big pantry, a cooktop island and a sunny corner sink are other nice extras in the spacious kitchen.
- Three bedrooms and a skylighted bonus room occupy the upper floor. The master bedroom has an arched entrance into its skylighted private bath.
- A half-bath and a spectacular recreation room that walks out to a patio are offered in the daylight basement.

Plan CDG-4018

Bedrooms: 3+	Baths: 2 full, 2 half

Living Area:

Upper floor	1,286 sq. ft.
Main floor	1,741 sq. ft.
Bonus room	250 sq. ft.
Partial daylight basement	664 sq. ft.
Total Living Area:	**3,941 sq. ft.**
Garage	784 sq. ft.
Exterior Wall Framing:	**2x6**

Foundation Options:

Partial daylight basement
(All plans can be built with your choice of foundation and framing. A generic conversion diagram is available. See order form.)

BLUEPRINT PRICE CODE:	**F**

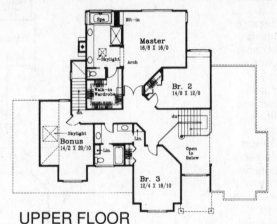

UPPER FLOOR

MAIN FLOOR

DAYLIGHT BASEMENT

TO ORDER THIS BLUEPRINT,
CALL TOLL-FREE 1-800-547-5570

Plan CDG-4018

PRICES AND DETAILS
ON PAGES 12-15

155

Grand Elegance

- This stately home offers grand elegance with a two-story-high entry, a superb master suite and a large island kitchen.
- Stone pillars and double doors offer an impressive welcome into the entry, which flows to the formal living areas.
- The bayed living room hosts a fireplace and opens to a rear deck. The dining room offers a built-in china cabinet.
- The vaulted family room also accesses the deck and looks through an open rail to the kitchen's spacious breakfast area.
- The generous kitchen also boasts a nifty corner pantry, a separate freezer and an oversized Jenn-Aire island. A large laundry room, a handy second stairway and garage access are all nearby.
- The spectacular master suite encompasses the upper floor. Highlights include a sitting room with an audio-visual center and a private bath with a spa tub and a separate shower. A quiet library, an enormous storage room and another storage area (not shown) above the garage are also upstairs.
- Two more bedrooms and a full bath are offered in the daylight basement. Space for a future recreation room with a woodstove alcove is also available.

Plan LMB-9812

Bedrooms: 4+	Baths: 3½
Living Area:	
Upper floor	988 sq. ft.
Main floor	2,447 sq. ft.
Daylight basement (finished)	658 sq. ft.
Total Living Area:	**4,093 sq. ft.**
Daylight basement (unfinished)	1,587 sq. ft.
Garage	902 sq. ft.
Exterior Wall Framing:	2x6
Foundation Options:	

Daylight basement

(All plans can be built with your choice of foundation and framing. A generic conversion diagram is available. See order form.)

BLUEPRINT PRICE CODE:	G

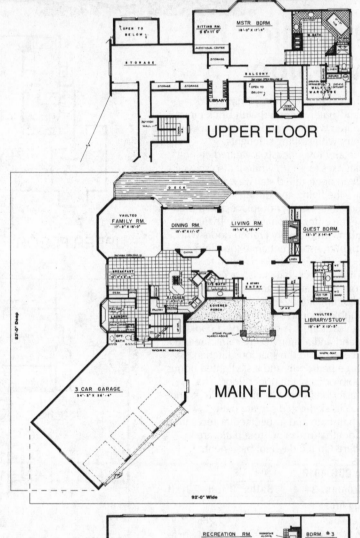

UPPER FLOOR

MAIN FLOOR

DAYLIGHT BASEMENT

TO ORDER THIS BLUEPRINT, CALL TOLL-FREE 1-800-547-5570

Plan LMB-9812

PRICES AND DETAILS ON PAGES 12-15

Outdoor Options

- Exciting indoor/outdoor interaction adds to the one-of-a-kind charm found in this sprawling hillside home.
- Unfolding from the inviting foyer, the breathtaking vaulted living room is warmed by a fireplace and brightened by a panoramic wall of glass that overlooks the backyard.
- The adjoining formal dining room offers a built-in buffet and sliding glass doors to one of the expansive outdoor decks. The island kitchen has a handy pass-through to the sunny eating nook, which also opens to the deck. Other conveniences include a roomy walk-in pantry, a nearby half-bath and an oversized laundry room.
- The main-floor bedroom features a large walk-in closet and private deck and bath access. The nearby library, with its built-in shelving and storage space, could serve as a guest room.
- Downstairs, two additional bedrooms share a hallway bath. A spacious activity room boasts plenty of windows and access to a backyard patio.

Plan LMB-9328

Bedrooms: 3+	Baths: 2½
Living Area:	
Main floor	2,052 sq. ft.
Daylight basement	2,052 sq. ft.
Total Living Area:	**4,104 sq. ft.**
Garage	541 sq. ft.
Exterior Wall Framing:	2x4

Foundation Options:

Daylight basement

(All plans can be built with your choice of foundation and framing. A generic conversion diagram is available. See order form.)

BLUEPRINT PRICE CODE:	**G**

MAIN FLOOR

DAYLIGHT BASEMENT

Beautiful Brick

- This home commands attention with a beautiful brick courtyard. Inside, soaring vaulted ceilings and interesting angles maintain the excitement.
- The entry's barrel-vaulted ceiling continues into the formal dining room. To the left, the sunken living room shows off a view of the front courtyard.
- The gourmet kitchen features a nifty cooktop island, a handy pantry, a bayed breakfast nook and an angled sink area with a bright window.
- The adjoining family room boasts a fireplace flanked by window seats. Three rear windows add more light, while a French door provides access to a backyard deck.
- Two secondary bedrooms, a full bath and a laundry room are located in a small wing near the garage.
- Isolated at the opposite end of the home, the vaulted master bedroom is highlighted by a gas fireplace, a large walk-in closet a spa bath and a private sun deck.
- The daylight basement includes two more bedrooms, another bath and a spectacular recreation room.

Plan I-4206-A

Bedrooms: 5+	Baths: 3½
Living Area:	
Main floor	2,942 sq. ft.
Partial daylight basement	1,264 sq. ft.
Total Living Area:	**4,206 sq. ft.**
Garage	768 sq. ft.
Exterior Wall Framing:	**2x6**

Foundation Options:

Partial daylight basement

(All plans can be built with your choice of foundation and framing A generic conversion diagram is available. See order form.)

BLUEPRINT PRICE CODE: **G**

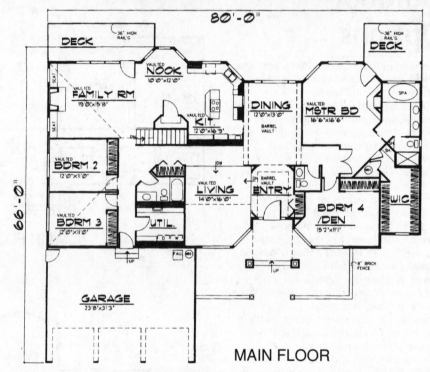

MAIN FLOOR

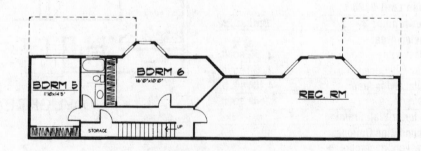

DAYLIGHT BASEMENT

TO ORDER THIS BLUEPRINT, CALL TOLL-FREE 1-800-547-5570

Plan I-4206-A

PRICES AND DETAILS ON PAGES 12-15

Entirely Exciting!

- Elegance and excitement describe this spacious, sloping-lot design.
- High vaulted ceilings are found throughout the primary living areas and in the master bedroom and foyer. The arched openings in the formal rooms add further drama, as do the fireplace in the living room and the French-door deck access in the dining room.
- The huge family room boasts an 11-ft. vaulted ceiling and interacts with the kitchen and breakfast nook while overlooking its own deck. A handsome fireplace adjoins a built-in wet bar and work desk.

- An oversized cooktop island with a vegetable sink and grill makes cooking a breeze in the roomy gourmet kitchen.
- The exquisite master suite is entered through double doors and features a private skylighted bath introduced by French doors. The bedroom bestows a romantic fireplace, a 10-ft. vaulted ceiling and a French door to the deck.
- Two secondary bedrooms on the main floor, two more in the daylight basement and a den are available to sleep more family or guests.
- A full bath, an oversized laundry room and an enormous recreation room with yet another fireplace are also located in the daylight basement.

Plan CDG-4017	
Bedrooms: 5+	**Baths:** 3½
Living Area:	
Main floor	2,622 sq. ft.
Partial daylight basement	1,715 sq. ft.
Total Living Area:	**4,337 sq. ft.**
Storage	120 sq. ft.
Garage	914 sq. ft.
Exterior Wall Framing:	2x6
Foundation Options:	

Partial daylight basement
(All plans can be built with your choice of foundation and framing. A generic conversion diagram is available. See order form.)

BLUEPRINT PRICE CODE:	G

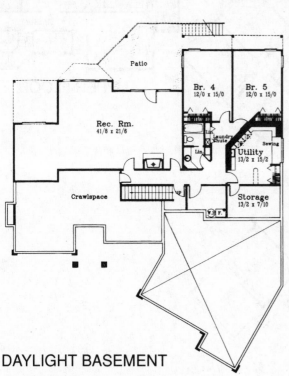

DAYLIGHT BASEMENT

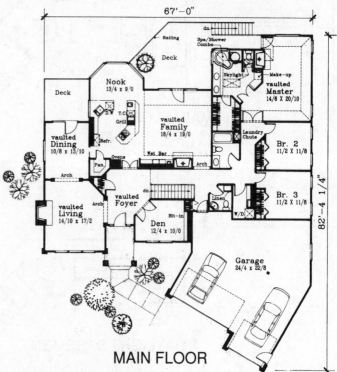

MAIN FLOOR

Hillside Estate

- The bright vaulted entry of this modern, spacious estate welcomes guests to the elegance found inside.
- A dramatic arch introduces the formal dining room, which features two built-in china cabinets. The nearby island kitchen has a pantry, a wet bar and a bright breakfast area with deck access. A dumbwaiter allows the kitchen to also serve the daylight basement.
- The unique vaulted living room is warmed by a stone fireplace. Sliding glass doors access a boomerang deck.

- Three bay-windowed main-floor bedrooms share a hallway bath.
- A turned staircase brightened by large windows leads to the upper-floor master bedroom, which boasts a corner fireplace and a private balcony. The master bath showcases a whirlpool bay, a designer shower, a dual-sink vanity and roomy walk-in closets. A skylighted library is nearby.
- The daylight basement offers a neat kitchenette, a bayed den, a hobby room and a fifth bedroom. An exciting spa solarium is located off the huge recreation room.

Plan LMB-9593

Bedrooms: 5+	Baths: 4½
Living Area:	
Upper floor	1,190 sq. ft.
Main floor	2,369 sq. ft.
Daylight basement	2,526 sq. ft.
Total Living Area:	**6,085 sq. ft.**
Garage	944 sq. ft.
Exterior Wall Framing:	2x6

Foundation Options:

Daylight basement

(All plans can be built with your choice of foundation and framing. A generic conversion diagram is available. See order form.)

BLUEPRINT PRICE CODE: G

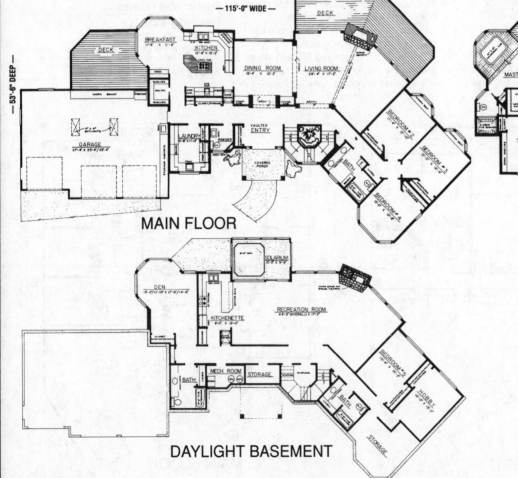

MAIN FLOOR

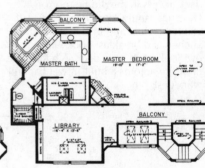

UPPER FLOOR

DAYLIGHT BASEMENT

Stately Manor

- Classical proportions, brick with corner quoins, and a railing-topped, covered front entry create a stately character.
- Once inside, the interior feels open, airy and bright, with only columns and railings separating the formal living and dining rooms, instead of closing them off with full walls.
- The kitchen overlooks the breakfast bay and family room, with second fireplace and French doors to the rear deck.
- The upper floor is highlighted by a vaulted master suite with dual walk-in closets and spacious master bath.

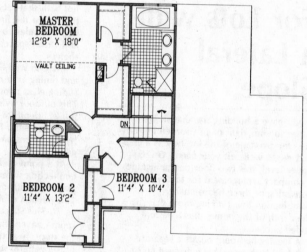

UPPER FLOOR

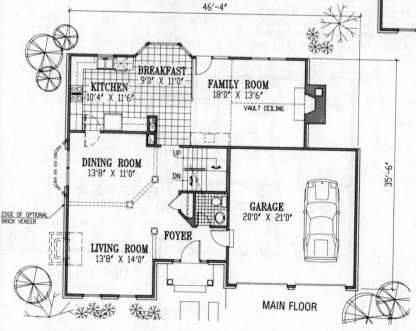

MAIN FLOOR

Plan CH-631-A	
Bedrooms: 3	**Baths:** 2 ½
Space:	
Upper floor	909 sq. ft.
Main floor	1,093 sq. ft.
Total Living Area	**2,002 sq. ft.**
Basement	990 sq. ft.
Garage	420 sq. ft.
Exterior Wall Framing	2x4
Foundation options:	
Standard Basement	
Daylight Basement	
Crawlspace	
(Foundation & framing conversion diagram	
available—see order form.)	
Blueprint Price Code	C

For Lots with a Lateral Slope

If you have a building site that slopes either to your right or to your left as you face the frontage of the lot, here is a plan that might well suit your needs. On its upper level, this two-floor design includes a compact arrangement for family living consisting of three bedrooms, a combination living/dining room that spans the depth of the home, plus a custom styled kitchen.

A master bedroom boasts a separate personal bathroom that is backed up to the plumbing wall common to the second full bath that serves the two bedrooms and the rest of the first floor plan. The main floor includes abundant built-in storage and closet space plus linen and utility shelves.

The end wall flanking the living room and dining area offers access through sliding glass doors to a cantilevered deck. This outdoor living area extends for the full 27′ depth of the house and projects for 8′ in width. Part of the area is covered by the extension of the overhang of the gable roof.

At a point midway in the floor plan and connecting with the central hallway, a staircase leads down to the lower level. This portion of the home consists of 810 sq. ft. This space is devoted to a laundry room conveniently located at the foot of the steps, near the access to the carport, plus a general storage area at the opposite side. The water heater and central heating system are enclosed in a separate room of their own.

The balance of the lower level is taken up with a 28′ x 13′ recreation room that is also served by a second fireplace. Sliding glass doors connect the party room with the covered carport. An attractive outside staircase leads from the driveway to the main entrance of the home, which is further defined by a masonry wall and open railing.

Here is a home that can well serve as a primary home fulfilling all your comfort needs. On the other hand, it could well be a second home suitable for later retirement.

Upper level:	1,192 sq. ft.
Lower level:	810 sq. ft.
Total living area:	2,002 sq. ft.

LOWER LEVEL
810 SQUARE FEET

GENERAL AREA
17′2″ x 11′10″

CARPORT
14′6″ x 27′0″

LAUNDRY

RECREATION
28′8″ x 13′0″

30′-0″ 14′-6″ 27′-0″

(Exterior walls are 2x6 construction)

UPPER LEVEL
1,192 SQUARE FEET

BEDROOM
12′0″ x 13′2″

BATH

BATH

LIN

CLOSET

KITCHEN
10′0″ x 8′7″

DINING
9′0″ x 9′0″

STOR

BEDROOM
11′0″ x 10′0″

CLOSET

BEDROOM
10′0″ x 10′0″

ENTRY

LIVING ROOM
14′0″ x 17′0″

44′-6″ 8′-0″ 27′-0″

Blueprint Price Code C
Plan H-2015-1

PRICES AND DETAILS
ON PAGES 12-15

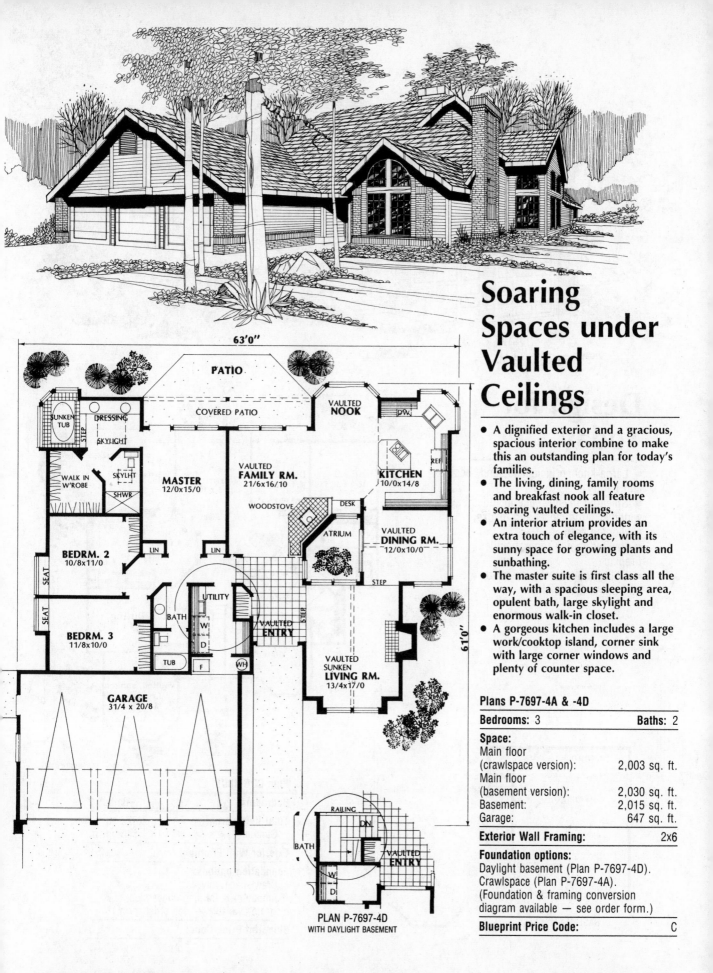

Soaring Spaces under Vaulted Ceilings

- A dignified exterior and a gracious, spacious interior combine to make this an outstanding plan for today's families.
- The living, dining, family rooms and breakfast nook all feature soaring vaulted ceilings.
- An interior atrium provides an extra touch of elegance, with its sunny space for growing plants and sunbathing.
- The master suite is first class all the way, with a spacious sleeping area, opulent bath, large skylight and enormous walk-in closet.
- A gorgeous kitchen includes a large work/cooktop island, corner sink with large corner windows and plenty of counter space.

Plans P-7697-4A & -4D

Bedrooms: 3	Baths: 2

Space:

Main floor (crawlspace version):	2,003 sq. ft.
Main floor (basement version):	2,030 sq. ft.
Basement:	2,015 sq. ft.
Garage:	647 sq. ft.

Exterior Wall Framing:	2x6

Foundation options:
Daylight basement (Plan P-7697-4D).
Crawlspace (Plan P-7697-4A).
(Foundation & framing conversion diagram available — see order form.)

Blueprint Price Code:	C

Floor plan labels: PATIO · COVERED PATIO · VAULTED NOOK · DW. · SUNKEN TUB · DRESSING · SKYLIGHT · WALK IN W'ROBE · SKYLHT · SHWR · MASTER 12/0x15/0 · VAULTED FAMILY RM. 21/6x16/10 · KITCHEN 10/0x14/8 · REF. · WOODSTOVE · DESK · ATRIUM · VAULTED DINING RM. 12/0x10/0 · BEDRM. 2 10/8x11/0 · LIN · LIN · SEAT · SEAT · UTILITY · BATH · W D · VAULTED ENTRY · STEP · BEDRM. 3 11/8x10/0 · TUB · F · WH · VAULTED SUNKEN LIVING RM. 13/4x17/0 · GARAGE 31/4 x 20/8 · 63'0" · 61'0"

PLAN P-7697-4D
WITH DAYLIGHT BASEMENT

Basement plan labels: RAILING · DN. · BATH · VAULTED ENTRY · W D

Design for Today

- Large kitchen includes island, desk and pantry.
- Splendid master suite includes bay window, large closet and deluxe, skylighted bath.
- Vaulted family room includes fireplace.
- Utility room is convenient to bedrooms and kitchen.

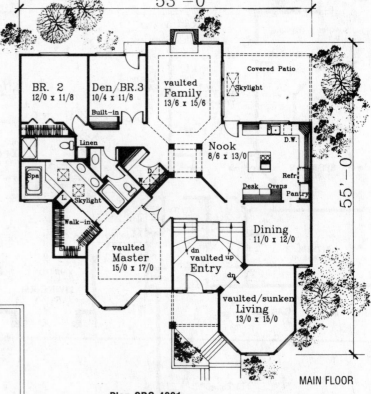

MAIN FLOOR

53'-0"

55'-0"

BR. 2
12/0 x 11/8

Den/BR.3
10/4 x 11/8

Built-in

vaulted Family
13/6 x 15/6

Covered Patio

Skylight

Linen

Nook
8/6 x 13/0

D.W.

Spa

Skylight

Desk Ovens

Refr.

Pantry

Walk-in

vaulted Master
15/0 x 17/0

dn vaulted up Entry

dn

Dining
11/0 x 12/0

vaulted/sunken Living
13/0 x 15/0

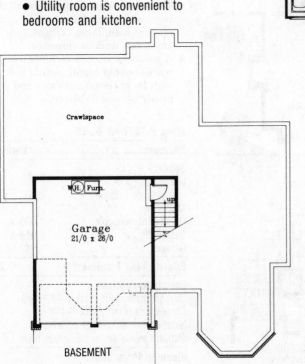

Crawlspace

W.H. Furn.

up

Garage
21/0 x 26/0

BASEMENT

Plan CDG-4001

Bedrooms: 2-3	Baths: 2
Total living area:	2,022 sq. ft.
Garage:	546 sq. ft.
Exterior Wall Framing:	2x6

Foundation options:
Crawlspace only.
(Foundation & framing conversion diagram available — see order form.)

Blueprint Price Code:	C

TO ORDER THIS BLUEPRINT,
CALL TOLL-FREE 1-800-547-5570

Plan CDG-4001

PRICES AND DETAILS
ON PAGES 12-15

Striking Hillside Design

Main floor:	1,899 sq. ft.
Lower floor:	127 sq. ft.
Total living area: (Not counting garage)	2,026 sq. ft.

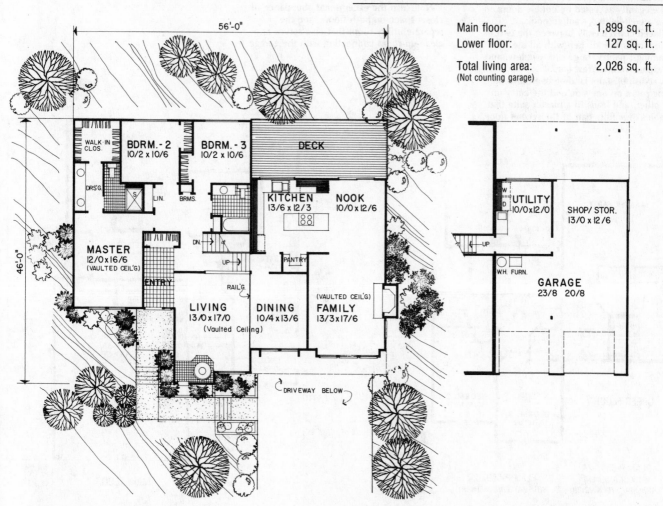

56'-0"

46'-0"

WALK-IN CLOS.

BDRM.-2
10/2 x 10/6

BDRM.-3
10/2 x 10/6

DECK

DRS'G.

S

LIN.

BRMS.

KITCHEN
13/6 x 12/3

NOOK
10/0 x 12/6

MASTER
12/0 x 16/6
(VAULTED CEIL'G)

DN.

UP

PANTRY

ENTRY

RAIL'G.

(VAULTED CEIL'G)

LIVING
13/0 x 17/0
(Vaulted Ceiling)

DINING
10/4 x 13/6

FAMILY
13/3 x 17/6

DRIVEWAY BELOW

W
D

UTILITY
10/0 x 12/0

SHOP/ STOR.
13/0 x 12/6

UP

W.H. FURN.

GARAGE
23/8 20/8

Blueprint Price Code C

Plan P-7597-2

PRICES AND DETAILS
ON PAGES 12-15

A Glorious Blend of New and Old

This three-bedroom, two and one-half-bath home is a glorious blend of contemporary and traditional lines. Inside, its 2,035 sq. ft. are wisely distributed among amply proportioned, practically appointed rooms. A vaulted entry gives way to a second reception area bordering on a broad, vaulted living room nearly 20' long.

With its walls of windows overlooking the back yard, this grand room's centerpiece is a massive woodstove, whose central location contributes extra energy efficiency to the home — upstairs as well as down. The dining room offers quiet separation from the living room, while still enjoying the warmth from its woodstove. Its sliding door accesses a large wraparound covered patio to create a cool, shady refuge.

For sun-seeking, another wraparound patio at the front is fenced but uncovered, and elegantly accessed by double doors from a well-lighted, vaulted nook.

Placed conveniently between the two dining areas is a kitchen with all the trimmings: pantry, large sink window, and an expansive breakfast bar.

A stylish upstairs landing overlooks the living room on one side and the entry on the other, and leads to a master suite that rambles over fully half of the second floor.

Adjacent to the huge bedroom area is a spacious dressing area bordered by an abundance of closet space and a double-sink bath area. Unusual extras include walk-in wardrobe in the third bedroom and the long double-sink counter in the second upstairs bath.

Note also the exceptional abundance of closet space on both floors, and the separate utility room that also serves as a clean-up room connecting with the garage.

Upper floor:	1,085 sq. ft.
Main floor:	950 sq. ft.
Total living area:	2,035 sq. ft.
(Not counting basement or garage)	

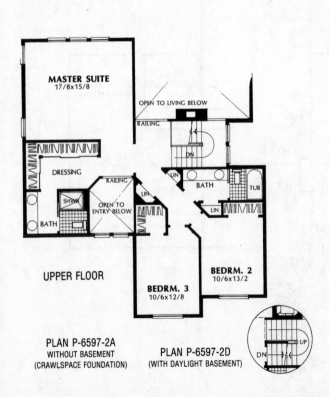

UPPER FLOOR

PLAN P-6597-2A
WITHOUT BASEMENT
(CRAWLSPACE FOUNDATION)

PLAN P-6597-2D
(WITH DAYLIGHT BASEMENT)

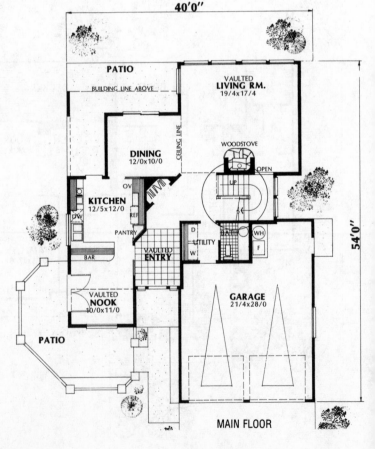

MAIN FLOOR

Blueprint Price Code C

Plans P-6597-2A & -2D

PRICES AND DETAILS ON PAGES 12-15

Expandable One-Story

- The hipped roof and covered entry give this well-appointed home a distinguished look.
- Inside, the foyer leads directly into the expansive Great Room, which boasts a vaulted ceiling, a fireplace with a built-in entertainment center, tall windows and access to the full-width deck with a hot tub.
- A half-wall separates the Great Room from the nook, which is open to the U-shaped kitchen. The impressive kitchen includes a snack bar, a walk-in pantry and a greenhouse window.
- The isolated main-floor master suite offers a vaulted ceiling, private access to the deck and the nearby hot tub, and a walk-in closet. The sumptuous master bath has a spa tub backlighted by a glass-block wall.
- Two more bedrooms on the lower level share another full bath. The optional expansion areas provide an additonal 730 sq. ft. of space.

Plan S-41792

Bedrooms: 3	Baths: 3
Living Area:	
Main floor	1,450 sq. ft.
Partial daylight basement	590 sq. ft.
Total Living Area:	**2,040 sq. ft.**
Garage	429 sq. ft.
Unfinished expansion areas	730 sq. ft.
Exterior Wall Framing:	2x6

Foundation Options:

Partial daylight basement
(Typical foundation & framing conversion diagram available—see order form.)

BLUEPRINT PRICE CODE: C

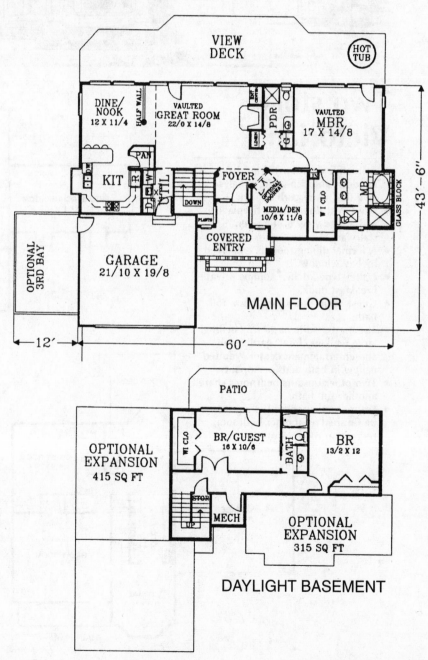

MAIN FLOOR

DAYLIGHT BASEMENT

Two story Victorian

- Attractive decorative trim, bay window, and fish-scale shingles give this home curb appeal.
- The Great Room has a fireplace and a nice view of the open stairway.
- A formal dining room is enhanced by bay window.
- Galley-type kitchen adjoins private breakfast nook.
- Guest room downstairs has a full bath.
- The master suite has a tray ceiling, large walk-in closet, garden tub and entertainment center. Vaulted ceiling in bath adds personality.
- Two other upstairs bedrooms share another full bath.
- Future bonus room (284 sq. ft.) can be finished as another bedroom, recreation room or office.

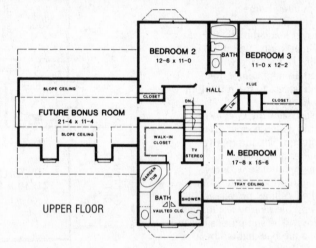

UPPER FLOOR

MAIN FLOOR

Plan C-8925

Bedrooms: 4	Baths: 3
Space:	
Upper floor:	1,020 sq. ft.
Main floor:	1,030 sq. ft.
Bonus area:	284 sq. ft.
Total living area:	2,334 sq. ft.
Basement:	1,018 sq. ft.
Garage:	484 sq. ft.
Exterior Wall Framing:	2x4

Foundation options:
Daylight basement.
Standard basement.
Crawlspace.
(Foundation & framing conversion diagram available — see order form)

Blueprint Price Code:	C

One-Story, Four-Bedroom Colonial

Here's gracious living at its best — North or South. Four bedrooms, two baths, a powder room, separate living and dining rooms, a galley kitchen, bay window breakfast area and large utility room make up the 2,053 sq. ft. of living area in this compact colonial.

Total living area: 2,053 sq. ft.
(Not counting basement or garage)

Specify daylight basement, crawlspace or slab foundation.

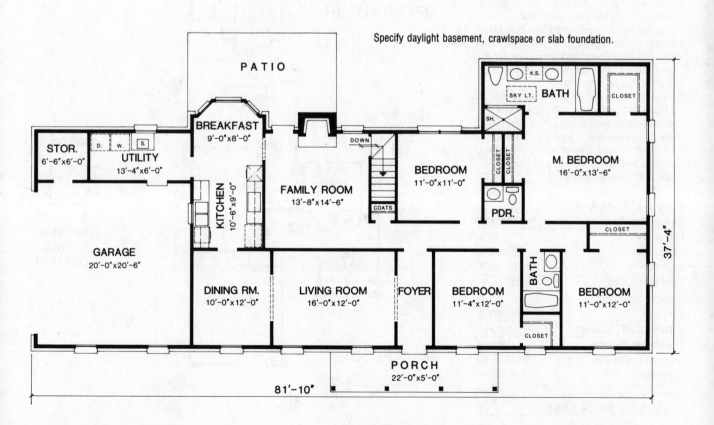

Blueprint Price Code C

Plan C-8635

Unique Family Living

- This smart-looking transitional design displays an exterior accented by half-round windows, pillars and brick trim.
- A lovely vaulted parlor or study off the entry is entered through double doors and can also function as a guest room.
- Adjoining the parlor is the formal dining room with a coffered ceiling and sliding glass doors that open to a covered backyard patio.
- The merging peninsula kitchen features a unique angled eating bar and a vaulted nook illuminated by skylights.
- Open to the kitchen is a spacious family room with a dramatic corner fireplace and sliding glass doors that lead to another covered patio.
- Upstairs, the vaulted master suite has an elegant double-door entrance and a private bath with a spa tub, a skylighted dressing area and a walk-in closet.
- Each secondary bedroom has a vaulted ceiling and private access to the compartmentalized bath.

Plans P-7733-4A & -4D

Bedrooms: 3+	Baths: 3
Living Area:	
Upper floor	960 sq. ft.
Main floor	1,107 sq. ft.
Total Living Area:	**2,067 sq. ft.**
Daylight basement	1,107 sq. ft.
Garage	441 sq. ft.
Exterior Wall Framing:	2x6
Foundation Options:	**Plan #**
Daylight basement	P-7733-4D
Crawlspace	P-7733-4A

(All plans can be built with your choice of foundation and framing. A generic conversion diagram is available. See order form.)

BLUEPRINT PRICE CODE:	C

UPPER FLOOR

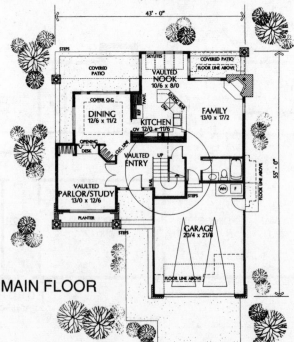

MAIN FLOOR

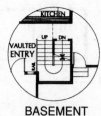

BASEMENT STAIRWAY LOCATION

Plans P-7733-4A & -4D

PRICES AND DETAILS ON PAGES 12-15

Spacious Contemporary

- Perfect for a sloping site overlooking splendid scenery, this home features a large deck, a patio, plenty of glass and a walk-out basement.
- Guests are welcomed by a roomy front porch with a decorative planter.
- The vaulted entry leads to a spectacular Great Room with vaulted ceiling, fireplace and rear window wall. The dining area is adjacent to the kitchen, which boasts an angled serving counter. French doors expand the entertaining area to include the spacious deck.
- The main-floor master suite offers a window seat, a walk-in closet and a skylighted dressing area.
- Two bedrooms and a full bath share the basement with a roomy family room, which boasts a second fireplace and sliders to a rear patio.

Plan P-6606-2D

Bedrooms: 3	Baths: 2½
Living Area:	
Main floor	1,140 sq. ft.
Daylight basement	935 sq. ft.
Total Living Area:	**2,075 sq. ft.**
Garage	451 sq. ft.
Exterior Wall Framing:	2x6

Foundation Options:

Daylight basement
(Typical foundation & framing conversion diagram available—see order form.)

BLUEPRINT PRICE CODE: **C**

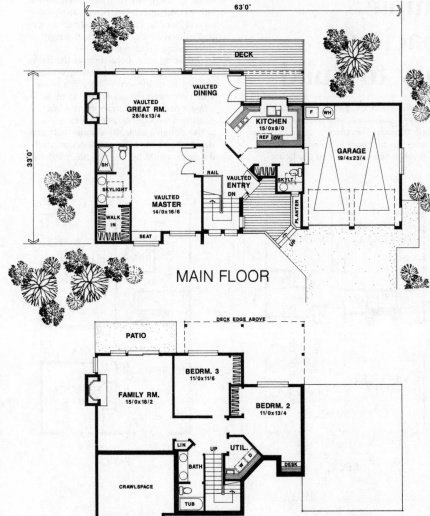

MAIN FLOOR

DAYLIGHT BASEMENT

Simple, Spacious, Easy to Build

For a simple, spacious, easy-to-construct home away from home, you should definitely consider this plan.

Entrance to the home is by way of the lower level or the side door to the living room, or both, where grade levels permit. This has the advantage of elevating the second floor to take advantage of a view that otherwise may be blocked out by surrounding buildings.

The living area, consisting of the living room, dining room and kitchen, occupies 565 sq. ft. of the main floor. The open room arrangement allows the cook to remain part of the family even when occupied with necessary chores.

The design's basically simple rectangular shape allows for easy construction, and the home could be built by any moderately experienced do-it-yourselfer. All you have to do is order the plan that fits your setting.

Plan H-833-5 has the garage entry to the street side. H-833-6 puts the garage under the view-side deck.

Upper floor:	1,200 sq. ft.
Lower level:	876 sq. ft.
Total living area: (Not counting garage)	2,076 sq. ft.

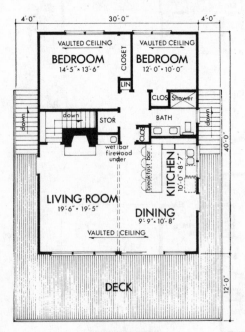

UPPER FLOOR
1200 SQUARE FEET

LOWER FLOOR
876 SQUARE FEET
PLAN H-833-5

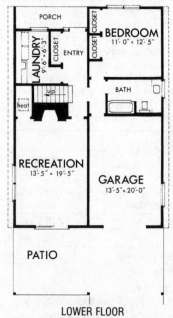

LOWER FLOOR
876 SQUARE FEET
PLAN H-833-6

Blueprint Price Code C

Plans H-833-5 & -6

Volume with Charm

- This charming two-story has an interesting variety of exterior elements and an open, airy interior.
- The two-story foyer has direct access to the main living areas. The formal spaces are oriented to the front of the home and include a dining room that overlooks a covered porch.
- A long view into the family room reveals a dramatic fireplace flanked by windows. The vaulted family room can also be viewed from the balcony above.
- A large kitchen and a vaulted breakfast room adjoin the family room. The breakfast room features a built-in work desk and a bayed sitting area. The kitchen offers a pantry closet and two convenient serving bars.
- A spectacular vaulted master suite is the perfect adult retreat. The bedroom opens to a private vaulted bath with a corner tub, a separate shower, dual sinks and a walk-in closet.

Plan FB-2081

Bedrooms: 4	Baths: 2½
Living Area:	
Upper floor	492 sq. ft.
Main floor	1,589 sq. ft.
Bonus room	226 sq. ft.
Total Living Area:	**2,307 sq. ft.**
Daylight basement	1,589 sq. ft.
Garage	400 sq. ft.
Storage	24 sq. ft.
Exterior Wall Framing:	2x4

Foundation Options:
Daylight basement
(Typical foundation & framing conversion diagram available—see order form.)

BLUEPRINT PRICE CODE: C

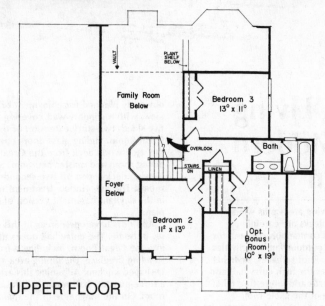

UPPER FLOOR

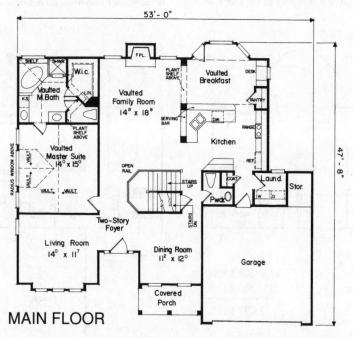

MAIN FLOOR

Open Living in a Modern Design

Spacious open living areas plus window-walls and wood decks are carefully combined in this contemporary home for both indoor and outdoor family activities and entertaining. Roof setbacks, skylights and windows over the high entry hall and strong fascia boards add interesting relief to the long slope of the gable roof.

In contrast, the rear wall of the home is obviously planned for enjoyment of a view, with a window-wall covering the five-sided, two-story extension of the Great Room. Sliding glass doors open onto the wide wood deck from the Great Room, dining room and master bedroom. Smaller viewing decks open off two second-floor rooms. The full-window treatment repeats in the daylight basement version of the plan.

All floors have open areas in this 2,089 sq. ft. home. The entry hall opens directly into the Great Room, including a free-standing fireplace, the dining area and the U-shaped kitchen. Adjoining this area are a three-quarters bathroom and the utility room. On the other side of the main floor is the master bedroom, including a walk-in wardrobe and a private bath with a window seat.

Open stairs lead off the entry hall to the 824 sq. ft. upper floor, which includes a large loft room overlooking the Great Room and warmed by a woodstove. A study, storage area, bathroom and two bedrooms are also included on the second floor.

The 1,210 sq. ft. daylight basement has a large recreation room with a wood stove, a fourth bedroom with walk-in closet, a full bath and an unfinished area that could become a workshop, crafts area or a guest room.

Exterior walls are 2x6 for energy efficiency.

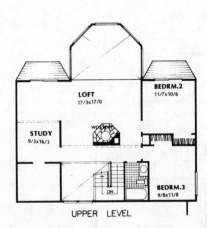

UPPER LEVEL

Main floor:	1,265 sq. ft.
Second floor:	824 sq. ft.
Total living area: (Not counting basement or garage)	2,089 sq. ft.
Daylight basement:	1,210 sq. ft.
Total with basement:	3,299 sq. ft.

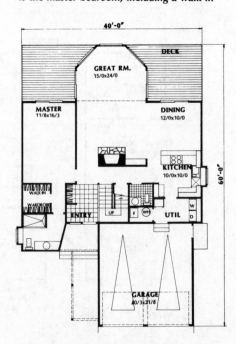

Blueprint Price Code E With Basement
Blueprint Price Code C Without Basement

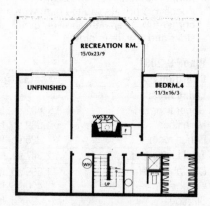

PLAN P-533-2D
WITH DAYLIGHT BASEMENT

PLAN P-533-2A
WITHOUT BASEMENT
(CRAWLSPACE FOUNDATION)

Plans P-533-2A & -2D

PRICES AND DETAILS ON PAGES 12-15

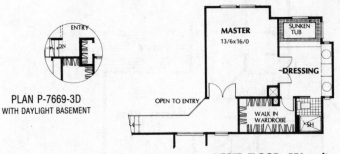

PLAN P-7669-3D
WITH DAYLIGHT BASEMENT

MASTER
13/6x16/0

SUNKEN TUB

DRESSING

OPEN TO ENTRY

WALK IN WARDROBE

SH

UPPER FLOOR 550 sq.ft.

"Adult Retreat" in Upstairs Master Suite

First floor:	1,545 sq. ft.
Second floor:	550 sq. ft.
Total living area:	2,095 sq. ft.
(Not counting basement or garage)	
Basement level:	1,102 sq. ft.

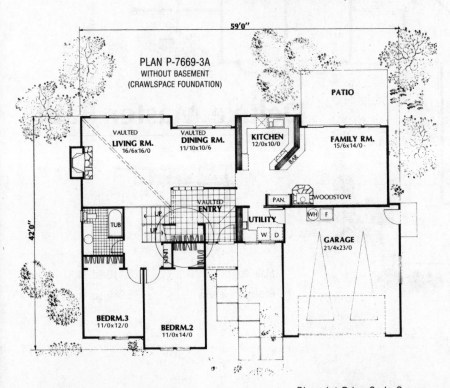

PLAN P-7669-3A
WITHOUT BASEMENT
(CRAWLSPACE FOUNDATION)

59'0"

42'0"

PATIO

VAULTED **LIVING RM.** 16/6x16/0

VAULTED **DINING RM.** 11/10x10/6

KITCHEN 12/0x10/0

FAMILY RM. 15/6x14/0

BAR

VAULTED **ENTRY**

UTILITY

PAN.

WOODSTOVE

WH F

W D

TUB

UP
UP

LINEN

GARAGE 21/4x23/0

BEDRM.3 11/0x12/0

BEDRM.2 11/0x14/0

Blueprint Price Code C

RAILING

DECK

DINING
12/0x13/10

SUNKEN
LIVING RM.
23/2x19/10

SH

LINEN DRESSING

SPA TUB
STEP

RAILING

DECK

TUB
BATH

WALK IN
W'ROBE

MASTER SUITE
13/6x15/0

WOOD

STEP

STEP

KITCHEN
13/6x11/0

ENTRY

SKYLIGHT

REF

PANTRY

UTILITY

W
D

BEDRM. 3
10/3x13/4

BEDRM. 2
10/3x10/10

WH

F

FRZR

SEAT

SEAT

GARAGE
31/4x25/4

Deluxe Master Bath

DW

REF

LIN

DN

FRZR

GARAGE

PLAN P-6600-4D
WITH DAYLIGHT BASEMENT

Main floor: 2,110 sq. ft.
Basement level: 2,080 sq. ft.

PLAN P-6600-4A
WITHOUT BASEMENT
(CRAWLSPACE FOUNDATION)

Total living area: 2,050 sq. ft.
(Not counting garage)

Blueprint Price Code C
Plans P-6600-4A & -4D

TO ORDER THIS BLUEPRINT,
CALL TOLL-FREE 1-800-547-5570

PRICES AND DETAILS
ON PAGES 12-15

Bold Contemporary Style

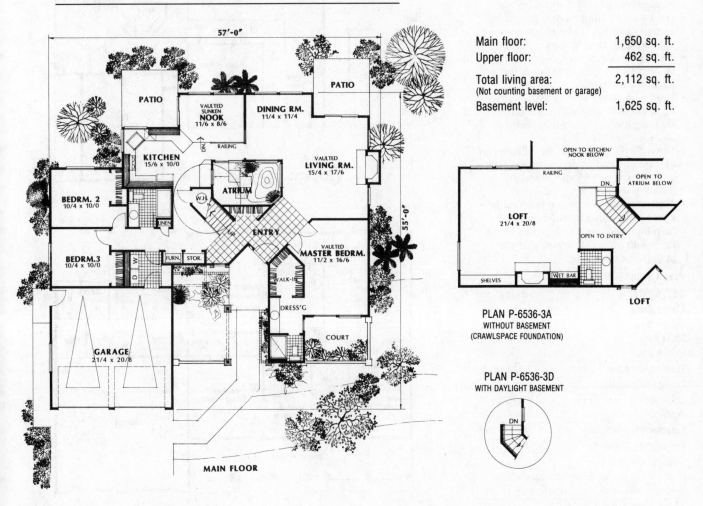

57'-0"

PATIO

VAULTED SUNKEN NOOK
11/6 x 8/6

DINING RM.
11/4 x 11/4

PATIO

KITCHEN
15/6 x 10/0

RAILING

DN

VAULTED LIVING RM.
15/4 x 17/6

ATRIUM

W.H.

BEDRM. 2
10/4 x 10/0

LINEN

ENTRY

55'-0"

BEDRM. 3
10/4 x 10/0

FURN. STOR.

VAULTED MASTER BEDRM.
11/2 x 16/6

DW

WALK-IN

DRESS'G

GARAGE
21/4 x 20/8

COURT

MAIN FLOOR

Main floor:	1,650 sq. ft.
Upper floor:	462 sq. ft.
Total living area:	2,112 sq. ft.
(Not counting basement or garage)	
Basement level:	1,625 sq. ft.

OPEN TO KITCHEN/ NOOK BELOW

RAILING

OPEN TO ATRIUM BELOW

DN.

LOFT
21/4 x 20/8

OPEN TO ENTRY

SHELVES

WET BAR

LOFT

PLAN P-6536-3A
WITHOUT BASEMENT
(CRAWLSPACE FOUNDATION)

PLAN P-6536-3D
WITH DAYLIGHT BASEMENT

DN

Blueprint Price Code C

TO ORDER THIS BLUEPRINT,
CALL TOLL-FREE 1-800-547-5570

Plans P-6536-3A & -3D

PRICES AND DETAILS
ON PAGES 12-15   **177**

Elegant Simplicity

- From the covered front porch to the main-floor master suite, this simple yet elegant home is filled with surprises.
- The vaulted dining room is graced by arched openings leading from the vaulted foyer and the family room.
- A sunny breakfast nook overlooks the vaulted family room and floods the kitchen with light.
- The family room offers a rear window wall, an inviting fireplace and built-in shelving topped by attention-getting plant shelves.
- The main-floor master suite includes an elegant tray ceiling and a vaulted bath with an oval whirlpool tub and an adjacent shower.
- A beautiful open staircase leads to the upper floor with a balcony overlook. Also included are two large bedrooms, each with a walk-in closet, plus an optional bonus space.

Plan FB-5019-WAVE

Bedrooms: 3	Baths: 2½
Living Area:	
Upper floor	502 sq. ft.
Main floor	1,414 sq. ft.
Bonus room	208 sq. ft.
Total Living Area:	**2,124 sq. ft.**
Daylight basement	1,414 sq. ft.
Garage	420 sq. ft.
Storage	28 sq. ft.
Exterior Wall Framing:	2x4
Foundation Options:	

Daylight basement
(Typical foundation & framing conversion diagram available—see order form.)

BLUEPRINT PRICE CODE: C

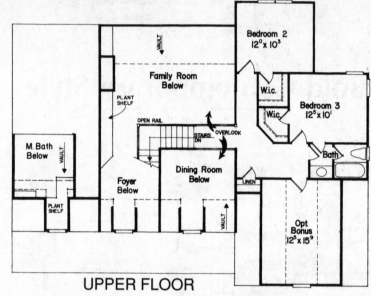

UPPER FLOOR

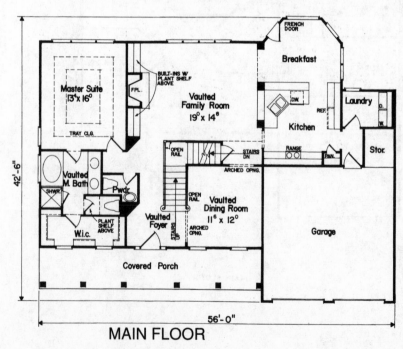

MAIN FLOOR

Plan FB-5019-WAVE

PRICES AND DETAILS ON PAGES 12-15

FRONT VIEW

Home Designed for Sloping Site

Here's a home that takes advantage of the natural contours of a sloping site. Besides the car storage and children's play area, the lower level of the home has a utility room, recreation area and a half-bath. Also notice the workshop complete with bench and overhead cabinets.

An abundance of storage is provided throughout in the form of a closet flanking the central hall and a storage area under the staircase. The full length of the daylight basement is used for a recreation room that also measures almost 14' wide. The latter room also includes a wet bar and fireplace.

The kitchen is convenient to the dining area as well as to the hall leading to the front entry. The generously sized living room connects with the dining area so that dining space may be expanded if needed. The gable wall includes sliding glass doors opening to the covered deck.

Bedrooms are placed to the rear in the quiet zone of the home. There, you will also find two complete bathrooms. One of the bathrooms is designed to serve the master bedroom, which also features a walk-in closet.

Overall size of the main floor area is 48' in length by 27' in depth. To this, add 9' for the extension of the covered deck. Living area of the main plan is 1,296 sq. ft.

An attractive exterior is achieved with the use of cedar for both the exterior siding and the shake roofing. A brick planter wall bordering the approach to the front porch

matches the masonry of the fireplace. Brick is also used to trim the pilaster supporting the front end of the dwelling.

Total living area: 2,125 sq. ft.

Blueprint Price Code C

Main Floor
48'-0" × 9'-0" — 27'-0"
WALK-IN CLOSET
BATH
KITCHEN 11'-3" × 9'-6"
DINING 11'-0" × 10'-0"
Shower
BATH
LIN LIN
LINEN
LIVING ROOM 16'-3" × 16'-5"
DECK
BEDROOM 11'-5" × 16'-3"
BEDROOM 10'-5" × 10'-7"
CLOSET
ENTRY

MAIN FLOOR 1296 SQUARE FEET

LAUNDRY 11'-6" × 9'-4"
LAV
STORAGE
SHOP
BENCH
WH
STORAGE
STOR
furnace
CARPORT 16'-0" × 27'-0"
BAR
RECREATION ROOM 30'-0" × 13'-6"

BASEMENT 829 SQUARE FEET

Built for All Seasons

- Spectacular rear viewing is yours in this exciting, yet homey design that provides comfort in all seasons.
- The heat-absorbing wall in the lower level and the fireplace-to-furnace "tie-in" circulation system help balance mild and cold days during the heating season.
- Two secondary bedrooms and extra storage space are also offered on the lower level.

- The main level features a bright and cheery L-shaped living and dining area with a brick column wall that absorbs heat from the sun.
- The upper side patio deck off the kitchen can be roofed and converted to a screened porch.
- The main level also houses the delightful master suite with dressing alcove and bath with step-up tub and corner mirrored wall.

Plan CPS-1045-SE

Bedrooms: 3	Baths: 2½

Space:

Lower floor:	1,095 sq. ft.
Main floor:	1,040 sq. ft.

Total living area:	**2,135 sq. ft.**
Garage:	624 sq. ft.

Exterior Wall Framing:	2x6

Foundation options:
Daylight basement.
(Foundation & framing conversion diagram available — see order form.)

Blueprint Price Code:	C

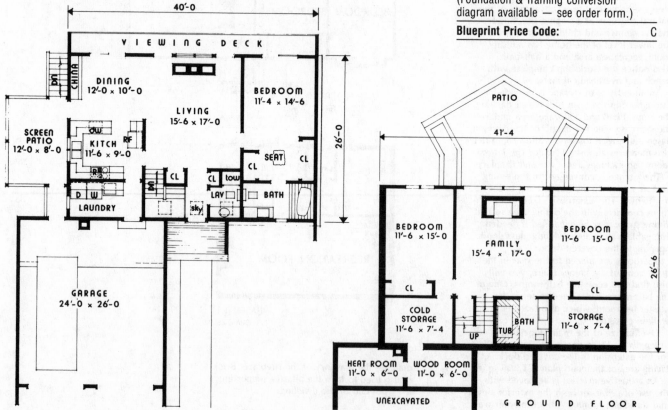

Plan CPS-1045-SE

PRICES AND DETAILS ON PAGES 12-15

Stately Multi-Level

- Off the split entry of this exciting multi-level home is a vaulted, sunken living room with fireplace and front boxed window.
- An open half wall makes the kitchen and bayed dining area loft-like above.

- The modern vaulted master suite has beautiful boxed window and bath with windowed jacuzzi tub.
- The lower level family room offers views and access to adjoining patio; an extra bedroom, bath and office or bonus space are also included.

Plan B-89007	
Bedrooms: 4	**Baths:** 3

Space:

Main floor:	1,536 sq. ft.
Lower level:	602 sq. ft.
Total living area:	**2,138 sq. ft.**
Basement:	360 sq. ft.
Garage:	420 sq. ft.

Exterior Wall Framing:	2x4

Foundation options:
Partial basement.
(Foundation & framing conversion diagram available — see order form.)

Blueprint Price Code:	C

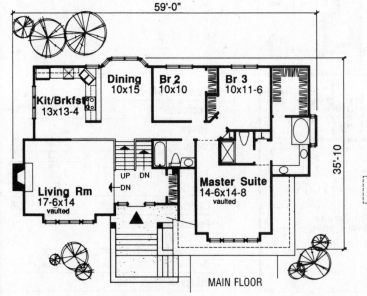

59'-0"

Dining
10x15

Br 2
10x10

Br 3
10x11-6

Kit/Brkfst
13x13-4

35'-10

UP   DN

DN

Living Rm
17-6x14
vaulted

Master Suite
14-6x14-8
vaulted

MAIN FLOOR

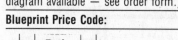

Patio

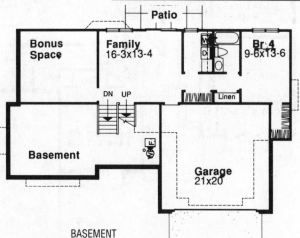

Bonus
Space

Family
16-3x13-4

Br 4
9-6x13-6

DN   UP

Linen

Basement

Garage
21x20

BASEMENT

Upstairs Suite Creates Adult Retreat

● This multi-level design is ideal for a gently sloping site with a view to the rear.

● Upstairs master suite is a sumptuous "adult retreat" complete with magnificent bath, vaulted ceiling, walk-in closet, private deck and balcony loft.

● Living room includes wood stove area and large windows to the rear. Wood bin can be loaded from outside.

● Main floor also features roomy kitchen and large utility area.

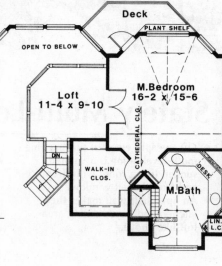

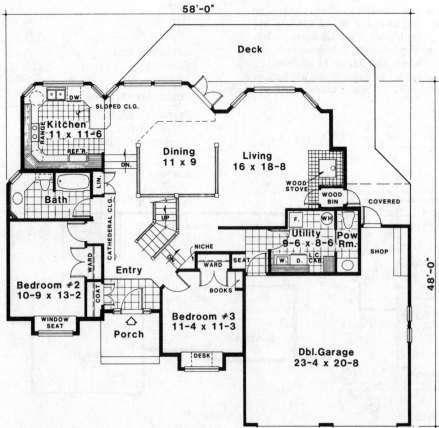

Plan NW-544-S

Bedrooms: 3	**Baths:** 2½

Space:	
Upper floor:	638 sq. ft.
Main floor:	1,500 sq. ft.
Total living area:	2,138 sq. ft.
Garage:	545 sq. ft.

Exterior Wall Framing:	2x6

Foundation options:
Crawlspace only.
(Foundation & framing conversion diagram available — see order form.)

Blueprint Price Code:	C

Home with High Style

- Sweeping rooflines attract attention to this stylish contemporary home.
- The vaulted entry is enhanced by a clerestory window above.
- Sunlight invades the main floor by way of a window wall in the living room and a sunspace off the patio or deck.
- A main-floor den could serve as a handy guest bedroom.
- The open family room shares a woodstove with the kitchen and nook.
- A formal dining room looks out on the home's natural surroundings.
- Upstairs, a large master bedroom features a private deck, a walk-in closet and a master bath with corner tub, separate shower and dual vanities.

Plan S-2001

Bedrooms: 3-4	Baths: 2½
Living Area:	
Upper floor	890 sq. ft.
Main floor	1,249 sq. ft.
Total Living Area:	**2,139 sq. ft.**
Basement	1,249 sq. ft.
Garage	399 sq. ft.
Exterior Wall Framing:	2x6

Foundation Options:

Daylight basement

Standard basement

Crawlspace

Slab

(Typical foundation & framing conversion diagram available—see order form.)

BLUEPRINT PRICE CODE: C

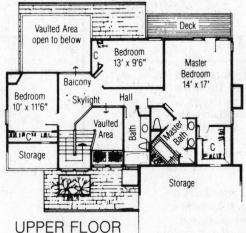

UPPER FLOOR

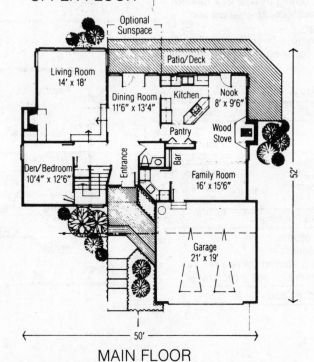

MAIN FLOOR

TO ORDER THIS BLUEPRINT,
CALL TOLL-FREE 1-800-547-5570

Plan S-2001

PRICES AND DETAILS
ON PAGES 12-15   **183**

Today's Tradition

- The traditional two-story design is brought up to today's standards with this exciting new design.
- The front half of the main floor is devoted to formal entertaining. The living and dining rooms offer symmetrical bay windows overlooking the wrap-around front porch.
- The informal living zone faces the rear deck and yard. It includes a family room with fireplace and beamed ceiling as well as a modern kitchen with cooktop island and snack bar.
- There are four large bedrooms and two full baths on the upper sleeping level.

Plan AGH-2143

Bedrooms: 4	Baths: 2½
Space:	
Upper floor:	1,047 sq. ft.
Main floor:	1,096 sq. ft.
Total living area:	**2,143 sq. ft.**
Daylight basement:	1,096 sq. ft.
Garage:	852 sq. ft.
Exterior Wall Framing:	**2x6**

Foundation options:
Daylight basement.
(Foundation & framing conversion diagram available — see order form.)

Blueprint Price Code: C

UPPER FLOOR

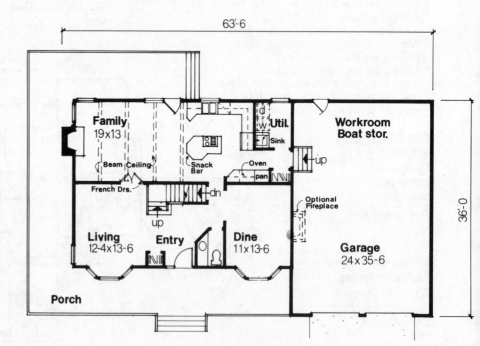

MAIN FLOOR

TO ORDER THIS BLUEPRINT, CALL TOLL-FREE 1-800-547-5570   Plan AGH-2143   *PRICES AND DETAILS ON PAGES 12-15*

REAR VIEW

A Striking Contemporary

A multiplicity of decks and outcroppings along with unusual window arrangements combine to establish this striking contemporary as a classic type of architecture. To adapt to the sloping terrain, the structure has three levels of living space on the downhill side. As one moves around the house from the entry to the various rooms and living areas, both the appearance and function of the different spaces change, as do the angular forms and cutouts that define the floor plan arrangement. Almost all the rooms are flooded with an abundance of daylight, yet are shielded by projections of wing walls and roof surfaces to assure privacy as well as to block undesirable direct rays of sunshine.

The design projects open planning of a spacious living room that connects with the dining and kitchen area. The home features four large bedrooms, two of which have walk-in closets and private baths. The remaining two bedrooms also have an abundance of wardrobe space, and the rooms are of generous proportions.

For energy efficiency, exterior walls are framed with 2x6 studs.

First floor:	1,216 sq. ft.
Second floor:	958 sq. ft.
Total living area: (Not counting basement or garage)	2,174 sq. ft.
Basement:	1,019 sq. ft.

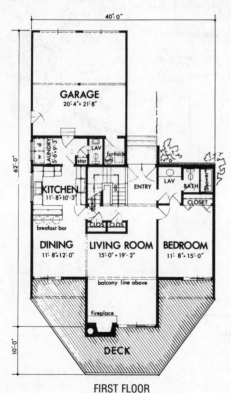

FIRST FLOOR
1216 SQUARE FEET

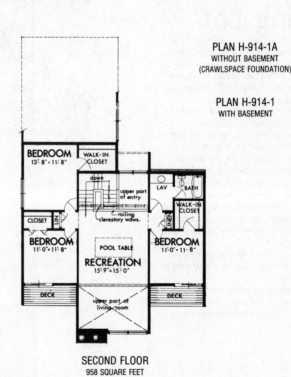

PLAN H-914-1A
WITHOUT BASEMENT
(CRAWLSPACE FOUNDATION)

PLAN H-914-1
WITH BASEMENT

SECOND FLOOR
958 SQUARE FEET

Traditional Design for Sloping Lot

Quaint shutters, rich brick accents and a bay window all come together to create a traditional all-American home. Designed specifically for a sloping lot, it has many other special features as well.

Inside, you'll find archways throughout the house reminiscent of old-time craftsmanship, with an eye to detail rarely found today. The floor plan itself is thoroughly up-to-date and combines the dramatic look of a multi-level with the easy livability of a one-level design. The entry opens to the formal living room, which is overlooked by the dining room and railed balcony four steps above. The rest of the living area is all conveniently located on this upper level.

The spacious master bedroom features dual vanities, a large walk-in closet and a luxurious spa tub.

Don't miss the nice-sized utility room with handy folding counter. You'll also find an extra large linen closet centrally located in the hallway.

Total living area: 2,174 sq. ft.
(Not counting garage)

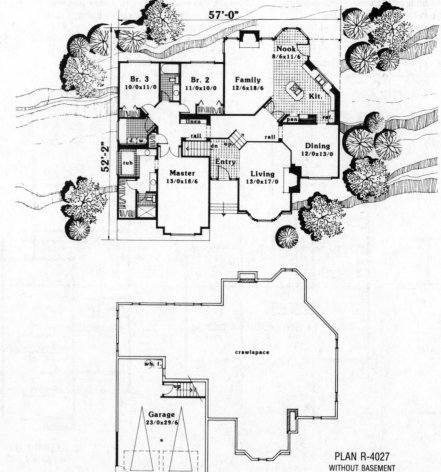

PLAN R-4027
WITHOUT BASEMENT
(CRAWLSPACE FOUNDATION)

TO ORDER THIS BLUEPRINT,
CALL TOLL-FREE 1-800-547-5570

Blueprint Price Code C
Plan R-4027

PRICES AND DETAILS
ON PAGES 12-15

Country Kitchen and Deluxe Master Bath

- Front porch, dormers and shutters give this home a decidedly country look on the outside, which is complemented by an informal modern interior.
- The roomy country kitchen connects with a sunny breakfast nook and utility area on one hand and a formal dining room on the other.
- The central portion of the home consists of a large family room with

a fireplace and easy access to a rear deck.
- The downstairs master suite is particularly impressive for a home of this size, a features a majestic master bath with two walk-in closets and double vanities.
- Upstairs, you will find two more ample-sized bedrooms, a double bath and a large storage area.

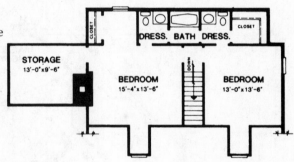

UPPER FLOOR

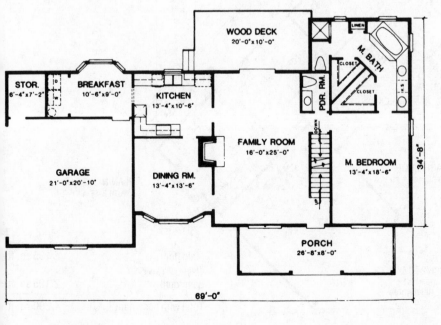

MAIN FLOOR

Plan C-8645

Plan C-8645	
Bedrooms: 3	Baths: 2½

Living Area:	
Upper floor	704 sq. ft.
Main floor	1,477 sq. ft.

Total Living Area:	**2,181 sq. ft.**
Daylight basement	Approx. 1,400 sq. ft.
Garage	438 sq. ft.
Storage	123 sq. ft.

Exterior Wall Framing:	2x4

Foundation Options:
Daylight basement
Crawlspace
Slab
(Typical foundation & framing conversion diagram available—see order form.)

BLUEPRINT PRICE CODE:	C

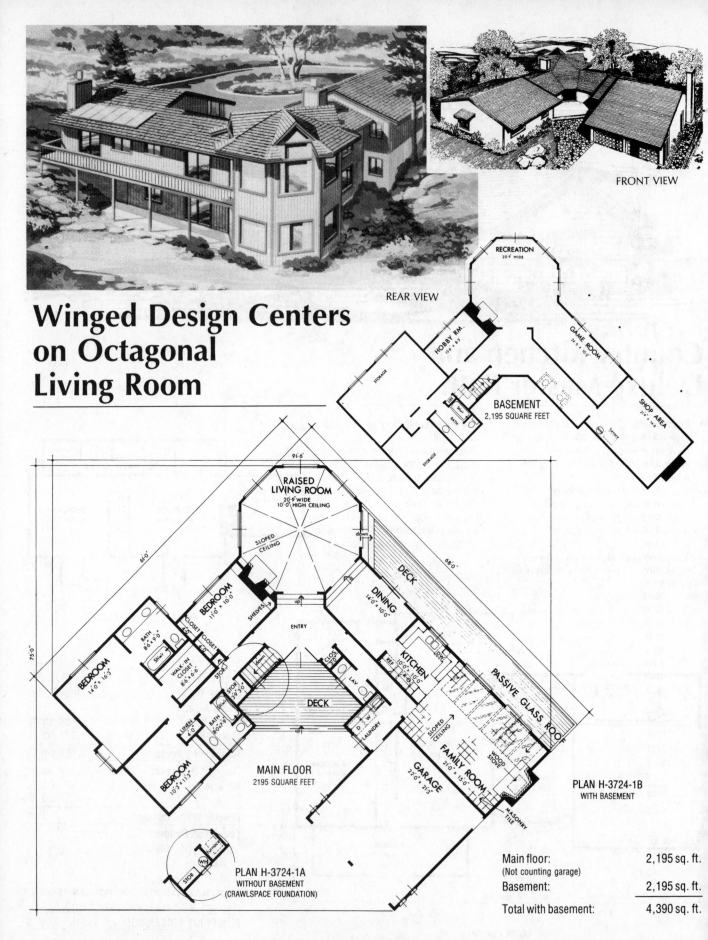

FRONT VIEW

REAR VIEW

Winged Design Centers
on Octagonal
Living Room

RECREATION 20'-9" WIDE

HOBBY RM.

STORAGE

BATH

STORAGE

BASEMENT
2,195 SQUARE FEET

GAME ROOM 24'-0" × 10'-0"

SHOP AREA

RAISED LIVING ROOM
20'-9" WIDE
10'-0" HIGH CEILING

SLOPED CEILING

91'-6"

61'-0"

DECK

68'-0"

DINING 14'-0" × 10'-0"

BEDROOM 11'-0" × 10'-0"

CLOSET CLOSET

SHELVES

ENTRY

KITCHEN 10'-0" × 10'-0"

BATH 8'-6" × 9'-0"

WALK-IN CLOSET 8'-6" × 6'-6"

75'-0"

BEDROOM 14'-0" × 16'-3"

LINEN

BATH 8'-6" × 7'-9"

STOR.

DECK

LAV

PASSIVE GLASS ROOF

CLOS.

D.W.

LAUNDRY

SLOPED CEILING

WOOD STOR.

BEDROOM 10'-3" × 11'-3"

MAIN FLOOR
2195 SQUARE FEET

FAMILY ROOM 21'-0" × 15'-0"

GARAGE 27'-0" × 21'-3"

MASONRY TILE

PLAN H-3724-1B
WITH BASEMENT

FURNACE

WH

STOR

PLAN H-3724-1A
WITHOUT BASEMENT
(CRAWLSPACE FOUNDATION)

Main floor: (Not counting garage)	2,195 sq. ft.
Basement:	2,195 sq. ft.
Total with basement:	4,390 sq. ft.

Blueprint Price Code G With Basement
Blueprint Price Code C Without Basement

TO ORDER THIS BLUEPRINT,
CALL TOLL-FREE 1-800-547-5570

Plans H-3724-1A & -1B

PRICES AND DETAILS
ON PAGES 12-15

Stunning One-Story Design

- This home gets off to a great start with a vaulted, skylighted foyer.
- The sunken living room simply sparkles, with its tray ceiling, fireplace and turret-like bay with high arched windows.
- The adjoining dining room also features a tray ceiling and a bay window.
- The unusual kitchen includes a built-in desk, a garden sink and an island cooktop with an eating bar.
- The adjacent nook and family room boast vaulted ceilings, an abundance of windows facing the rear patio and a woodstove tucked into one corner.
- A plant shelf provides an elegant introduction to the bedroom hall, where double doors open to a den.
- Also entered through double doors, the master bedroom is highlighted by a tray ceiling, a rear window wall and access to the patio. The magnificent master bath includes a raised, skylighted ceiling and a step-up garden spa tub.

Plans P-7754-3A & -3D

Bedrooms: 2+	Baths: 2
Living Area:	
Main floor (crawlspace version)	2,200 sq. ft.
Main floor (basement version)	2,288 sq. ft.
Total Living Area:	**2,200/2,288 sq. ft.**
Daylight basement	2,244 sq. ft.
Garage	722 sq. ft.
Exterior Wall Framing:	2x4
Foundation Options:	**Plan #**
Daylight basement	P-7754-3D
Crawlspace	P-7754-3A

(All plans can be built with your choice of foundation and framing. A generic conversion diagram is available. See order form.)

BLUEPRINT PRICE CODE: **C**

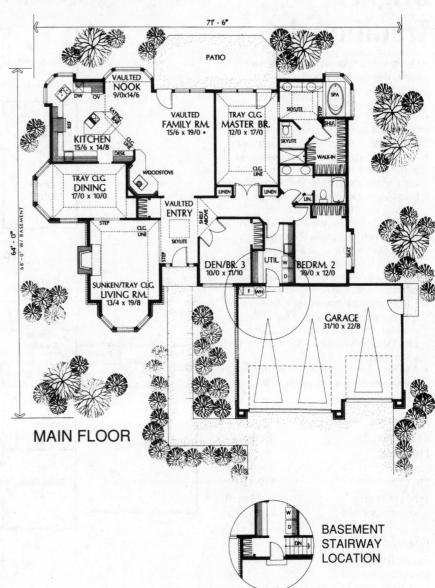

MAIN FLOOR

BASEMENT STAIRWAY LOCATION

Bright Traditional

- Designed to take advantage of natural light, this attractive home offers plenty of windows to take in the front and backyard views.
- Visitors are welcomed in the two-story foyer and ushered into the spacious living and dining rooms that adjoin it.
- A fireplace flanked by large windows highlights the vaulted family room at the back of the home. The adjacent breakfast room features a vaulted ceiling, overhead plant shelves, a handsome bay window and a pantry.
- The kitchen continues the open, airy feeling of the home and is separated from the breakfast room by a serving bar. A convenient powder room and laundry room are removed to the side.
- The main-floor master suite features a tray ceiling and a vaulted bath with an oval tub, a separate shower, a high plant shelf and a dual-sink vanity with knee space.
- A bridge connects the two bedrooms on the upper floor and overlooks the family room and the foyer.

Plan FB-5062-MATT

Bedrooms: 3	Baths: 2½
Living Area:	
Upper floor	560 sq. ft.
Main floor	1,660 sq. ft.
Total Living Area:	**2,220 sq. ft.**
Daylight basement	1,660 sq. ft.
Garage	419 sq. ft.
Exterior Wall Framing:	2x4

Foundation Options:
Daylight basement
(Typical foundation & framing conversion diagram available–see order form.)

BLUEPRINT PRICE CODE:	C

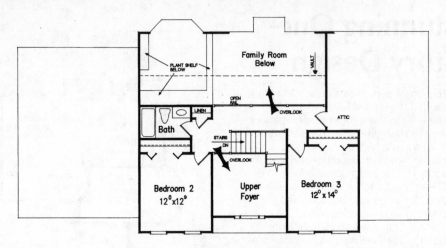

UPPER FLOOR

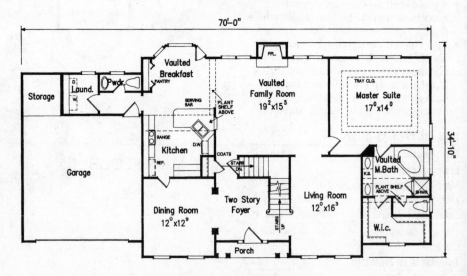

MAIN FLOOR

TO ORDER THIS BLUEPRINT, CALL TOLL-FREE 1-800-547-5570

Plan FB-5062-MATT

PRICES AND DETAILS ON PAGES 12-15

Chalet Style for Town or Country

- The exterior features exposed beams, board siding and viewing decks with cut-out railings to give this home the look of a mountain chalet.
- Inside, the design lends itself equally well to year-round family living or part-time recreational enjoyment.
- An expansive Great Room features an impressive fireplace and includes a dining area next to the well-planned kitchen.
- The upstairs offers the possibility of an adult retreat, with a fine master bedroom with private bath and large closets, plus a loft area available for many uses.
- Two secondary bedrooms are on the main floor, and share another bath.
- The daylight basement level includes a garage and a large recreation room with a fireplace and a half-bath.

Plan P-531-2D

Bedrooms: 3	Baths: 2½
Living Area:	
Upper floor	573 sq. ft.
Main floor	1,120 sq. ft.
Daylight basement	532 sq. ft.
Total Living Area:	**2,225 sq. ft.**
Garage	541 sq. ft.
Exterior Wall Framing:	2x6

Foundation Options:
Daylight basement
(Typical foundation & framing conversion diagram available—see order form.)

BLUEPRINT PRICE CODE: C

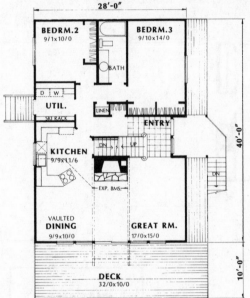

MAIN FLOOR

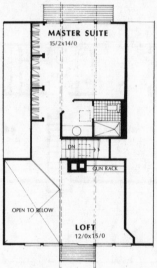

UPPER FLOOR

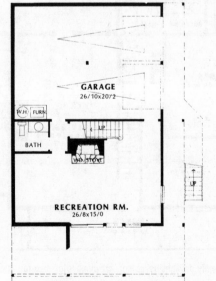

DAYLIGHT BASEMENT

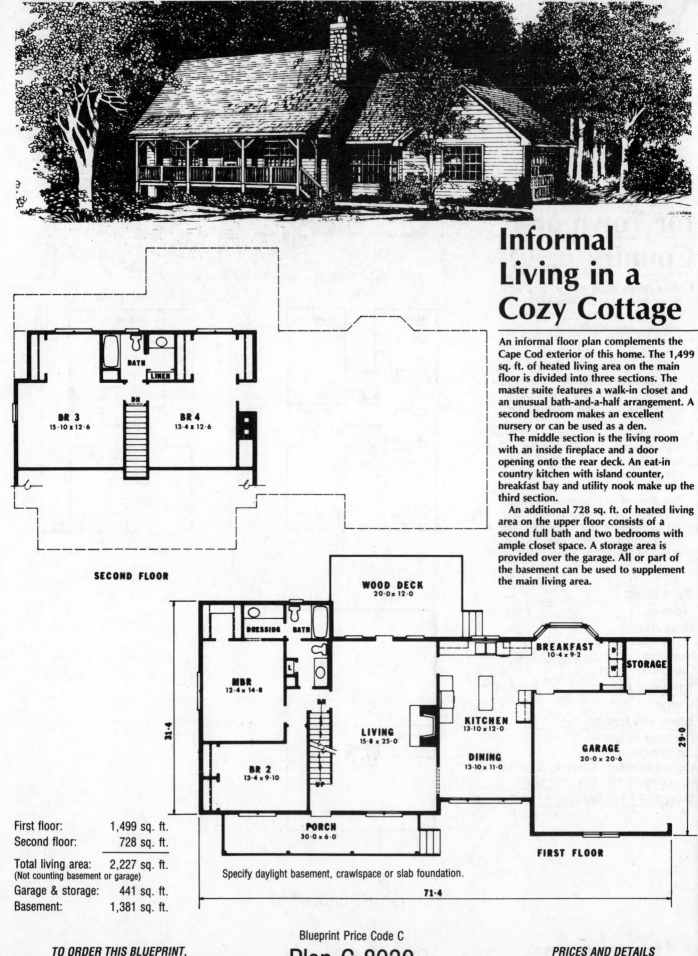

Informal Living in a Cozy Cottage

An informal floor plan complements the Cape Cod exterior of this home. The 1,499 sq. ft. of heated living area on the main floor is divided into three sections. The master suite features a walk-in closet and an unusual bath-and-a-half arrangement. A second bedroom makes an excellent nursery or can be used as a den.

The middle section is the living room with an inside fireplace and a door opening onto the rear deck. An eat-in country kitchen with island counter, breakfast bay and utility nook make up the third section.

An additional 728 sq. ft. of heated living area on the upper floor consists of a second full bath and two bedrooms with ample closet space. A storage area is provided over the garage. All or part of the basement can be used to supplement the main living area.

SECOND FLOOR

BATH
LINEN
BR 3
15·10 x 12·6
BR 4
13·4 x 12·6
DN

FIRST FLOOR

WOOD DECK
20·0 x 12·0
DRESSING
BATH
MBR
12·4 x 14·8
BR 2
13·4 x 9·10
LIVING
15·8 x 25·0
KITCHEN
13·10 x 12·0
DINING
13·10 x 11·0
BREAKFAST
10·4 x 9·2
STORAGE
GARAGE
20·0 x 20·6
PORCH
30·0 x 6·0
31·4
29·0
71·4

Specify daylight basement, crawlspace or slab foundation.

First floor:	1,499 sq. ft.
Second floor:	728 sq. ft.
Total living area:	2,227 sq. ft.
(Not counting basement or garage)	
Garage & storage:	441 sq. ft.
Basement:	1,381 sq. ft.

Blueprint Price Code C

Plan C-8030

Traditional Lines, Up-to-date Interior

Multi-paned and arched windows, expanses of brick facing, wide board siding and a sharply pitched gable roofline merge into this two-story, 2,234-sq. ft. house that is both traditional and pleasantly up-to-date.

A skylight in the vaulted ceiling lightens the entry wall. Several steps to the right lead you into the vaulted-ceiling living room and the adjacent dining area. The front window has a window seat, and a sliding door in the dining area leads to one of two patios.

The family room, with a woodstove, flows together with the nook and the L-shaped kitchen for a spacious family activity or casual entertaining area. The nook includes a pantry and a built-in desk. The hall bathroom and utility room complete the 1,154-sq. ft. main floor.

The center dormer projection on the house, clad in brick, encloses a staircase to the 1,080-sq. ft. second floor. Railings set off an open space between landings and the two-story expanse of windows. A low wall along the upper hallway allows you to look into the living room below.

The master suite has a walk-in wardrobe/dressing area and a bathroom. Three more bedrooms share the twin-lavatory hall bathroom. The house also is available in a daylight basement version.

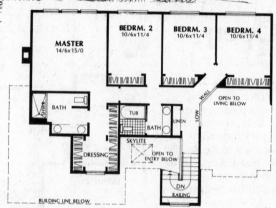

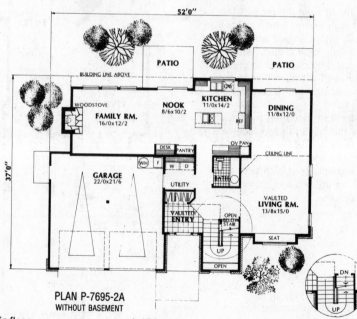

PLAN P-7695-2A
WITHOUT BASEMENT

Main floor:	1,154 sq. ft.
Upper floor:	1,080 sq. ft.
Total living area: (Not counting basement or garage)	2,234 sq. ft.

PLAN 7695-2D
WITH DAYLIGHT BASEMENT

Basement level:	1,154 sq. ft.

Blueprint Price Code C

Plans P-7695-2A & -2D

PRICES AND DETAILS
ON PAGES 12-15

Lofty, Open Spaces

- Lofty hip roofs accented by gable extensions and brick pillars prepare you for the open living spaces inside this comfortable contemporary home. A covered walkway leads to the vaulted entry, which is brightened by a skylight.
- To the left, the open living and dining rooms each boast tall, arched windows and vaulted ceilings with exposed beams.
- Straight ahead from the entry is the vaulted family room, which offers a woodstove on an angled stone hearth. The adjoining nook is also vaulted, and features a sliding door out to the wide patio. The well-planned kitchen has a bright corner sink and a cooktop serving bar.
- The master suite occupies the back corner of the house and includes a large walk-in wardrobe, a skylighted dressing area and a raised spa tub.
- A compartmentalized bath with a dual-sink vanity services the remaining three bedrooms.

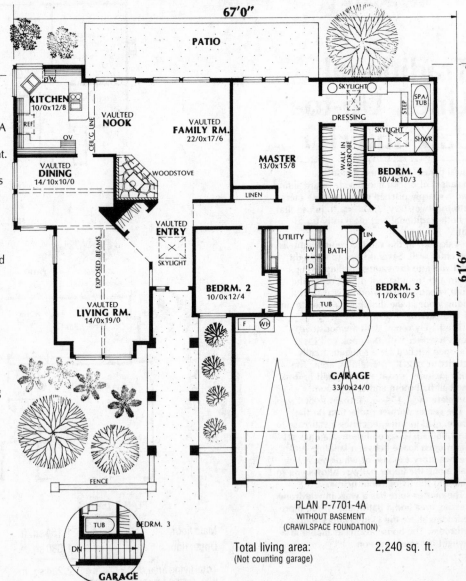

PLAN P-7701-4D
WITH DAYLIGHT BASEMENT

Main floor:	2,340 sq. ft.
Basement:	2,340 sq. ft.

PLAN P-7701-4A
WITHOUT BASEMENT
(CRAWLSPACE FOUNDATION)

Total living area: 2,240 sq. ft.
(Not counting garage)

Blueprint Price Code C

Plans P-7701-4A & -4D

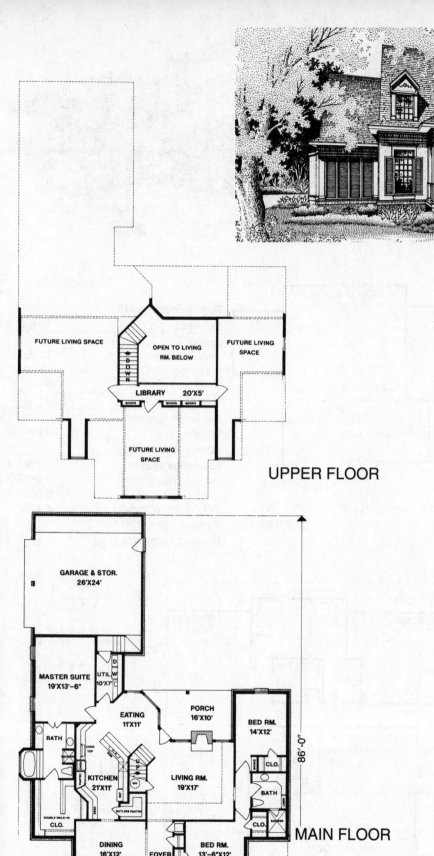

FUTURE LIVING SPACE

OPEN TO LIVING
RM. BELOW

**FUTURE LIVING
SPACE**

DOWN

LIBRARY 20'X5'

BOOKS BOOKS BOOKS

**FUTURE LIVING
SPACE**

UPPER FLOOR

GARAGE & STOR.
26'X24'

MASTER SUITE
19'X13'–6"

UTIL
10'X7'

BATH

EATING
11'X11'

PORCH
16'X10'

BED RM.
14'X12'

COOK TOP

CLO.

KITCHEN
21'X11'

LIVING RM.
19'X17'

UP

BATH

BUTLERS PANTRY

DOUBLE WALK-IN
CLO.

CLO.

DINING
16'X12'

FOYER

BED RM.
13'–6"X12'

MAIN FLOOR

PORCH
24'X8'

59'-0"

86'-0"

Rural and Refined

- This refined and graceful two-story is at home in the country or in the city.
- Visitors are given a warm welcome by the railed, covered front porch.
- A quiet balcony library overlooks the dramatic two-story living room, with its fireplace and access to a rear porch.
- Nine-foot ceilings give a spacious feeling to the rest of the home.
- An angled counter separates the gourmet kitchen from the sunny, angled eating area. The formal dining room is also easily serviced from the kitchen, which boasts a butler's pantry, a second pantry and a built-in desk.
- An enormous walk-in closet is found in the isolated master suite. The master bath has an enticing garden tub, a separate shower and dual vanities.
- A hall bath with an oversized shower is shared by two additional bedrooms.
- The upstairs attic areas could easily accommodate future expansion.

Plan THD-220-0	
Bedrooms: 3	**Baths:** 2
Living Area:	
Upper floor	96 sq. ft.
Main floor	2,159 sq. ft.
Total Living Area:	**2,255 sq. ft.**
Daylight basement	2,159 sq. ft.
Garage and storage	664 sq. ft.
Future expansion area	878 sq. ft.
Exterior Wall Framing:	2x6

Foundation Options:
Daylight basement
Crawlspace
Slab
(Typical foundation & framing conversion diagram available—see order form.)

BLUEPRINT PRICE CODE: C

TO ORDER THIS BLUEPRINT,
CALL TOLL-FREE 1-800-547-5570

Plan THD-220-0

PRICES AND DETAILS
ON PAGES 12-15 **195**

Impressive Contemporary

- A wide, sweeping facade introduces this striking contemporary design.
- Inside, the good impression continues, with the sight of a huge Great Room with a large masonry fireplace.
- The large passive sun room can serve as a breakfast room, family room or arboretum, while at the same time collecting and redistributing the sun's heat throughout the house.
- The bedroom adjoining the sun room features a luxurious private bath and huge walk-in closet. Another downstairs bedroom is next to a second full bath.
- The upstairs offers enormous potential as a special retreat for kids or adults, a studio, office, exercise area, additional bedroom or "dormitory" for kids' overnighters.
- Also note the large utility area and the abundance of storage space throughout the home.

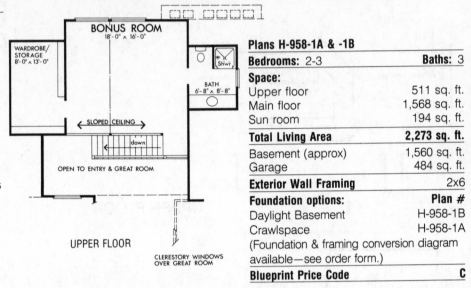

UPPER FLOOR

CLERESTORY WINDOWS
OVER GREAT ROOM

Plans H-958-1A & -1B	
Bedrooms: 2-3	**Baths: 3**
Space:	
Upper floor	511 sq. ft.
Main floor	1,568 sq. ft.
Sun room	194 sq. ft.
Total Living Area	**2,273 sq. ft.**
Basement (approx)	1,560 sq. ft.
Garage	484 sq. ft.
Exterior Wall Framing	2x6
Foundation options:	**Plan #**
Daylight Basement	H-958-1B
Crawlspace	H-958-1A
(Foundation & framing conversion diagram available—see order form.)	
Blueprint Price Code	**C**

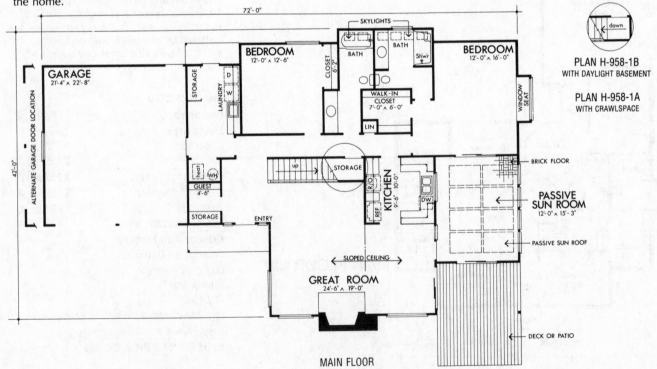

PLAN H-958-1B
WITH DAYLIGHT BASEMENT

PLAN H-958-1A
WITH CRAWLSPACE

MAIN FLOOR

Decorative and Distinctive

- A decorative covered front entry and shuttered windows create a distinctive facade for this traditional two-story.
- The two-story foyer is flanked by two large formal spaces. The dining room features a lovely bay window and easy access to the kitchen.
- A coat closet and a powder room are located off the hall that leads to the family room. This spacious family activity area is warmed by a nice fireplace and has a beautiful French door that provides outdoor access.
- The adjoining kitchen has a serving bar that extends to the family room as well as to the sunny breakfast area. A pantry and a laundry room are discreetly placed near the entrance to the garage.
- The upper floor houses four bedrooms, three with walk-in closets. The master bedroom has a private, vaulted bath.

Plan FB-2279

Bedrooms: 4	Baths: 2½
Living Area:	
Upper floor	1,190 sq. ft.
Main floor	1,089 sq. ft.
Total Living Area:	**2,279 sq. ft.**
Daylight basement	1,089 sq. ft.
Garage	410 sq. ft.
Storage	66 sq. ft.
Exterior Wall Framing:	2x4

Foundation Options:

Daylight basement

Crawlspace

Slab

(Typical foundation & framing conversion diagram available—see order form.)

BLUEPRINT PRICE CODE:	C

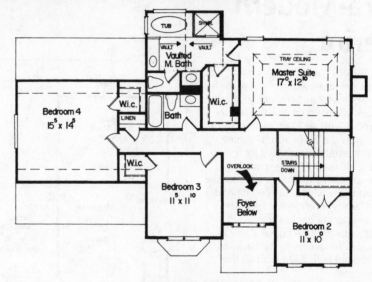

UPPER FLOOR

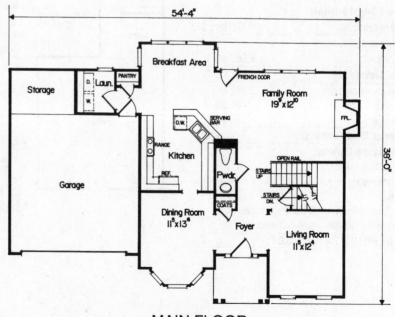

MAIN FLOOR

Ultra-Modern Interior

- The traditional exterior of this home conceals an ultra-modern floor plan.
- The foyer, brightened by sidelights and a transom window, reveals the sunken living room with an 11-ft. ceiling and a rear window wall. The formal dining room is entered through elegant arches.
- The fantastic family living spaces include an island kitchen, a gazebo-like breakfast room with a tray ceiling and a vaulted family room with a fireplace and access to the backyard.
- The regal master suite boasts a tray ceiling, private access to the backyard and a vaulted bath filled with all the latest luxuries.
- Two more bedrooms, two full baths and a vaulted bedroom or optional sitting room complete this unique design.

Plan FB-5010-GRAN

Bedrooms: 3+	Baths: 3
Living Area:	
Main floor	2,282 sq. ft.
Total Living Area:	**2,282 sq. ft.**
Daylight basement	2,282 sq. ft.
Garage	441 sq. ft.
Storage	70 sq. ft.
Exterior Wall Framing:	2x4

Foundation Options:

Daylight basement
Crawlspace
Slab
(Typical foundation & framing conversion diagram available—see order form.)

BLUEPRINT PRICE CODE:	C

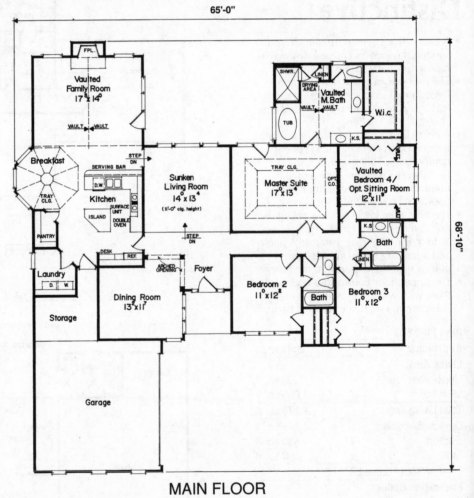

MAIN FLOOR

TO ORDER THIS BLUEPRINT, CALL TOLL-FREE 1-800-547-5570

Plan FB-5010-GRAN

PRICES AND DETAILS ON PAGES 12-15

PLAN H-2107-1B

Solarium for Sloping Lots

This plan is available in two versions. Plan H-2107-1B, shown above, is most suitable for a lot sloping upward from front to rear, providing a daylight front for the lower floor. The other version, Plan H-2107-1 (at right), is more suitable for a lot that slopes from side to side.

Either way, this moderately sized home has a number of interesting and imaginative features. Of these, the passive sun room will provoke the most comment. Spanning two floors between recreation and living rooms, this glass-enclosed space serves the practical purpose of collecting, storing and redistributing the sun's natural heat, while acting as a conservatory for exotic plants, an exercise room, or any number of other uses. A link between the formal atmosphere of the living room and the carefree activities of the recreation area is created by this two-story solarium by way of an open balcony railing. Living, dining, and entry blend together in one huge space made to seem even larger by the vaulted ceiling spanning the entire complex of rooms.

PLAN H-2107-1

MAIN FLOOR
1505 SQUARE FEET

PLAN H-2107-1B
DAYLIGHT BASEMENT

PLAN H-2107-1
WITH STANDARD BASEMENT
(BOTH VERSIONS INCLUDE
2X6 EXTERIOR WALL CONSTRUCTION)

Main floor:	1,505 sq. ft.
Lower level:	779 sq. ft.
Total living area: (Not counting garage)	2,284 sq. ft.

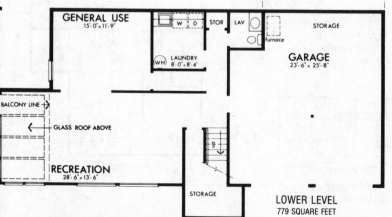

LOWER LEVEL
779 SQUARE FEET

Blueprint Price Code C

Plans H-2107-1 & -1B

Four-Bedroom Contemporary Style

Steeply pitched, multi-level gable rooflines accented by diagonal board siding and tall windows add imposing height to this contemporary, 2,289 sq. ft. home. With most of the 1,389 sq. ft. main floor devoted to the living, dining and family rooms, and a long patio or wood deck accessible off the nook, the home lends itself ideally to family activities and gracious entertaining.

Directly off the spacious foyer is the vaulted-ceiling living room and dining area, brightened with high windows and warmed by a log-sized fireplace. The wide U-shaped kitchen, nook and family room, with wood stove, join and extend across the back half of the main floor. With doors off the nook and utility room leading to a large patio, this area combines for large, informal activities. Also off the front entry hall is a full bathroom, a den or fourth bedroom, and the open stairway, brightened by a skylight, leading to the upper floor.

The master bedroom suite, occupying about half of the upper floor, has a wide picture window, walk-in dressing room/ wardrobe, and a skylighted bathroom with sunken tub and separate shower. The other two bedrooms share the hall bathroom. A daylight basement version of the plan further expands the family living and recreation areas of this home.

Main floor:	1,389 sq. ft.
Upper floor:	900 sq. ft.
Total living area:	2,289 sq. ft.
(Not counting basement or garage)	
Basement level:	1,389 sq. ft.

MAIN FLOOR

PLAN P-7627-4A
WITHOUT BASEMENT

PLAN P-7627-4D
WITH DAYLIGHT BASEMENT

UPPER FLOOR

Blueprint Price Code C

Plans P-7627-4A & -4D

TO ORDER THIS BLUEPRINT, CALL TOLL-FREE 1-800-547-5570

PRICES AND DETAILS ON PAGES 12-15

Three-Bedroom Split-Entry

- This lovely split-entry combines contemporary and traditional styling in an affordable floor arrangement.
- The main/upper level houses the sleeping rooms, two baths, convenient laundry facilities, and the main living areas.
- A formal dining room is divided from the foyer by an open handrail; the room can also overlook the front yard through a large, boxed window wall.
- The adjacent living room boasts a handsome fireplace and sliders to the rear patio.
- A large, versatile bonus space and a garage are found on the lower level.

50'-0"

Patio

Master Br
12x17

Living Rm
14x14

Brkfst
11x7-6

Br 2
12x11-6

Br 3
11x12

W
D

DN   UP

Dining
12-2x12-8

34'-4"

MAIN FLOOR

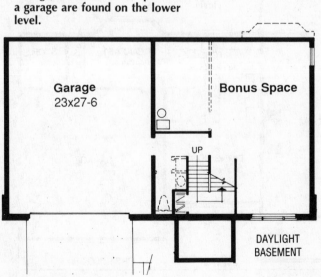

Garage
23x27-6

Bonus Space

UP

DAYLIGHT
BASEMENT

Plan B-90014

Bedrooms: 3	**Baths:** 2-2½

Space:	
Main/upper floor:	1,549 sq. ft.
Basement:	750 sq. ft.

Total living area:	2,299 sq. ft.
Garage:	633 sq. ft.

Exterior Wall Framing:	2x4

Foundation options:
Daylight basement.
(Foundation & framing conversion diagram available — see order form.)

Blueprint Price Code:	C

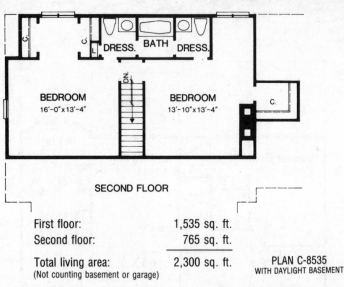

SECOND FLOOR

First floor:	1,535 sq. ft.
Second floor:	765 sq. ft.
Total living area:	2,300 sq. ft.

(Not counting basement or garage)

PLAN C-8535
WITH DAYLIGHT BASEMENT

Traditional Touches Dress Up a Country Cottage

Multipaned windows, shutters and a covered porch embellish the traditional exterior of this country cottage. The floor plan incorporates a central Great Room. A raised-hearth stone fireplace forms part of a wall separating the Great Room from the kitchen.

The large country kitchen features an island and abundant counter space. The breakfast room includes a bay window. A large dining room faces the front.

First-level master bedroom has its own super bath with separate shower, garden tub, twin vanities and walk-in closets. Two large bedrooms, separate dressing areas and compartment tub occupy the second level.

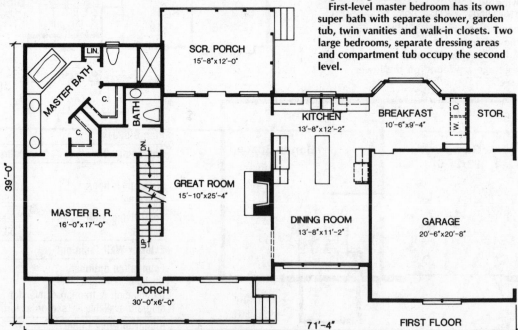

FIRST FLOOR

Blueprint Price Code C

Plan C-8535

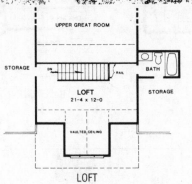

UPPER GREAT ROOM

STORAGE

BATH

LOFT
21-4 x 12-0

STORAGE

VAULTED CEILING

LOFT

Gracious Traditional

- This traditional-style ranch is perfect for a corner building lot. Long windows and dormers add distinctive elegance.
- The floor plan has a popular "split-bedroom" design. The master bedroom is secluded away from the other bedrooms.
- The large Great Room has a vaulted ceiling and stairs leading up to a loft.
- The upstairs loft is perfect for a recreation area, and has a full bath.

- The master bedroom bath has a large corner tub and his and hers vanities. A large walk-in closet provides plenty of storage space.
- The two other bedrooms have large walk-in closets, desks, and a shared bath.
- The kitchen and private breakfast nook are located conveniently near the utility/garage area.

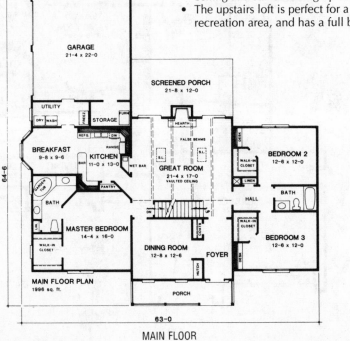

MAIN FLOOR

Plan C-8920	
Bedrooms: 3	**Baths:** 3
Living Area:	
Upper floor	305 sq. ft.
Main floor	1,996 sq. ft.
Total Living Area:	**2,301 sq. ft.**
Daylight basement	1,996 sq. ft.
Garage	469 sq. ft.
Exterior Wall Framing:	2x4
Foundation Options:	
Daylight basement	
Crawlspace	
(Typical foundation & framing conversion diagram available—see order form.)	
BLUEPRINT PRICE CODE:	C

Distinctive Contemporary

- Distinctive rooflines and elegant windows give this home an eye-catching, contemporary look.
- The interior offers a vaulted family room with fireplace, built-in shelving, a rear patio and an open stairway to the upper level.
- The nook and island kitchen share an eating bar and patio of their own.
- Formal living and dining rooms combine at the front of the home, both with raised ceilings.
- The main-floor master suite is entered through elegant double doors; it has a nearby washer/dryer and private bath with isolated toilet, separate shower and step-up spa.
- A study/loft shares the upper level with two additional bedrooms.

Plans P-7750-3A & -3D

Bedrooms: 3	Baths: 2 ½
Space:	
Upper floor	616 sq. ft.
Main floor	1,685 sq. ft.
Total Living Area	**2,301 sq. ft.**
Daylight Basement	1,685 sq. ft.
Garage	699 sq. ft.
Exterior Wall Framing	**2x6**
Foundation options:	**Plan #**
Crawlspace	P-7750-3A
Daylight Basement	P-7750-3D
(Foundation & framing conversion diagram available—see order form.)	
Blueprint Price Code	**C**

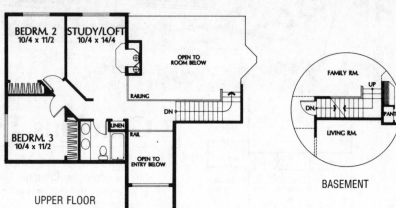

UPPER FLOOR

BASEMENT

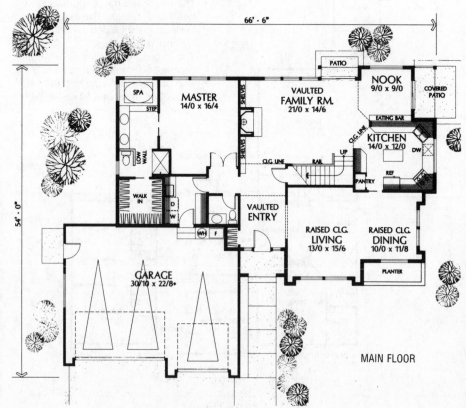

MAIN FLOOR

Plans P-7750-3A & -3D

PRICES AND DETAILS ON PAGES 12-15

Spacious and Inviting

The four-column front porch, picture window, siding, brick, stone and cupola combine for a pleasing exterior for this three-bedroom home.

Extra features include a fireplace, screen porch, deluxe master bath and a large separate breakfast room.

Total living area: 2,306 sq. ft.
(Not counting basement or garage)

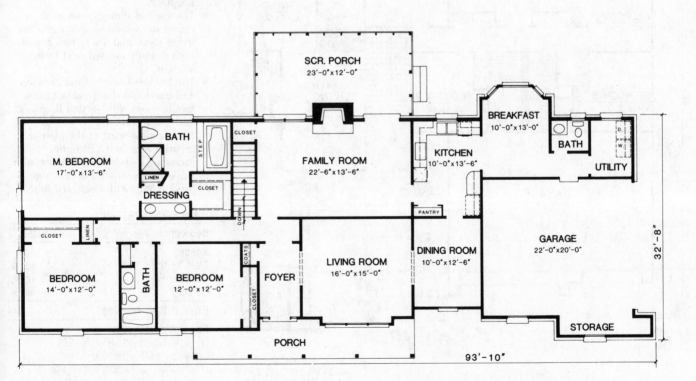

Specify daylight basement, crawlspace or slab foundation.

Blueprint Price Code C
Plan C-8625

PRICES AND DETAILS
ON PAGES 12-15

Atrium Attraction

- A central atrium allows each of the main living spaces to enjoy an oasis of color and light within this spacious contemporary home.
- The entry opens to a dramatic view of the atrium and the sunken living room with vaulted ceiling and fireplace.
- The vaulted dining room, with round-top windows, looks into the living room and the atrium and is conveniently located next to the kitchen.
- The kitchen has an island cooktop and overlooks the breakfast nook, family room with second fireplace, and the atrium.
- The sleeping wing of the plan incorporates four bedrooms, including a lavish master suite with walk-in closet, patio access and private bath with oversized tub.

Plans P-7581-2A, -2D

Bedrooms: 4	Baths: 2

Space:	
Main floor:	2,315 sq. ft.
Basement:	2,270 sq. ft.
Garage:	789 sq. ft.

Exterior Wall Framing:	2x4

Foundation options:
Daylight basement. (P-7581-2D)
Crawlspace. (P-7581-2A)
(Foundation & framing conversion diagram available — see order form.)

Blueprint Price Code:	C

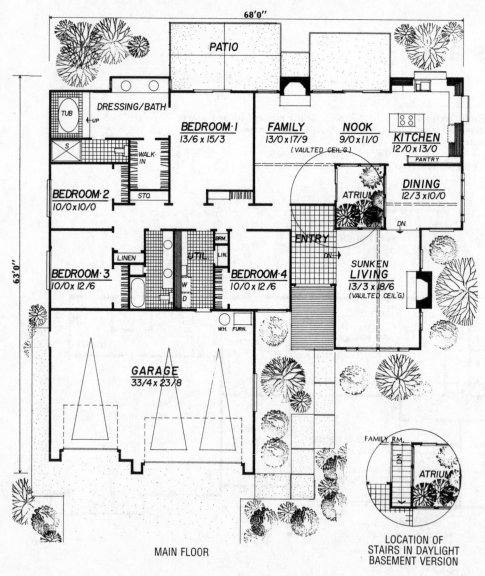

MAIN FLOOR

LOCATION OF STAIRS IN DAYLIGHT BASEMENT VERSION

TO ORDER THIS BLUEPRINT,
CALL TOLL-FREE 1-800-547-5570

Plans P-7581-2A, -2D

PRICES AND DETAILS ON PAGES 12-15

Great Family Living Areas

- The covered front porch and multi-windowed facade give this home its countrypolitan appeal and comfort.
- Inside, a wonderful kitchen, breakfast nook and family room combination steals the show. The step-saving kitchen includes a large pantry closet, an over-sized worktop island/snack bar and a built-in desk. The bay-windowed breakfast nook steps down to the vaulted family room with fireplace.
- The formal living room includes an optional fireplace, while the dining room has an optional bay window.
- A half-bath is just off the foyer, as is a study. The laundry room is convenient to both the kitchen and the garage .
- The upper floor features a spectacular master suite, offering a vaulted ceiling in the sleeping area, a dressing area with a walk-in closet and a skylighted bath with a corner platform tub.
- The blueprints for this plan include details for finishing the exterior with brick or with wood siding.

Plan CH-240-A

Bedrooms: 4-5	Baths: 2½
Living Area:	
Upper floor	1,019 sq. ft.
Main floor	1,300 sq. ft.
Total Living Area:	**2,319 sq. ft.**
Basement	1,300 sq. ft.
Garage	384 sq. ft.
Exterior Wall Framing:	2x4

Foundation Options:
Daylight basement
Standard basement
Crawlspace
(Typical foundation & framing conversion diagram available—see order form.)

BLUEPRINT PRICE CODE:	C

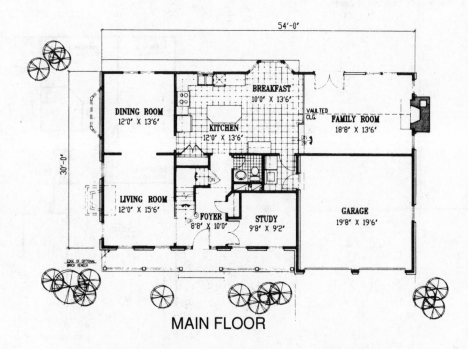

UPPER FLOOR

MAIN FLOOR

"Adult Retreat" Includes Reading Loft

Main floor:	1,610 sq. ft.
Upper floor:	715 sq. ft.
Total living area:	2,325 sq. ft.
(Not counting basement or garage)	

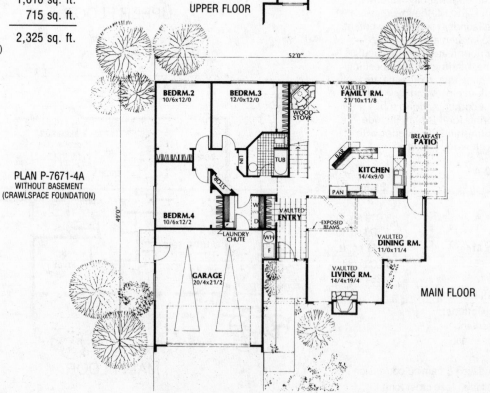

READING LOFT 12/0x11/0

MASTER SUITE 13/0x17/2

LINEN

BOOKS

DN

SH

TUB 7/0x3/6

SKYLIGHTS

DRESSING

WALK IN WARDROBE

OPEN TO ENTRY

UPPER FLOOR

FAMILY ROOM

PLAN P-7671-4D
WITH DAYLIGHT BASEMENT
BASEMENT LEVEL: 1634 sq. ft.

PLAN P-7671-4A
WITHOUT BASEMENT
(CRAWLSPACE FOUNDATION)

52'0"

49'0"

BEDRM.2 10/6x12/0

BEDRM.3 12/0x12/0

WOOD STOVE

VAULTED FAMILY RM. 21/10x11/8

BREAKFAST PATIO

LIN

TUB

KITCHEN 14/4x9/0

BAR

PAN

STOR.

BEDRM.4 10/6x12/2

W

D

VAULTED ENTRY

EXPOSED BEAMS

VAULTED DINING RM. 11/0x11/4

LAUNDRY CHUTE

WH

F

GARAGE 20/4x21/2

VAULTED LIVING RM. 14/4x19/4

MAIN FLOOR

Blueprint Price Code C

Charming Design for Hillside Site

- Split-level design puts living room on entry level, other rooms up or down a half-flight of steps.
- Kitchen includes work/eating island and combines with dining/family room for informal living.
- Vaulted master suite includes private bath and large closet.
- Daylight basement includes two bedrooms, bath, utility area and a rec room.

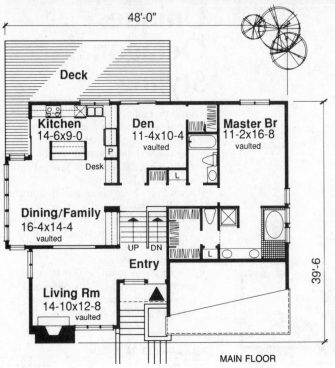

48'-0"

39'-6"

Deck

Kitchen 14-6x9-0

Den 11-4x10-4 vaulted

Master Br 11-2x16-8 vaulted

P Desk

Dining/Family 16-4x14-4 vaulted

UP DN

Entry

Living Rm 14-10x12-8 vaulted

L

MAIN FLOOR

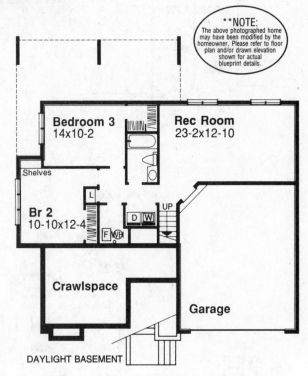

NOTE:
The above photographed home may have been modified by the homeowner. Please refer to floor plan and/or drawn elevation shown for actual blueprint details.

Bedroom 3 14x10-2

Rec Room 23-2x12-10

Shelves

Br 2 10-10x12-4

L

F W

D W

UP

Crawlspace

Garage

DAYLIGHT BASEMENT

Plan B-89037

Bedrooms: 3+	Baths: 3

Living Area:

Main floor	1,422 sq. ft.
Partial daylight basement	913 sq. ft.

Total Living Area:	**2,335 sq. ft.**
Garage	480 sq. ft.

Exterior Wall Framing:	2x6

Foundation Options:

Partial daylight basement
(Typical foundation & framing conversion diagram available—see order form.)

BLUEPRINT PRICE CODE:	C

TO ORDER THIS BLUEPRINT,
CALL TOLL-FREE 1-800-547-5570

Plan B-89037

PRICES AND DETAILS
ON PAGES 12-15

209

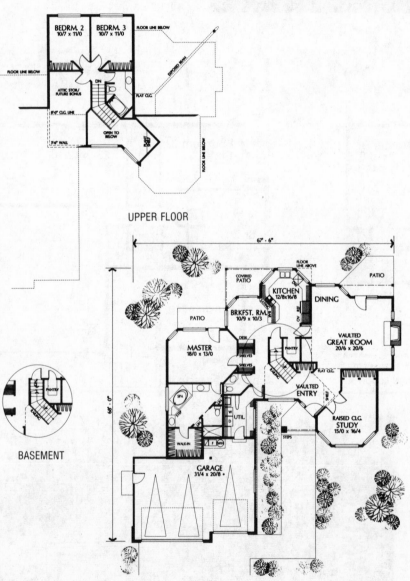

UPPER FLOOR

BASEMENT

MAIN FLOOR

Unique Octagonal Styling

- Volume ceilings and multiple angled windows add style and luxury to this two-level, brick-accented home.
- The vaulted entry reveals double doors that access the study with raised ceiling and a large bay window.
- A vaulted Great Room and dining area share a fireplace and a patio view.
- A second patio joins the bayed kitchen and breakfast room, which share an eating bar. A large pantry is secluded near the stairway.
- The spacious main-level master bedroom offers a private patio and generous bath with walk-in closet, spa tub and separate vanities.

Plans P-6613-3A & -3D

Bedrooms: 3	Baths: 2 ½
Space:	
Upper floor	410 sq. ft.
Main floor	1,925 sq. ft.
Total Living Area	**2,335 sq. ft.**
Basement	1,925 sq. ft.
Garage	648 sq. ft.
Exterior Wall Framing	2x6
Foundation options:	**Plan #**
Daylight Basement	P-6613-3D
Crawlspace	P-6613-3A
(Foundation & framing conversion diagram available—see order form.)	
Blueprint Price Code	C

Loaded with Features

• Great Room has fireplace and long windows to add to its elegance. Also has a nice view of open stair.

• Galley-type kitchen between formal dining room and secluded breakfast nook.

• Downstairs bedroom with full bath is perfect for guests or mother-in-law.

• Master bedroom is large and has trey ceiling. TV-stereo center allows for more useable floor space.

• Master bath has corner tub, shower, and window seat. Vaulted ceiling gives bath a spacious feeling.

• Optional bonus room can be used as a playroom, office or bedroom.

Plan C-8910

Bedrooms: 4	Baths: 3

Finished space:

Upper floor	1,025 sq. ft.
Main floor	1,033 sq. ft.
Bonus area:	284 sq. ft.
Total living area	**2,342 sq. ft.**
Garage:	484 sq. ft.

Features:
Great Room
Large breakfast nook
Guest bedroom
Deluxe master bedroom suite

Exterior Wall Framing	2x4

Foundation options:
Daylight basement.
Standard basement.
Crawlspace.
Slab.

Blueprint Price Code	C

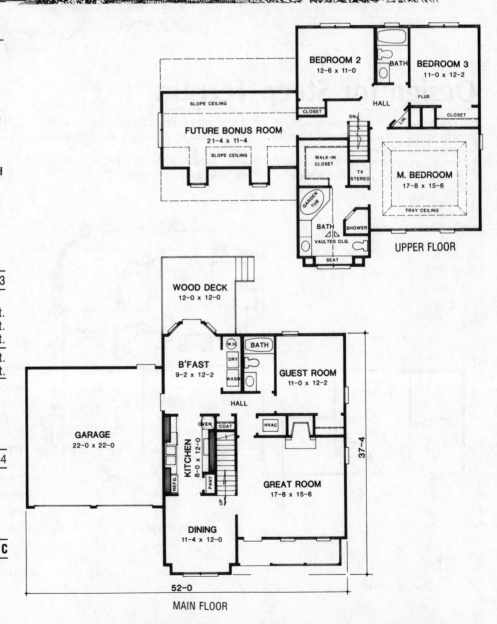

UPPER FLOOR

MAIN FLOOR

Design for Steep Terrain

- A railing separates the sunken living room from the vaulted dining room for a great visual flow of space.
- The kitchen is highlighted by a corner window sink, an island and a walk-in pantry.

- The master suite includes a luxury bath illuminated by a skylight and a spacious walk-in closet.
- The partial basement could be omitted for building on flat lots.

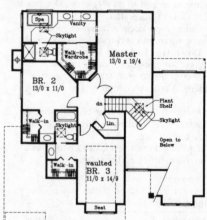

UPPER FLOOR

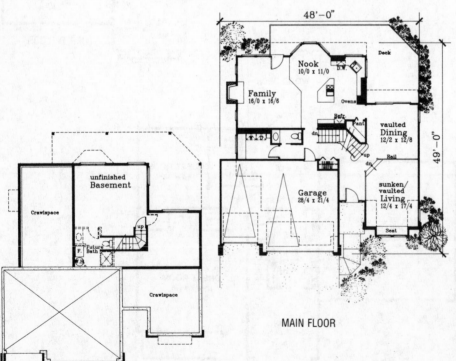

MAIN FLOOR

BASEMENT

Plan CDG-2009

Bedrooms: 3	**Baths:** 2½

Living Area:	
Upper floor	1,113 sq. ft.
Main floor	1,230 sq. ft.

Total Living Area:	**2,343 sq. ft.**
Partial daylight basement	606 sq. ft.
Garage	604 sq. ft.

Exterior Wall Framing:	2x6

Foundation Options:
Partial daylight basement
(Typical foundation & framing conversion diagram available—see order form.)

BLUEPRINT PRICE CODE:	C

Country-Style Comfort

The large front porch and charming window treatments give added appeal to this country-style design. Inside, the vaulted foyer leads to the luxurious master bedroom, the dining room, or the Great Room at the rear of the home.

The Great Room features vaulted ceilings, with exposed beams and a balcony above lending a rustic feel. A raised-hearth fireplace, built-in wet bar and access to a backyard deck add extra livability and comfort. The adjoining breakfast room is brightened by a bay window, and a breakfast bar supplements the formal eating area.

The master suite includes a walk-in closet, oversized vanity, and a garden tub. Vaulted ceilings highlight the bathing area, which also features a large linen closet and a shower.

An open stairway leads to the second floor, with views of the Great Room below. Each of the upstairs bedrooms has a walk-in closet, plus there's a large storage room for overflow. A full bath completes the second floor.

First floor:	1,494 sq. ft.
Second floor:	853 sq. ft.
Total living area: (Not counting basement or garage)	2,347 sq. ft.
Basement:	897 sq. ft.
Garage:	484 sq. ft.
Porch:	250 sq. ft.
Deck:	200 sq. ft.

SECOND FLOOR

FAMILY (BELOW)

STORAGE
13·4 x 11·2

OPEN RAIL   FLUE

BALCONY   L   CLOS.

BATH

BR 3
13·4 x 11·0

OPEN   DN

BR 2
13·4 x 13·10

CLOSET

32-0

38-0

FIRST FLOOR

WOOD DECK
20'-0" x 10'-0"

BREAKFAST
13'-0" x 8'-0"

GARAGE
22'-0" x 22'-0"

HEARTH

GREAT ROOM
23'-6" x 14'-0"
VAULTED CEILING

FALSE BEAMS

WET BAR

KITCHEN
13'-0" x 10'-0"

STORAGE

LINEN

BALCONY ABOVE

UTILITY

WASH DRY

POWDER

UP

BATH

GARDEN TUB

CLOSET

DINING ROOM
13'-0" x 12'-6"

PORCH

SHOWER

FOYER

DOWN

M. BEDROOM
14'-0" x 18'-0"

PORCH

55'-0"

67'-6"

Specify daylight basement or crawlspace foundation.

Blueprint Price Code C

Plan C-8655

Roomy Four-Bedroom Home

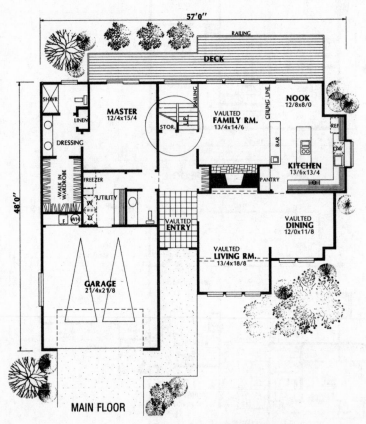

MAIN FLOOR

57'0"

RAILING
DECK

SHWR
LINEN
MASTER
12/4x15/4
DRESSING
WALK IN WARDROBE
FREEZER
UTILITY
WH
STOR.
RAILING
CEILING LINE
VAULTED FAMILY RM.
13/4x14/6
BAR
NOOK
12/8x8/0
REF
KITCHEN
13/6x13/4
DW
PANTRY
VAULTED ENTRY
VAULTED DINING
12/0x11/8
VAULTED LIVING RM.
13/4x18/8

GARAGE
21/4x21/8

48'0"

PLAN P-7592-2A
WITHOUT BASEMENT

Main floor:	1,685 sq. ft.
Upper floor:	665 sq. ft.
Total living area:	2,350 sq. ft.

(Not counting basement or garage)

MASTER   DN   UP   FAMILY RM.

PLAN P-7592-2D
WITH DAYLIGHT BASEMENT

Basement level:	1,634 sq. ft.
Storage:	484 sq. ft.

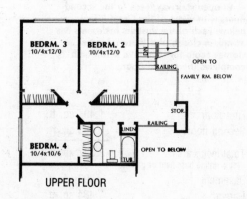

BEDRM. 3
10/4x12/0
BEDRM. 2
10/4x12/0
RAILING
OPEN TO FAMILY RM. BELOW
STOR.
BEDRM. 4
10/4x10/6
LINEN
RAILING
OPEN TO BELOW
TUB

UPPER FLOOR

Blueprint Price Code C

Plans P-7592-2A & -2D

Time-Tested Traditional Includes Deluxe Master Suite

This 2,360 square foot traditional design features a master suite with a walk-in closet as well as a deluxe compartmentalized bath with another walk-in closet, linen closet, double vanity, vaulted ceiling, large glass area, garden tub and separate shower stall. Two additional bedrooms with ample closets and a second full bath and linen closet are included on the 1,146 square foot upper floor.

The formal foyer is flanked by a dining room on one side and a study on the other. Behind the dining room is a U-shaped kitchen with breakfast bay. Double doors onto the rear patio, a raised-hearth fireplace, a half bath and a coat closet are included in the living room. The large utility room behind the garage completes the 1,214 square foot mainfloor.

Multi-paned windows, shutters, lap siding and a formal entrance combine for a traditional exterior.

First floor:	1,214 sq. ft.
Second floor:	1,146 sq. ft.
Total living area:	2,360 sq. ft.
(Not counting basement or garage)	

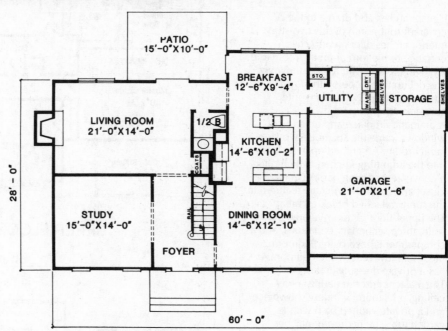

Specify daylight basement or crawlspace foundation.

FIRST FLOOR

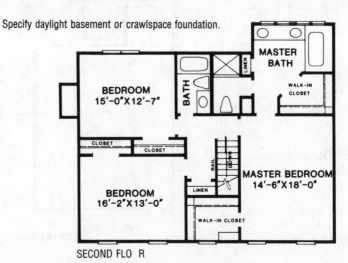

SECOND FLOOR

Blueprint Price Code C
Plan C-8350

TO ORDER THIS BLUEPRINT,
CALL TOLL-FREE 1-800-547-5570

PRICES AND DETAILS
ON PAGES 12-15   215

Appealing Arches

- Elegant arches add drama to the covered front porch of this two-story.
- Interior arches offer an attractive entrance to the formal dining room and the living room, which flank the foyer.
- The decorative niche off the foyer attractively displays your favorite conversation pieces.
- A dramatic fireplace and an array of windows frame the spacious two-story family room. An arched opening leads into the adjoining kitchen, which offers a convenient serving bar. A pantry closet and open shelving are featured in the sunny attached breakfast area.
- The upper floor includes a large master suite, three secondary bedrooms, and a compartmentalized bath. Bedroom 2 has a window seat, while Bedroom 4 has a private dressing area.
- The master bedroom flaunts a tray ceiling, a beautiful window showpiece and a private vaulted bath with a garden tub. The bedroom may be extended to include a sitting area.

Plan FB-2368

Bedrooms: 4	Baths: 2½
Living Area:	
Upper floor	1,168 sq. ft.
Main floor	1,200 sq. ft.
Total Living Area:	**2,368 sq. ft.**
Daylight basement	1,200 sq. ft.
Garage	504 sq. ft.
Exterior Wall Framing:	2x4

Foundation Options:
Daylight basement
Slab
(Typical foundation & framing conversion diagram available—see order form.)

BLUEPRINT PRICE CODE: C

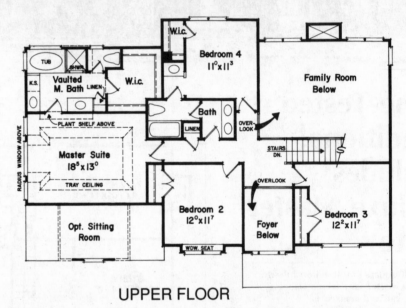

UPPER FLOOR

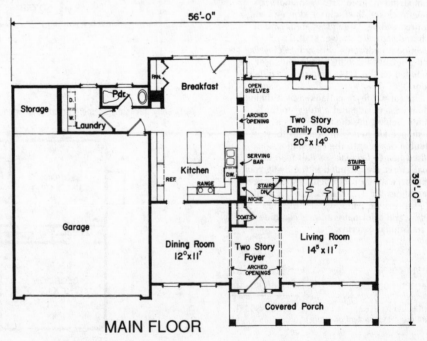

MAIN FLOOR

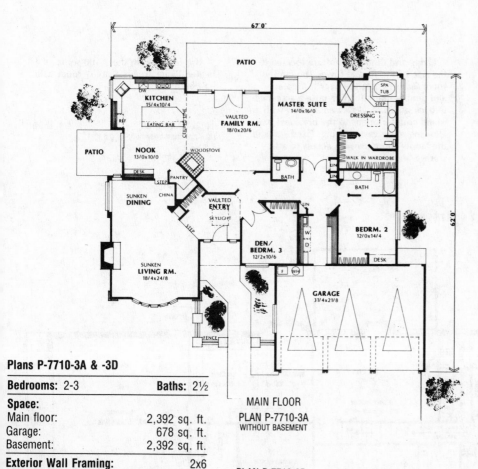

67'0"

PATIO

KITCHEN
15/4x10/4

EATING BAR

VAULTED
FAMILY RM.
18/0x20/6

MASTER SUITE
14/0x16/0

SPA TUB

DRESSING

PATIO

NOOK
13/0x10/0

WOODSTOVE

DESK

STEP

PANTRY

WALK IN WARDROBE

SUNKEN
DINING

CHINA

VAULTED
ENTRY

BATH

BATH

SKYLIGHT

DEN/
BEDRM. 3
12/2x10/6

BEDRM. 2
12/0x14/4

SUNKEN
LIVING RM.
18/4x24/8

DESK

GARAGE
31/4x21/8

FENCE

62'0"

MAIN FLOOR
PLAN P-7710-3A
WITHOUT BASEMENT

PLAN P-7710-3D
WITH DAYLIGHT BASEMENT

PANTRY

BASEMENT

Plans P-7710-3A & -3D

Bedrooms: 2-3	Baths: 2½

Space:

Main floor:	2,392 sq. ft.
Garage:	678 sq. ft.
Basement:	2,392 sq. ft.

Exterior Wall Framing:	2x6

Foundation options:
Daylight basement, Plan P-7710-3D.
Crawlspace, Plan P-7710-3A.
(Foundation & framing conversion
diagram available — see order form.)

Blueprint Price Code:	C

Deluxe Living Spaces

- Visitors approaching the front entry are welcomed by a courtyard with a wrought-iron fence and brick columns.
- The front door opens to a large entry magnified by a vaulted ceiling and skylight.
- The large, sunken living/dining area is great for formal entertaining.
- A huge kitchen/nook combination includes an island eating bar which adjoins the spacious, vaulted family room.
- The magnificent master suite includes an incredible bath with spa tub, separate shower and a large walk-in wardrobe closet.
- Daylight basement version doubles the space.

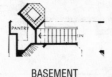

Master Suite Features Luxurious Bath

This lovely French Provincial design features a master suite with a deluxe compartmentalized bath which includes a vaulted ceiling with sky lights, garden tub, shower, linen closet and a separate dressing room with double vanity and large walk-in closet. Two additional bedrooms with ample closet space share a second compartmentalized bath.

Living and dining rooms are located to the side of the formal foyer. The family room features a raised hearth fireplace and double doors leading onto a screened-in back porch. A U-shaped kitchen with an island counter opens to the breakfast bay allowing more casual living. Fixed stairs in the family room provide access to attic storage above.

Also included in the 2,400 sq. ft. of heated living area is a utility room with half bath.

Total living area: 2,400 sq. ft.
(Not counting basement or garage)

Specify daylight basement, crawlspace or slab foundation when ordering.

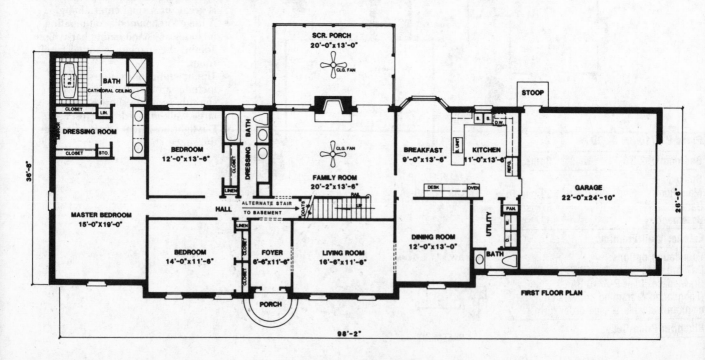

Blueprint Price Code C

Plan C-8363

Functional, Engaging Split-Level

This functional split-level home offers all the amenities today's homeowner is looking for in only 2,404 sq. ft.

A covered entry porch provides an escape from the elements in inclement weather, while the foyer serves as a traffic hub inside this engaging home. From it, you can enter the vaulted living room, the formal dining room, or the kitchen/nook area. Notice that the nook commands a sweeping view of the spacious family room below.

Also located downstairs, through a double-door entry, is an ample-sized den, which could also serve as a fourth bedroom.

Upstairs, double doors usher you into the spacious master bedroom that overlooks the backyard. Featured within the master bath is an elegant tiled spa tub nestled within a window bay. A generous walk-in wardrobe awaits you to the rear of the bath.

Take note of the three-car garage with its liberal parking space, another added plus in this home's favor.

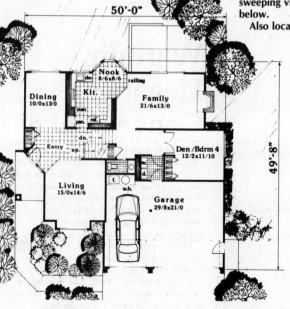

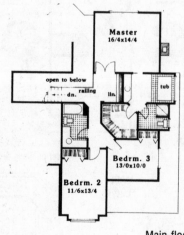

PLAN R-4032
WITHOUT BASEMENT
(CRAWLSPACE FOUNDATION)

Main floor:	1,389 sq. ft.
Upper floor:	1,015 sq. ft.
Total living area: (Not counting garage)	2,404 sq. ft.

TO ORDER THIS BLUEPRINT,
CALL TOLL-FREE 1-800-547-5570

Blueprint Price Code C
Plan R-4032

PRICES AND DETAILS
ON PAGES 12-15 **219**

50'-0"

46'-0"

Patio

Kitchen
10/6x15/0

Nook
10/0x10/0

dw

Dining
12/0x13/0

Family
16/0x13/0

ovens
Pantry

W. D.

Linen

spa

railing

up

up

dn

sunken
Living
13/0x17/0

Entry

Den/Study
11/0x13/6

Master
16/8x12/0

**MAIN
FLOOR**

PLAN R-4034
WITHOUT BASEMENT
(CRAWLSPACE FOUNDATION)

Exterior walls are 2x6 construction.

up

furn wh

Garage
27/6x23/0

Bedrm 2
10/0x11/3

Bedrm 3
10/0x11/3

Linen

dn

Landing

Open To
Below

**UPPER
FLOOR**

Warmth,
Elegance,
Convenience

The children and guest bedrooms are
upstairs and the master bedroom suite is
downstairs — for a special "adult retreat."
This gorgeous two-story brick home has all
the major living space on the main floor
and the two extra bedrooms above,
making it an ideal home for retired
couples as well as families.

On the main level, a nice kitchen with a
nook connects to the family room. The
master suite has a large walk-in closet, a
spa, and a double vanity. The house also
includes a den/study. French doors off the
dining room lead to a patio in the
backyard.

This is definitely a nice, warm, elegant
home which will be appreciated by all.

Main floor:	1,964 sq. ft.
Upper floor:	442 sq. ft.
Total living area:	2,406 sq. ft.
(Not counting garage)	

Blueprint Price Code C

Plan R-4034

FRONT VIEW

Making the Most of a Daylight Basement

This striking plan will interest those who need a fairly large home on a hillside building site. Notice the unique way in which the two-car garage is attached at an angle. This creates a convenient rear entry through the laundry room from the garage. Access to all parts of the dwelling is convenient via the central hallway.

A sun deck runs the full length of the home, and the dining room and family room have access to the porch through sliding doors. All rooms along this side of the home have a view to the rear.

An open stairway leads from the entry to the lower level where three spacious bedrooms, a storage area, and a second optional laundry are located.

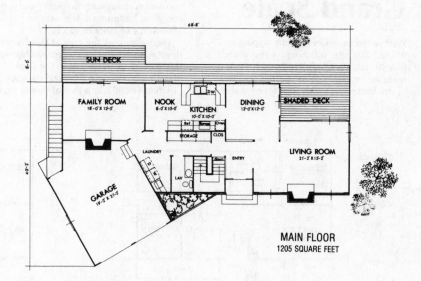

MAIN FLOOR
1205 SQUARE FEET

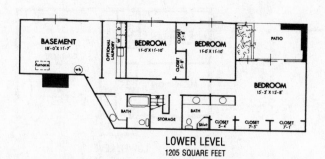

LOWER LEVEL
1205 SQUARE FEET

Main floor:	1,205 sq. ft.
Lower level:	1,205 sq. ft.
Total living area:	2,410 sq. ft.
(Not counting garage)	

Gracious Living on a Grand Scale

Well suited to either a gently sloping or flat building site, this home is also geared to a conservative building budget. First, it saves money through the partial enclosure of the lower level with foundation walls. A

portion of the lower level that is surrounded by concrete walls is devoted to a 15'-10" x 13'-0" bedroom or optional den with wardrobe closet, a spacious recreation room with fireplace, and a third complete bathroom along with an abundance of storage space.

The balance of the area at this level is devoted to a two-car garage. Access from this portion of the home to the floor directly above is via a central staircase.

In Plan H-2082-2, a formal dining room

and large kitchen provide two places for family eating.

Plan H-2082-1 includes a combination family room and U-shaped kitchen in one open area. Spatial continuity is further extended into the cantilevered deck that projects over the garage driveway below and is accessible through sliding glass doors off the family room.

This system of multi-level planning offers economy in building where grading would otherwise be required.

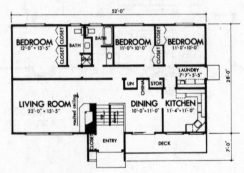

PLAN H-2082-2
MAIN FLOOR
1500 SQUARE FEET

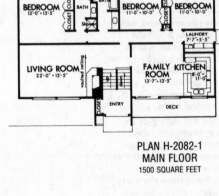

PLAN H-2082-1
MAIN FLOOR
1500 SQUARE FEET

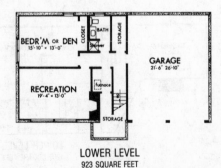

LOWER LEVEL
923 SQUARE FEET

Main floor:	1,500 sq. ft.
Lower level:	923 sq. ft.
Total living area: (Not counting garage)	2,423 sq. ft.

Blueprint Price Code C

Plans H-2082-1 & -2

Old-Fashioned Charm

- A trio of dormers add old-fashioned charm to this modern design.
- Both the living room and the dining room offer vaulted cellings, and the two rooms flow together to create a sense of even more spaciousness.
- The open kitchen, nook and family room combination features a sunny alcove, a walk-in pantry and an inviting wood stove.
- A first-floor den and a walk-through utility room are other big bonuses.
- Upstairs, the master suite includes a walk-in closet and a deluxe bath with a spa tub and a separate shower and water closet.
- Two more bedrooms, each with a window seat, and a bonus room complete this stylish design.

Plan CDG-2004

Bedrooms: 4	**Baths:** 2½

Living Area:

Upper floor	928 sq. ft.
Main floor	1,317 sq. ft.
Bonus room	192 sq. ft.
Total Living Area:	**2,437 sq. ft.**
Partial daylight basement	780 sq. ft.
Garage	537 sq. ft.
Exterior Wall Framing:	2x6

Foundation Options:

Partial daylight basement

Crawlspace

(Typical foundation & framing conversion diagram available—see order form.)

BLUEPRINT PRICE CODE:	**C**

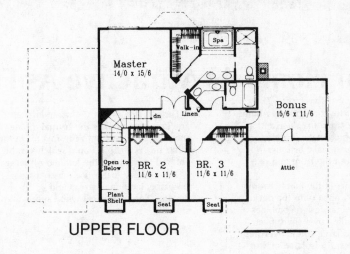

UPPER FLOOR

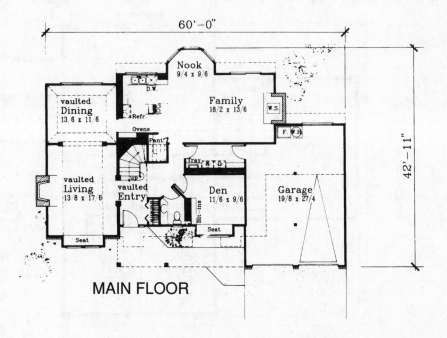

MAIN FLOOR

Rear of Home As Attractive As Front

The rear of this rustic/contemporary home features a massive stone fireplace and a full-length deck which make it ideal for mountain, golf course, lake or other locations where both the front and rear offer scenic views.

Sliding glass doors in the family room and breakfast nook open onto the deck. The modified A-Frame design combines a 20'6" cathedral ceiling over the sunken family room with a large studio over the two front bedrooms. An isolated master suite features a walk-in closet and compartmentalized bath with double vanity and linen closet. The front bedrooms include ample closet space and share a unique bath-and-a-half arrangement.

On one side of the U-shaped kitchen and breakfast nook is the formal dining room which opens onto the foyer. On the other side is a utility room which can be entered from either the kitchen or garage.

The exterior features a massive stone fireplace, large glass areas and a combination of vertical wood siding and stone.

SECOND FLOOR

Specify daylight basement, crawlspace or slab foundation when ordering.

First floor:	2,192 sq. ft.
Second floor:	248 sq. ft.
Total living area:	2,440 sq. ft.

(Not counting basement or garage)

TO ORDER THIS BLUEPRINT,
224 **CALL TOLL-FREE 1-800-547-5570**

Blueprint Price Code C
Plan C-7710

PRICES AND DETAILS
ON PAGES 12-15